EDITH WHARTON

A Study of the Short Fiction

Also available in Twayne's Studies in Short Fiction Series

Twayne's Studies in Short Fiction

Gordon Weaver, General Editor
Oklahoma State University

EDITH WHARTON
Photograph courtesy of Yale University, Beinecke Rare Book and Manuscript Library.

EDITH
WHARTON

——— *A Study of the Short Fiction* ———

Barbara A. White
University of New Hampshire

TWAYNE PUBLISHERS • NEW YORK
Maxwell Macmillan Canada • Toronto
Maxwell Macmillan International • New York Oxford Singapore Sydney

Twayne's Studies in Short Fiction Series No. 30

Twayne Publishers
Macmillan Publishing Company
866 Third Avenue
New York, NY 10022

Maxwell Macmillan Canada, Inc.
1200 Eglinton Avenue East
Suite 200
Don Mills, Ontario M3C 3N1

Macmillan Publishing Company is part of the Maxwell Communication
Group of Companies.

Library of Congress Cataloging-in-Publication Data
White, Barbara Anne.
    Edith Wharton : a study of the short fiction / Barbara A. White.
        p.   cm. — (Twayne's studies in short fiction ; no. 30)
    Includes bibliographical references (p.   ) and index.
    ISBN 0–8057–8340–7 (alk. paper)
    1. Wharton, Edith, 1862–1937—Criticism and interpretation.
2. Short story.   I. Title.   II. Series.
PS3545.H16Z93   1991
813'.52—dc20   91-24547
                                                         CIP

The paper used in this publication meets the minimum requirements
of American National Standard for Information Sciences—Permanence
of Paper for Printed Library Materials, ANSI Z39.48-1984. ∞™

10 9 8 7 6 5 4 3 2

Printed in the United States of America.

Copyediting supervised by Barbara Sutton.
Book production by Janet Z. Reynolds.
Typeset by Compset, Inc., Beverly, Massachusetts.

For Harvey

Contents

Preface

Edith Newbold Jones Wharton told stories for seventy years. As a child in the 1860s she escaped her aristocratic playmates to make up tales; as an adolescent and soon-to-be debutante in New York she wrote a novella. In 1891 Wharton published her first short story and embarked on a writing career that would take her far from society life and marriage to sportsman Teddy Wharton. She would meet the artists she had always admired (in contrast to the idle rich with whom she grew up), get divorced, and spend the last third of her life as an independent writer in France. Wharton's novels garnered money and prizes—*The House of Mirth* (1905) became a best-seller and *The Age of Innocence* (1920) won a Pulitzer Prize—but her short stories were also acclaimed. Admiring audiences ranged from her mother to her friend Henry James to the reviewers, who for the most part gave excellent notices.[1]

Despite Wharton's reputation as a story writer during her lifetime, she is seldom mentioned in books on the short story published in the last fifty years. There are at least two explanations for this oddity, the first having to do with the history of the short story and the second with Wharton's general literary reputation. As to the short story, Wharton lived at the wrong time. She came too late to pioneer in the form and too early to participate in the formal experiments of the 1920s. As we will see, Wharton's theory of the story was quite traditional. She emphasized unity of effect in the French tradition of Flaubert and Maupassant and would scarcely have understood the modern rejection of plot and artifice.[2] In practice Wharton was a transitional figure, just as she was as a novelist, bridging the Victorian and modern eras. She anticipated the new story of the twenties in her pessimism, use of fallible narrators, and very un-Jamesian economy.[3] But in accounts of the short story this transitional period has been little studied.

The tales of Henry James could not be entirely neglected because of his high stature as a writer. After her death in 1937 Wharton's literary reputation waned, a not uncommon occurrence, and she then became a victim of the downgrading of female writers that was especially severe in the late 1940s, 1950s, and 1960s.[4] If Wharton could not be attacked as a sentimentalist, she could either be put in her place as the supposed imitator of a man (James) or damned with faint praise. The Twentieth Century Views collection of essays on Wharton, published in 1962, is remarkable for its seeming attempt to demolish its subject. The often mean-spirited essays by famous critics tell us more about the ethos of the time than about Edith Wharton. We learn, for instance, that the "biting old dowager of American letters" wrote her "little" books out of "personal maladjustment" (her unhappy marriage), for in women "a manifestation of something like genius may be stimulated by some exceptional emotional strain, but will disappear when the stimulus has passed."[5] It becomes clear that Wharton survived in the canon of American literature, when so many other women disappeared, only because of the adaptability of *The House of Mirth* and *The Age of Innocence* to the critics' preoccupation with the "American dream." Another Wharton novel is described as "a relapse into 'psychological problems'" and the rest of her work dismissed for lacking a "conception of America as a unified and dynamic economy" and failing to "understand America as it is."[6] The short stories are hardly mentioned.

In the late 1960s there occurred almost simultaneously two important developments that would shift the focus to Wharton's achievement as a whole and begin the restoration of her literary reputation. These events were the contemporary women's movement and the opening of Wharton's papers at Yale University. Feminist literary criticism has challenged stereotypes of Wharton as a hidebound traditionalist and directed attention to aspects of her work that were previously ignored, leading to Sandra Gilbert and Susan Gubar's recent conclusion that Wharton's fiction may constitute "the most searching—and searing—feminist analysis of the construction of 'femininity' produced by any novelist in this century."[7] The opening of the Wharton papers has given us a better sense of Wharton as a person than we were allowed by her reserved autobiography, *A Backward Glance* (1934). Her correspondence and manuscripts destroy the image of the cold, unfeeling lady of letters and reveal her childhood miseries, severe nervous illnesses, and passionate love affair with journalist Morton Fullerton. The biographies based on Wharton's papers, *Edith Wharton* (1975) by R. W. B. Lewis and *A Feast of Words: The Triumph of Edith Wharton* (1977) by Cynthia Griffin Wolff, are solid accomplishments that may be said to have inaugurated a new era in Wharton criticism.

So far in the new era critical attention has focused on the novels, although other genres, such as Wharton's interesting travel narratives, are gradually being considered. One of Wharton's bibliographers calls the short stories "the single most neglected aspect of her literary achievement."[8] Indeed, this book is the first full-length study of the stories. I thus consider it introductory and have restricted its scope to the eighty-five published short stories.[9] Much work remains to be done with Wharton's novellas, which ought to be examined as a group, and her stories in manuscript (though most of these are incomplete and offer no surprises). Part 1 of this book provides a critical interpretation of the published stories, and Part 2 contains writings by Wharton wherein she discusses her theory and practice of the short story. A sampling of previous criticism of Wharton's stories can be found in Part 3. The idea is to furnish an overview of the short stories that will not only include analysis of individual tales and exploration of characteristic themes and techniques but also take into account Wharton's intentions and the range of responses to her writing.

Criticism of the published stories has often been organized thematically, as illustrated in the critical selections in Part 3 that comment on Wharton's marriage stories and her ghost stories. Although this division is sometimes useful, it is perhaps time to stress the basic homogeneity of the stories, the fact that the artist tales may concern personal relationships more than art, and that marriages may be disrupted by ghosts. The stories of any particular time period resemble each other more than the art or marriage or ghost stories of another era. I have thus chosen to taken a chronological approach in Part 1. Wharton did not develop much as a short-story writer, and she consistently produced about the same ratio of good, bad, and indifferent stories. But she did change emphases from the early years when she was establishing herself as an artist and experimenting with narrative point of view, to the prewar period when she employed male narrators and showed a new concern with economic institutions; after the war she gradually returned to female characters and narrators and many of the early themes. The first section of my essay in Part 1 is a consideration of Wharton's general short-story practice in terms of her theory, with illustrative analysis of three stories. The second section deals roughly with her early stories (twenty-four stories from 1891 to 1902), the third section with the middle period (thirty-five stories from 1902 to World War I), and the fourth with the later period (twenty-six stories from 1915 to her death in 1937).[10] I say "roughly" because I have not been rigid in adhering to this division and the reader is advised to check the index for particular stories.

Many of my friends have helped with this project, though none should be held responsible for the conclusions I have drawn. I am especially grateful to Josephine Donovan and Mary Moynihan for enjoyable talks about Wharton. Thanks also to the friends who provided the motive—Melody Graulich made me read Wharton and Carol Barringer inspired me—and to the friends who provided the means—Harvey Epstein tamed the word processor and Susan Franzosa shared an eventful trip to New Haven. I appreciate the assistance of the following: Alfred Bendixen; Liz Traynor Fowler; Lucy Freibert; Judith Funston; Stephen Garrison; Susan Goodman; Ellen McNally; Lisa Maloney; the University of New Hampshire; Gordon Weaver; and Annette Zilversmit. Finally, I want to thank Watkins/Loomis Agency, Inc. for allowing me to quote from Wharton's published work, and the Collection of American Literature, the Beinecke Rare Book and Manuscript Library, Yale University for permitting quotation from the Edith Wharton papers.

Notes

1. Her mother tried to write down her childhood tales as she made them up, so Wharton tells us in the unpublished autobiographical manuscript, "Life and I," Edith Wharton Papers, Beinecke Library, Yale University, 11. A portion of "Life and I" has been published in *The Ghost Stories of Edith Wharton* (New York: Scribner's, 1973) as "An Autobiographical Postscript," 275–76. For annotations of selected reviews, see Marlene Springer, *Edith Wharton and Kate Chopin: A Reference Guide* (Boston: G. K. Hall, 1976). A survey of Wharton's reputation as a short-story writer may be found in Patricia R. Plante, "Edith Wharton as Short Story Writer," *Midwest Quarterly* 4 (July 1963): 363–79. Although this survey can be useful, it strongly accentuates the negative (probably because it was written when Wharton's reputation was at its lowest).

2. Compare, for instance, Wharton's comments on plot and unity of effect with Sean O'Faolain's in *The Short Story* (London: Collins, 1948), 154–55: "[I]t is an interesting matter to consider just how much anecdote even a good story can stand without appearing artificial." Of course, Wharton was still writing short stories in the 1920s and could have experimented with form. In fact, some critics (such as Wright—see next note) imply that she must have been terribly old-fashioned and conservative not to have adopted the new ways. But it should be remembered that she was sixty at the time and that most writers are not expected to change styles late in life.

3. These characteristics are associated with the stories of the 1920s by Austin McGiffert Wright in *The American Short Story in the Twenties* (Chicago: University of Chicago Press, 1961). Wright puts Wharton in an earlier period along with writers like Freeman and Garland and compares them with Hemingway and Porter and other innovators of the twenties. His conclusions actually show, however, that Wharton belongs in between the two groups. If some of his generalizations about the earlier writers, such as their fondness for plot, apply to Wharton, others do not. For instance, Wright claims that first-person narrators were rare in the early period and that in all the stories he selected for his sample the narrators were observers rather than protagonists (281); but Wharton is clearly an exception.

4. See, for instance, my discussion of the critical reputations of Carson McCullers, Jean Stafford, and other writers of the time in *Growing Up Female: Adolescent Girlhood in American Fiction* (Westport, Conn.: Greenwood Press, 1985), 89–136, 187–93.

5. The quotations are taken from the following essays collected in *Edith Wharton: A Collection of Essays*, ed. Irving Howe (Englewood Cliffs, N.J.: Prentice-Hall, 1962): Alfred Kazin, "Edith Wharton" (1942), 89, 94; Lionel Trilling, "The Morality of Inertia" (1956), passim; Edmund Wilson, "Justice to Edith Wharton" (1947), 27–28. Considering that she often presents her hapless heroines as being objectified as pieces of furniture, it is interesting that Wharton is also called "finished as a Sheraton sideboard" by Vernon L. Parrington, "Our Literary Aristocrat" (1921), 151. The editor of the volume attempts to be fair in his "Introduction: The Achievement of Edith Wharton," 1–18.

6. Wilson, 23; Kazin, 93; Parrington, 154. The connections between the insistence on "Americanness" and the exclusion of female writers from the literary canon is made in Nina Baym, "Melodramas of Beset Manhood: How Theories of American Fiction Exclude Women Authors," *American Quarterly* 33 (Summer 1981): 123–39.

7. Sandra M. Gilbert and Susan Gubar, "Angel of Devastation: Edith Wharton on the Arts of the Enslaved," in *Sex Changes*, vol. 2 of *No Man's Land: The Place of the Woman Writer in the Twentieth Century* (New Haven: Yale University Press, 1989), 128. Gilbert and Gubar point out, of course, that Wharton cannot be considered a "feminist," as most people would probably define the term today.

8. Alfred Bendixen, "Wharton Studies, 1986–1987: A Bibliographic Essay," *Edith Wharton Newsletter* 5 (Spring 1988): 8.

9. R. W. B. Lewis includes 86 stories in *The Collected Short Stories* (New York: Charles Scribner's Sons, 1968), but one of these, "Her Son" (1932), should be considered a novella, as Lewis later acknowledged. See R. W. B. Lewis, *Edith Wharton: A Biography* (New York: Harper & Row, 1975), 522. Subsequent references to this biography will be noted in the text.

10. The 24 early stories include the stories collected in *A Greater Inclination* (1899) and *Crucial Instances* (1901), those referred to by Lewis as "early

uncollected stories" (1891–1900), and "The House of the Dead Hand," which was not published until 1904 but was written in 1898. The 35 stories of the middle period include "The Letter" (1904), "The Introducers" (1905), "Les Metteurs en Scène" (1908), and the stories collected in *The Descent of Man* (1904), *The Hermit and the Wild Woman* (1908), *Tales of Men and Ghosts* (1910), and *Xingu* (1916), with the exception of "Coming Home," the only story written after the start of the war. The 26 late stories include "Coming Home" (1915), "Writing a War Story" (1919), and the stories collected in *Here and Beyond* (1926), *Certain People* (1930), *Human Nature* (1933), *The World Over* (1936), and *Ghosts* (1937).

Part 1

THE SHORT FICTION

Wharton's Telling of the Short Story: Theory and Practice

It is as much the lack of general culture as of original vision which makes so many of the younger novelists, in Europe as in America, attach undue importance to trifling innovations. Original vision is never much afraid of using accepted forms; and only the cultivated intelligence escapes the danger of regarding as intrinsically new what may be a mere superficial change, or the reversion to a discarded trick of technique.[1]

This is a typical statement from Edith Wharton's *The Writing of Fiction*, which appeared in 1925 when she was over sixty. Wharton catalogs the younger writers' faults and complains about the supposedly new stream of consciousness technique; she considers it a reversion to an old French trick and, rightly or wrongly, rejects it as being insufficiently selective. Associating herself with the "accepted forms," Wharton promotes instead the "strength of tradition" and "the old way of selection and design"(*WF*, 154–55).

Her comments must have sounded old-fashioned in the 1920s. Another explanation for her lack of visibility and prestige as a short-story writer, in addition to her sex and the other reasons I discussed in my preface, may be her refusal to seem modern and experimental. In some ways Wharton was only posing as the conservative grande dame upholding tradition: the grande dame was writing stories at the time about a Christian missionary losing his faith and a shabby farmer having sex with a ghost; as she always managed to remind the younger novelists, she was the same Edith Wharton who at the beginning of her career had been admonished, "Have you never known a respectable woman? If you have, in the name of decency write about her!"[2] But if the attitudes and subject matter were modern, the form was not.

In "Telling a Short Story," the second chapter of *The Writing of Fiction*, Wharton advocates the well-made story.[3] The writer must have a plan and choose every detail to fit; the first page must contain the germ of the last. The "old way of selection and design" is even more important in the short story than it is in the novel because of the story's compactness. Only great skill in "the disengaging of crucial moments from the welter of existence" allows the writer to be economical without violating the need for verisimilitude (*WF*, 14). As Wharton notes in another essay of the writer's creation of dialogue, "His [*sic*] characters must talk as they would in reality, and yet everything not relevant to his tale must be eliminated. The secret of success lies in his instinct of selection."[4]

In selecting details that produce a sense of reality, or "the impression of vividness, of *presentness*" that Wharton finds essential to the short story, the writer should follow two rules: "The effect of compactness and instantaneity sought in the short story is attained mainly by the observance of two 'unities'—the old traditional one of time, and that other, more modern and complex, which requires that any rapidly enacted episode shall be seen through only one pair of eyes." The unity of time, she explains, means that there should be no lapses of time long enough to suggest change in the characters. The unity of vision, for which she duly acknowledges Henry James, has a corollary—"never to let the character who serves as reflector record anything not naturally within his register." Writers who fail to choose the reflector carefully and understand the mind chosen may disturb the larger design by attributing to the reflector "incongruities of thought and metaphor."

As she presents her literary theory, Wharton occasionally cautions us that there is no formula for writing good short stories and rules are made to be broken. Yet the reader receives the overall impression that there *are* rules—there is, after all, a "never"—and that the short story has become a rather fixed form. Wharton might have accomplished even more than she did with the short story had her conception of form been less rigid. Her ideas about point of view could be particularly restrictive, as I will later discuss. Although in nearly all her eighty-five stories she adhered to the principle that the episode be seen through only one pair of eyes, the exceptions are revealing; fully half of her very best stories admit other points of view.[5] Is this coincidence, or could there be a liberating effect in bending one's own rules?

At any rate, in "Telling a Short Story," Wharton the critic seems to sense that her statements emphasize some aspects of her theory at the expense of others. She notes that "in writing of the short story I may have seemed to dwell too much on the need of considering every detail in its plan and development" (*WF*, 75). In the last section of the essay she suddenly comes up with various "dangers" that short-story authors might succumb to in the very attempt to write with economy and plan. They might produce a mere sketch or summary, having left out the most significant dimensions; they might fail to look deeply enough into a subject and so acquire the "indolent habit of decorating its surface." Now Wharton stresses the slowness of the creative process, the need for meditation and patience. If an author were to hold a story situation in mind, letting it grow slowly and gradually "reveal all its potentialities," the resulting tale "would have the warm scent and flavor of a fruit ripened in the sun instead of the insipidity of one forced in a hothouse."

This metaphor is not an isolated one. The second half of "Telling a Short Story" contains a remarkable succession of organic metaphors. Not only does the story become a fruit offered to the reader "as a natural unembellished fragment of experience, detached like a ripe fruit from the tree," it is also an essence extracted and distilled from a plant and a jewel that must be presented from just the right angle to make it "give out all its fires." The writer "broods" until the story emerges from the egg, and Wharton repeats the term "ab ovo." Lastly, the story is like a fire or explosion. The most frequently quoted part of Wharton's essay seems to be her relation of an anecdote from Benvenuto Cellini's autobiography. When Cellini and his father sat at the hearth and saw a salamander in the fire, the father boxed the son's ears so that he would never forget what he had seen. Wharton views the anecdote as a lesson for the short-story writer: you must make a vivid beginning, but don't box your reader's ear unless you have a salamander, that is, something worth telling, waiting in the flames. Sometimes the "blaze" or "flash" seems more like a veritable explosion, as Wharton compares the short story to the novel and contends that the story must "suggest illimitable air within a narrow space" because "the trajectory is so short that flash and sound nearly coincide."

These romantic metaphors are all the more striking in a text seemingly devoted to order, form, tradition, and even the classical "unities." Wharton characteristically took what she wanted from disparate traditions: she was the author of Gothic romance as well as the novelist of manners.[6] However, one might expect a believer in Edgar Allan Poe's theory of "pre-established design" to use Poe's figures, so that the story would correspond to a skillfully constructed invention or an intricate picture with a "decorated surface."[7] One might also expect the woman who was fascinated by architecture, wrote *The Decoration of Houses* (1897), and treasured her friendship with Henry James to pick up on James's comparison of the art of fiction to the building of a house. Interestingly, she does so but principally in connection with the novel, "that slowly built-up monument in which every stone has its particular weight and thrust to carry." In a 1907 letter to novelist Robert Grant, Wharton contrasts her abilities as novelist and as short-story writer, using this metaphor. In 1925, in *The Writing of Fiction*, she employs the house image in discussing the novel and natural growth images in the chapter on the short story. According to Wharton, one builds a novel and hatches a short story.

That which is hatched—or ripened or exploded—in a story is what Wharton calls the "situation." Situation as "the main concern of the short story" distinguishes it from the novel, where the main concern is character, specifically character developed over time. Although Wharton does not define exactly what she means by "situation," she clearly intends it to include but not be restricted to plot. She sees plot in any rigid sense, "in the sense of an elaborate puzzle into which a given number of characters have to be arbitrarily fitted," as an outdated convention(*WF*, 82). But her own practice, in addition to her approving references to plot-oriented stories by authors like Guy de Maupassant, Rudyard Kipling, and Robert Louis Stevenson, shows that she considered stories where the situation consists principally of action to be acceptable versions of the short story.

Wharton's postwar comedies rely heavily on plot, and stories like "Velvet Ear-pads" (1926), composed around the same time as *The Writing of Fiction*, are dominated by farcical action. She also liked to write Mediterranean melodramas. Early examples, such as "The Confessional" (1901) and "The Letter" (1904), may be considered by-products of her research on historical Italy for her first novel, *The Valley of Decision* (1902); but she produced later stories, like "Dieu D'Amour" (1928), in the same vein. These stories often degenerate into "elaborate puzzles" in which Wharton forgets a few of the crucial pieces. Sometimes her attention is more fully engaged, as in "A Venetian Night's Entertainment" (1903), a colorful account of a con game in eighteenth-century Venice. Perhaps this story, absolutely all plot, succeeds in being entertaining because it attempts no more.

In general, however, Wharton sought a story "situation" that would include, in addition to plot, a significant subject or theme and the consciousness of the character from whose viewpoint the events are seen. This practice made it difficult for her to summarize her stories. In a 1909 letter she warns an editor that when she tries it, "I produce a very bald and often erroneous effect, and I can only ask you to believe that the part I leave out is *always* what constitutes for me the psychological value of the story."[8] Wharton's best stories are so much of a piece that it is hard to explain the situation without repeating the whole story. When one can summarize, the story may seem ludicrous. "The Journey" (1899) concerns a woman traveling on a train with her husband's body; because she fears being put off the train, she keeps secret the fact that he has died during the journey. Nothing else happens. Although it is truly effective, the story does not sound promising.

Occasionally, different critics will summarize a Wharton story so variously that one wonders if they have read the same work. Critic A describes "Roman Fever" (1934), one of Wharton's most widely anthologized stories, as "a very light little comedy" about "the decorum of the great days." Critic B finds it a "bleak story about the fallen condition of women in patriarchal culture."[9] If I had to characterize "Roman Fever" in one sentence, I would call it a story simultaneously light and bleak about the impossibility of escaping the past. All three descriptions obviously fail to convey what Wharton calls "the psychological value of the story." Some further attention to "Roman Fever" may help illuminate Wharton's application of the main points of her theory: her emphasis on situation as the main concern of the short story and her insistence on a well-made story that is at the same time an organic product.

The action in "Roman Fever" has taken place in the past. All that occurs in the present is that two American widows spend an afternoon on the terrace of a Roman restaurant recalling their youth in Rome. They had been in love with the same man. Mrs. Slade was engaged to him and eventually married him, while Mrs. Ansley fell ill, suddenly left Rome, and married someone else. Now they have returned with their grown-up daughters who at the beginning of the story go off in search of adventure. At first Mrs. Slade and Mrs. Ansley reminisce in a desultory way "with a sort of diffused serenity."[10] Gradually the tension builds, as the jealous Mrs. Slade obsessively probes the past and forces her friend's revelation, in the last line of the story, that young Babs Ansley was fathered by Mr. Slade.

The story is eminently well made. Wharton has her unities of time and vision, as the story is revealed primarily from the point of view of Mrs. Slade,[11] and every detail fits perfectly into the whole. The first page, where we hear Babs's laughing farewell, contains the germ of the last. The hints that prepare us for the surprise ending are beautifully placed throughout the story; they arise from very natural-sounding dialogue, as we discover that Babs is older than the Slade girl and seems too vivacious to be the daughter of such dull people as Mrs. Slade considers the Ansleys. We do not suspect Mrs. Ansley's hurried marriage because the competitive Mrs. Slade views it solely as an attempt to beat her to the altar. Wharton cleverly plants the clues so that at the end of the story, just as at the end of a good mystery, the reader exclaims, "Of course! I should have known all along."

However, the story does not exist solely for an ending in the manner of O. Henry. Part of Wharton's skill lies in forcing the reader to imagine the agonies of Mrs. Slade's "Of course!" The situation in "Roman Fever" includes not only the anecdote and punch line but the complex consciousness of Mrs. Slade. Ironically, although Wharton rejected "stream of consciousness" as a technique because she viewed it as precluding selectivity, she was always adept at reproducing inner consciousness. She could give the general effect of a mind at work, moving from insight to rationalization and back, while making the thoughts of the reflectors sound like their speech;[12] one never forgets, for instance, that Mrs. Slade is a society matron (she thinks that Mrs. Ansley "twenty-five years ago, had been exquisitely lovely—no, you wouldn't believe it, would you? . . . though, of course, still charming, distinguished" [2:835; Wharton's ellipses]).

Summary makes Mrs. Slade sound unpleasant in her envy and competitiveness, and in some ways she is; but the reader is asked to empathize with her, even while being supplied with the details that undercut her version of reality. Wharton believed that "reading should be a creative act as well as writing." She counted on her readers "meeting me halfway" and "filling in the gaps in my narrative." Although Wharton made these comments in an essay on the ghost story, Jean Frantz Blackall argues convincingly that she used ellipsis frequently in all her stories to force the reader to fill in the gaps. She wanted to go beyond reproducing the rhythms of thought and "entice the reader to enter into imaginative collaboration with the writer."[13] The reader must "complete the thought, fathom the joke, enter into the emotional vibrations of the characters" (156). Many Wharton stories invite readers to share the subjective experience of the main character (at the same time that they judge it), and the story can be characterized in terms of the experience. Thus "Autres Temps . . ." (1911) is no more about changing social mores than how it feels to be a pariah, "After Holbein"

(1928) no more about New York society than how it feels to be old and losing grip on one's mind and body.

In "Roman Fever" we experience with Mrs. Slade how it feels to be haunted by one's past, to be no longer able to suppress it as it demands resolution. Mrs. Slade would like to forget her youth in Rome, just as she has tried to forget her son who died in boyhood because "the thought of the boy had become unbearable" (2: 836). Yet she cannot help "brooding" (2: 838) and obsessively questioning Mrs. Ansley about the past. She has an inkling of the awful truth, which she would like to avoid, but "simply can't bear it any longer—!" (2: 840) and feels compelled to "get the whole thing off my mind" (2: 842). Every time her friend replies vaguely or changes the subject Mrs. Slade resolves to stop pressing, and then something, usually her jealousy, urges her on. It makes her sum up to her advantage ("I had him for twenty-five years. And you had nothing") and provokes the final revelation that Mrs. Ansley had Barbara (2: 843).

Mrs. Slade realizes her jealousy has become a kind of sickness. She feels "self-disgust" at her inability to think more kindly of her friend: "Would she never cure herself of envying her?" (2: 839). Her error lies in underestimating the extent and power of the disease. Typically, Wharton supplies the reader with greater understanding without going outside Mrs. Slade's consciousness. Mrs. Slade would prefer a more exciting daughter, like Babs: "She wished that Jenny would fall in love—with the wrong man, even; that she might have to be watched, outmaneuvered, rescued. And instead, it was Jenny who watched her mother, kept her out of draughts, made sure she had taken her tonic" (2: 836). Later, while she confesses to Mrs. Ansley that she doesn't understand why she got an angel instead of a dynamo, she does recognize that "if I were a chronic invalid I'd—well, I think I'd rather be in Jenny's hands" (2: 838). By now the reader realizes that Mrs. Slade has been lucky in her daughter (not all ironies of fate in Wharton's fiction turn out bleak and depressing). Mrs. Slade is indeed a "chronic invalid" whom Jenny has been wise to watch and will now have to nurse.

Of course, nearly every Wharton story extends beyond the personal to the social realm, and Mrs. Slade's advanced case of "Roman fever" is not restricted to her alone but forms part of a veritable epidemic. Mrs. Ansley has clearly been affected. Not only was she so ill in her youth as to be confined to her bed, but she still suffers from envy and

competitiveness. Wharton employs various techniques to reveal the reactions of non-point-of-view characters. Sometimes she gives them a
personal emblem by which the reader can gauge their feelings. In Mrs.
Ansley's case, as a recent article has shown, that emblem is knitting.[14]
Although Mrs. Slade misinterprets her friend's attention to knitting as
indifference ("She can knit—in the face of *this*!" [2: 838]), Mrs. Ansley
uses it to control her growing agitation and fend off Mrs. Slade's prob-
ing, for Mrs. Ansley too wants to preserve her illusions of the past.
Finally, when Mrs. Slade pushes too far, the knitting "slid in a panic-
stricken heap to the ground" (2: 840) and Mrs. Ansley actively joins
battle. She cannot resist asserting her superiority by telling Mrs. Slade
she feels sorry for her and, finally, playing her trump card as she "began
to move ahead of Mrs. Slade toward the stairway" (2: 843). Mrs. Ansley
ends one up but as sick as Mrs. Slade. Mrs. Slade was correct when
she reflected at the beginning of the story that "the similarity of their
lot had again drawn them together" (2: 835).[15] They both have Roman
fever.

   Wharton's title, as is often the case with her titles, reflects the controlling metaphor of the story, in this instance illness and disease. The
disease of Mrs. Slade and Mrs. Ansley is common enough to have a
name. In their grandmothers' day, the two recall, Roman fever meant
the chill one caught in Rome after sunset; that illness killed Henry
James's Daisy Miller after she disgraced herself meeting an adventurer
in the Colosseum. Wharton evokes James's story in setting up the
event in the past that led to the conception of Babs Ansley. The young
Mrs. Ansley had told Mrs. Slade about a great-aunt who loved the same
man as her younger sister and sent her sister out to the Forum at night,
whereupon she caught the fever and died. Taking this story to heart,
Mrs. Slade sent Mrs. Ansley a note purporting to be from Mr. Slade
asking her to meet him in the Colosseum; instead of getting rid of her
rival, this ploy led Mrs. Ansley to answer the note and summon Mr.
Slade to the Colosseum, whereupon Babs was conceived. One can thus
see how Critic A views the story as light and comic, satirizing the "decorum of the great days." In this reading, one of the post-Jamesian
meanings of Roman fever can be the fever of mating. Wharton was no
doubt amused by her evocation of full-blown intercourse in the Colosseum where Daisy Miller had her more innocent assignation.

   But there is also Critic B's view of the story as a bleak account of the
"fallen condition of women in patriarchal culture," where women's "al-
legiance must always be to men and never to one another" (Donovan,

82). From Mrs. Ansley's great-aunt to Mrs. Ansley and Mrs. Slade themselves, women are shown wracked by the disease of jealousy and competition. It made the great-aunt kill her sister and poisoned Mrs. Slade's and Mrs. Ansley's lives. Even after Mr. Slade's death, this sickness has kept them from taking pleasure in one another; they remain "Mrs. Slade" and "Mrs. Ansley," defined through their ties to men, and still competing. Mrs. Slade projects this script onto the next generation, as she imagines Jenny and Babs vying for one of their dates; she can only attribute the girls' companionship to Jenny's being used as a "foil" (2: 838). Wharton gives us no hints as to whether the girls themselves already suffer from the scourge of Roman fever.

The Roman setting is, of course, not only essential in providing a context for the disease but also completely appropriate to a story about the past. Wharton ranks with the greatest short-story writers in her creation of setting and atmosphere. She possessed such skill in evoking place that sometimes a brief visit would provide her enough material for a brilliant setting, as in "The Seed of the Faith" (1919), based on her trip to Morocco. Wharton knew Rome and had visited the city just before composing "Roman Fever" (Lewis, 522), but the greatest requisite of this story is that the setting not be overdone. Thus Wharton contents herself with telling the reader Mrs. Slade and Mrs. Ansley can see the Palatine, the Forum, and the Colosseum from the terrace of their restaurant. There are no long descriptions or paeans to the glory of Rome. In the beginning of the story the city seems a mere decorative backdrop. Only gradually, as the past wells up to overwhelm the two women, does the reader come to feel the presence of the Roman past and realize that Rome is an integral part of the story. For the women "too many memories rose from the lengthening shadows of those august ruins" (2: 838). They literally as well as figuratively view the ruins of the past; the "dusky secret mass of the Colosseum" that seems to loom over them at the end of the story has long been an actor in their drama (2: 843).

The fact that the Roman setting is so woven into the fabric of the story reminds us of Wharton's desire for the story to be an organic growth. Her success in making "Roman Fever," like all her best stories, "a fruit ripened in the sun" could be inferred simply from the interesting language critics have used to discuss it. John Gerlach, whose subject is surprise endings and not at all Wharton's literary theory or general practice, finds the conclusion of "Roman Fever" successful in "making the story whole" and "deepening" it: "The ending

11

clarifies and binds together the beginning and the middle, revealing what in retrospect is both latent and inevitable. Indirection was only apparent; what is calm is so only as a means of concealing volcanic truth."[16] Wharton's own metaphors can also be found in R. W. B. Lewis's account of her late work. He thinks "a fresh kind of power can be felt welling up." "Roman Fever" and a few other works were written out of an imagination stirred by light within (527) and reveal "a serenity that pervades the narrative in a long atmospheric glow" (524).

An element of Wharton's short-story theory and practice that is more complex than I have yet indicated is her treatment of point of view. In an article on narrative technique, Michael J. O'Neal quotes a lengthy passage from "Roman Fever" and argues that it would be an oversimplification to declare the passage narrated from the point of view of Mrs. Slade and label it selective omniscience.[17] He thinks Wharton creates a "multi-layered point of view" by blending several voices, including those of Mrs. Slade, a distanced author-narrator, and "society," the voice of the late nineteenth-century New York society that has shaped the characters' attitudes (270). This is a bit subtler than Wharton's brisk remarks in "Telling a Short Story" would indicate.

Perhaps Wharton made only perfunctory comments on point of view because she believed James had already exhausted the topic. At any rate, she stresses the mechanical, as in her insistence on never letting the characters who serve as reflectors record anything beyond their registers. But, as O'Neal points out, Wharton at her best makes the reflecting mind seem open, "not a closed mind, locked within its own idiom, having the negative virtue of avoiding incongruities" (271). She does say the reflecting mind should be "so situated, and so constituted, as to take the widest possible view." In order to examine some of the effects she produces with point of view, I will consider two more Wharton stories in this chapter, "The Other Two" (1904) and "The Pretext" (1908). The former is a much-anthologized story that Lewis considers her best; the latter has scarcely been noticed.

With "The Other Two" one enters familiar Wharton territory: the story takes place in New York, has a male reflector, and concerns marriage and divorce. It illustrates as well as "Roman Fever" does how Wharton conceives "situation." The situation is simply that a man has married a twice-divorced woman. Nothing happens; nothing is resolved. We do not even get the gradual revelation of complicated past actions, as in "Roman Fever." Lewis says, "[I]t has scarcely any plot—

it has no real arrangement of incidents, there being too few incidents to arrange—but consists almost entirely in the leisurely, coolly comic process by which a situation is revealed to those involved in it . . . in particular to Waythorn, his wife's third husband" (1: xiv).

If there is scarcely any plot, the story is structured around two "crucial moments," to use Wharton's term, that she takes great pains to set up. We will recall that Wharton admonishes the writer to find "the real meaning of a situation" by "letting it reveal all its potentialities." One potentiality of "a man has married a twice-divorced woman" is that the divorced husbands will refuse to stay properly divorced. The wife may not be able to separate them in either her mind or her drawing room— and thus the two crucial moments, the first when Alice Waythorn forgets that it was her second husband who took cognac and pours a shot into Waythorn's coffee, and the second, at the end of the story, when all the husbands show up for tea.

The technical difficulties of leading up to these scenes are obvious, and it is a tribute to Wharton's skill that she succeeds in making them seem natural. The ending, a total success, is well prepared for, as one ex has visited the Waythorn residence several times to see his daughter and the other has been conducting business with Waythorn. The cognac presents more of a difficulty because Waythorn must know the habits of the second husband, Varick, and Wharton has to resort to Waythorn's accidentally having lunch in the same restaurant and witnessing Varick pour cognac in his coffee. Her reliance on coincidence is one aspect of her writing that has frequently been criticized.[18] She usually tries to disguise it, in some stories not very successfully; in this case she cleverly makes it part of the situation. That is, Waythorn "had known when he married that his wife's former husbands were both living, and that amid the multiplied contact of modern existence there were a thousand chances to one that he would run against one or the other" (1: 388). But Waythorn has never quite absorbed this truth or, as we say, "realized the situation." In the beginning he had a simple view, having "fancied that a woman can shed her past like a man" (1: 393), but in the course of the story he discovers the true complexities of having married a divorced woman.

As his situation is fully revealed to him, Waythorn completely changes his view of Alice. At the beginning of the story he relishes seeing her "under his own roof" in "his house" (1: 380); the rooms seem "full of bridal intimacy" (1: 382). He admires her "composure" (1: 380) and "the unperturbed gaiety which kept her fresh and elastic"

(1: 381). But when the first husband has to be admitted to visit the daughter, Waythorn, in a rather blatant sexual image, broods about his front door having "admitted another man who had as much right to enter it as himself" (1: 383). Whereas he had previously admired Alice's composure, he begins to view her as untroubled by the encounters with the ex-husbands and thus a bit insensitive. Wharton's first crucial moment, with the cognac, is exquisite, worth all the stage managing. As Alice pours his coffee, Waythorn admires her hair. He thinks "how light and slender she was" and feels himself "yielding again to the joy of possessorship. They were his, those white hands with their flitting motions, his the light haze of hair the lips and eyes" (1: 386). Suddenly she pours the cognac in his coffee.

From this instant, Waythorn's view of Alice turns almost entirely negative. He even constructs a new past for her. Although she had implied that her first husband was brutal and he knows her second committed adultery, he concludes from his perception of Haskett's shabbiness and his new knowledge of Varick's finances that Alice deliberately engineered an economic rise through her husbands (Waythorn is a stockbroker). Waythorn outwardly complies with the situation, accepting a cup of tea at the end of the story, along with other comforts his wife knows how to provide; he even begins to "reckon up the advantages which accrued from it, to ask himself if it were not better to own a third of a wife who knew how to make a man happy than a whole one who had lacked opportunity to acquire the art" (1: 394). But he can never again delight in his wife. Toward the end of "The Other Two" Waythorn conjures up another sexual image: "She was 'as easy as an old shoe'—a shoe that too many feet had worn. . . . Alice Haskett—Alice Varick—Alice Waythorn—she had been each in turn, and had left hanging to each name a little of her privacy, a little of her personality, a little of the inmost self where the unknown god abides" (1: 393). This passage, which is striking enough to be quoted by everyone who discusses the story, gains in interest when we recall that Waythorn had originally thought Alice "fresh and elastic" (1: 381).

In the course of the story Alice does not change, but Waythorn's view of her moves from one extreme to another. For a change in perception to form the substance of a story is typical of Wharton's practice throughout her career. "The Other Two" bears a strong resemblance to a very early work, "The Lamp of Psyche" (1895), in which the title directly reflects the theme; the mythical Psyche, having been forbidden to look at her lover Cupid, lost him after she took a lamp and

examined him while he slept. Wharton's heroine, Delia Corbett, lives blissfully in Paris with her "perfect" second husband until she takes a closer look at his past (1: 45). When they visit Boston, her aunt asks what Corbett, an American, did in the Civil War. Corbett says he cannot remember why he stayed home, and Delia decides he is a coward. She gradually modifies her view of him until "for the passionate worship which she had paid her husband she substituted a tolerant affection" (1: 57). There is no indication that Corbett is truly a coward, rather than a wealthy idler who was never expected to fight, but in either case he cannot survive being viewed in Boston light.

The same holds true of Alice Waythorn, the connection being made by Waythorn's sense of "groping about with a dark-lantern in his wife's past" (1: 391). "The Other Two" is a more subtle and complex story, however. Wharton reveals some unsureness in her earlier work in setting up the situation and establishing the point of view. She occasionally discusses what she calls Delia's "foibles" directly with the reader, even in one instance apologizing for Delia's having been infatuated with Corbett before her first husband died: "The high-minded reader may infer from this that I am presenting him, in the person of Delia Corbett, with a heroine whom he would not like his wife to meet; but how many of us could face each other in the calm consciousness of moral rectitude if our inmost desire were not hidden under a convenient garb of lawful observance?" (1: 43)

In "The Other Two" the author has distanced herself, in line with her developing literary theory by which she came to scorn the "slovenly habit" of authors "tumbling in and out of their characters' minds, and then suddenly drawing back to scrutinize them from the outside" (*WF,* 89). One occasionally hears the voice of the author-narrator in "The Other Two"; for instance, in the "old shoe" passage Wharton enthusiasts will recognize in the phrase "the inmost self where the unknown god abides" a familiar image more akin to Wharton than her hero.[19] But the author-narrator voice is muted in this story, more successfully "blended" in O'Neal's sense than in "The Lamp of Psyche." Instead of directly pointing out Waythorn's "foibles," as she does Delia's (1: 43–44), Wharton hints at the limitations of his vision. She provides the means, through his description of his wife's actions, for alternative views.

Waythorn comes to believe, as I have indicated, that Alice has hardly been affected by the encounters with her ex-husbands. Old shoe that she is, she easily adjusts to fit any situation; she lacks Waythorn's "sensibility which made him suffer so acutely" (1: 388). But Alice's actions belie this interpretation. When she has to announce her first husband's impending visit, she looks worried, neglects to smile, has trembling lips, and turns red under Waythorn's gaze (1: 382). We have only his assertion that after he finally tells her to forget about it and "her lips waver back into a smile," she has truly forgotten (1: 383). In fact, all the indications of disturbance beneath the placid surface are repeated during other incidents—the wavering smile, the trembling, and the blush (1: 386, 392). Thus the reader is prepared for the end of the story where Alice acts the smiling hostess for the three men, and Wharton can suggest with great economy the feelings under the polished veneer. When Alice sees the first husband she makes use of her smile in "veiling a slight tremor of surprise" (1: 395). As the second enters her view, "Her smile faded for a moment, but she recalled it quickly, with a scarcely perceptible side-glance at Waythorn" (1: 396).

Alice's actions reveal a person very different from the one Waythorn sees—a desperate woman struggling to perform the increasingly difficult, finally impossible task of pleasing Waythorn. The serenity and smiles can be interpreted as the result of a rather horrifying assertion of self-control in the attempt to give Waythorn what he wants. Only once does Alice allow a "flame of anger" to pass over her face and, of course, "she subdued it instantly" (1: 391). The "side-glance" to check her progress at pleasing has become second nature to her. Waythorn blames Alice: the "old shoe" passage, narrated very closely from his point of view, gives the impression that in leaving a bit of her personality hanging on each of her former names Alice has cheated Waythorn of his due. But when she is viewed independently of Waythorn, the passage suggests an identity in shreds. Wharton also manages to place Alice's disintegration within a larger context, intimating that it is less a personal peculiarity than a social problem. Alice's twelve-year-old daughter used to be "straight," but now "she's too anxious to please—and she don't always tell the truth" (1: 390). Is the cause really the French governess, as the girl's father thinks, or initiation into womanhood?

Of course, this broader context is beyond Waythorn. He dimly perceives some of the contradictions of patriarchal marriage. For instance, he sees that the requirement that the wife serve the husband and adapt herself to his desires conflicts with the requirement that she be fresh and unused. Alice does so well at the "art" of "how to make a man happy" because she has learned it: "he knew exactly to what training

she owed her skill" (1: 394). But Waythorn cannot cure himself of looking at the situation through the eyes of other men; he even wonders
what men from other classes, his footman and clerks, think about it.
Waythorn can only speak the language of patriarchy, in particular of
Wall Street, and Wharton thereby provides another clue to the limitations of his vision.

I have already quoted several passages that speak to Waythorn's "joy
of possessorship" (1: 386), his appreciation of Alice as another beautiful
ornament to adorn "his" house. One can hardly miss this aspect of a
character who refers to owning a third of a wife. In fact, Alice becomes
to Waythorn more a piece of real estate than an ornament. He accepts
her first husband "as a lien on the property" (1: 392) and finally compares himself "to a member of a syndicate. He held so many shares in
his wife's personality and his predecessors were his partners in the
business" (1: 393). With Waythorn a stockbroker Wharton can let the
financial metaphors run riot. The story is full of puns and wordplay, as
in most of her best work. For instance, before he married Alice, Waythorn "discounted" the gossip about her—an uncommon lapse for a
man who counts everything (1: 381). As he comes increasingly to discuss his marriage as a "transaction" (1: 393), the reader begins to doubt
his reconstruction of Alice's past. Perhaps she shed her first two husbands in order to get ahead financially; she could be an early version
of the repellent Undine Spragg in Wharton's *The Custom of the Country*
(1913), who steps on husbands as rungs in a ladder.[20] However, there
is no evidence in the story that Alice's motives are economic and every
indication that the market-mad Waythorn conceives the world in financial terms.

The dominance of the marketplace in "The Other Two," which was
published in 1904, recalls *The House of Mirth*, which came out the following year. In the novel, often considered Wharton's best, Lily Bart
proves a more delicate ornament than Alice Haskell/Varick/Waythorn;
when she refuses to be bought and sold in the mart, this flower is
destroyed. The novel and story even share some specifics: Alice's
daughter is named Lily, and her second husband Gus (an important
character in *The House of Mirth*). Wharton had no consistent practice
regarding the relationship between her novels and short stories. As
Richard H. Lawson points out, one should be "cautious about viewing
the stories as seeds of the novels, for sometimes the story is a byproduct of the novel-planning and novel-writing process—a byproduct that
saw print before the novel."[21] Whether seed or by-product, the stories

usually bear the very loose relationship to the novels of having been composed in a parallel frame of mind. During the period of "The Other Two" and *The House of Mirth* Wharton's imagination was focused on marriage as a social and financial institution that reduces women to property.

Literary critics have not taken a sympathetic view of *The House of Mirth*'s Waythornish businessmen, even Lawrence Selden, the principal male character, who thinks as he strolls up Madison Avenue with Lily "that she must have cost a great deal to make, that a great many dull and ugly people must, in some mysterious way, have been sacrificed to produce her."[22] But most critics have fully accepted Waythorn's perspective, arguing that he comes to a "more complete understanding of Alice" and experiences a "final illumination" with his perception of her as an old shoe.[23] It is easier to overlook Waythorn's limitations than it is Selden's if only because *The House of Mirth* contains various points of view; what a different novel it would be if we saw Lily only through Selden's eyes!

Besides the fact that events in "The Other Two" are filtered solely through Waythorn, it is clear that he comes to adopt and express some of Wharton's own opinions (Waythorn is an anagram of Wharton-y, a joke she probably intended).[24] We know that Wharton had ambivalent feelings toward divorce, particularly during this period of her life when she was considering it for herself. She makes Waythorn learn that divorce cannot be as "easy" as he (and presumably Alice, because she obtained two) had originally thought. But this does not mean that Waythorn's vision is not also sharply limited in the ways we have already noted. The axiom that one should always question the reflector's version of reality in a Wharton short story has a corollary that the more obvious, the more Wharton-y, a viewpoint seems, the more it needs to be questioned.

A good illustration is "The Pretext," a story that has been universally misinterpreted. Most of the small amount of critical attention given this story has been devoted to the biographical connections: Wharton wrote it as she embarked on a love affair with journalist Morton Fullerton, and she got the idea from her friend Henry James. In a letter written in January 1908 James relinquishes his rights in "our petite donnée," which they had discussed the year before. A young English acquaintance of James had attended Harvard and apparently fallen in love with a professor's wife, leading him to defy his family and break his engagement. Wharton and James imagined for the "original limited anecdote" a "crown and consummation," in which an English relative visits the professor's wife to remonstrate with her and is greatly startled by her "impossibility."[25]

James does not explain why the wife is so impossible, but Millicent Bell sums up Wharton's finished story as follows. The young man has named the wife as the reason for breaking his engagement. But when the English relative meets the wife she realizes "that, of course, some other woman is the *real* reason; she sees at a glance the 'impossibility' for that role of this middle-aged image of American propriety." The relative informs the wife, who "imagines that his love for her has been the cause" of the breakup, that the young man "has simply used her as a 'pretext.'"[26] No wonder Lewis finds the story an oblique statement about Wharton's relationship with Fullerton (Lewis, 193). Morton Fullerton was slightly younger; he openly pursued women and at the beginning of their affair had just gotten engaged to his cousin, whom he soon abandoned. Wharton was understandably anxious. As we might expect, "The Pretext" is told from the point of view of the middle-aged woman, and in spite of the complications of the donnée and involved "consummation," the action is almost entirely internal, our interest engaged by the changing emotions of the reflector.

The story begins brilliantly as Mrs. Margaret Ransom, wife of a university lawyer, "springs" upstairs to her bedroom after the visit of Guy Dawnish, the young Englishman she and her husband have befriended during his year's stay in New England. Although Margaret remains "slender" and "light of foot" and feels "girlish" after her talk with Guy (1: 632), she sees in her mirror thinning hair and a lined face: "It was [a] face which had grown middle-aged while it waited for the joys of youth" (1: 632). If she steps back from the mirror, the lingering pink from her blush disguises the wrinkles and if she lets her hair down . . . "but was it right to try to make one's hair look thicker and wavier than it really was?" (1: 633).

Wharton has great fun contrasting Margaret's new sensual awareness with the remnants of her "rigid New England ancestry" (1: 633). Even her looking glass is a "cramped eagle-topped mirror above her plain prim dressing table"; naturally it has an "unflattering surface," for that is the only kind of "meager concession to the weakness of the flesh" allowed by the puritanical town of Wentworth. When poor Margaret tries to "collect herself," as she has been taught from childhood, she realizes her sensations have never before been scattered but "had lain in neatly sorted and easily accessible bundles on the high shelves of a perfectly ordered moral consciousness. And now—now that for the first time they *needed* collecting—now that the little winged and scattered bits of self were dancing madly down the vagrant winds of fancy, she knew no spell to call them to the fold again" (1: 633).

Margaret's husband interrupts her fantasies to summon her to a university dinner where he will be speaking. He cannot imagine why she would have locked the bedroom door, and her hair is a mess—she looks like a bad woman from New York. During her husband's speech Margaret nearly faints from the heat and is led outside by Guy Dawnish to the banks of the campus river. Here in a wonderful scene in a sort of classical moonlit glade, described very differently from the rest of Wentworth, the two say good-bye, for Guy must return to England. Wharton succeeds completely in keeping Guy's feelings and motives vague, as the plot requires, yet making the encounter wholly realistic. There is a great deal of shy, furtive touching of hands and of stammers and pauses (plus a veritable cascade of Wharton ellipses). Guy has something he wants to tell Margaret but she, guilty and fearful, begs him not to speak. She can hardly hear him anyway because "her heart was beating so violently that there was a rush in her ears like the noise of the river after rain, and she did not immediately make out what he was answering." Amusingly, "as she recovered her lucidity she said to herself that, whatever he was saying, she must not hear it" (1: 643). The scene comes to a close as, in a Wharton pun, "the 'speaking' was at an end" and Margaret's husband appears (1: 644).

The second half of the story details Margaret's changing reactions to this incident, which she thinks of as her one hour of life. Sometimes she feels lonely and regrets not having had an affair with Guy. In a phrase Wharton also applied to herself, she is a woman "to whom *nothing had ever happened*" (1: 646). Yet in another sense everything has happened. Her romance has "given her a secret life of incommunicable joys, as if all the wasted springs of her youth had been stored in some hidden pool, and she could return there now to bathe in them" (1:646). This remarkable metaphor is part of a pattern of cool/wet vs. hot/dry imagery that informs the story and is typical of Wharton. She excelled at cold and hot imagery in her short stories and such novels as *Ethan Frome* (1911) and *Summer* (1917). We have already seen that earlier in "The Pretext" Margaret and Guy seek the river as they escape the hot, stuffy dinner and Mr. Ransom's speech—Mr. Ransom who is "thick and yet juiceless, in his dry legal middle age" (1: 636).

Margaret finds it difficult to preserve her secret life without reinforcement; she realizes that the "miracle" by the river that has "sweet-ened and illumined her life" (1: 646) may have been for Guy a less important moment in which he meant to express only his gratitude. But when she discovers that he has broken his engagement, she be-lieves she has been loved and feels "bathed in a tranquil beauty. The days flowed by like a river beneath the moon—each ripple caught the brightness and passed it on" (1: 649). Invigorated by dips in her "hid-den pool," Margaret can take a new interest in her formerly dull duties as lawyer's wife and member of the Higher Thought Club of Went-worth. At this point the English relative arrives and, unable to believe that Margaret is really the Mrs. Robert Ransom named by Guy, informs her she has been used as a pretext. As the story ends, Margaret drags herself upstairs to her mirror and sees "no trace of youth left in her face—she saw it now as others had doubtless always seen it. If it seemed as it did to Lady Caroline Duckett, what look must it have worn to the fresh gaze of young Guy Dawnish?" (1: 654). Margaret observes herself for a long time—"she wished to clear her eyes of all illusions"—and then imagines the empty rest of her life, a desert of years to come.

The "pretext" has been given two interpretations, one by several different critics that Guy named Margaret to protect his real lover and another by Millicent Bell that there is no other woman and Guy just needed an excuse to break an unwanted engagement.[27] In fact, Mar-garet thinks of both possibilities at the end of the story (1: 654). But when one seriously considers either alternative, it becomes obvious just how farfetched the whole idea of the pretext is. We are being asked to believe that a young man deliberately lies about a woman who has befriended him and whom he obviously likes. Considering Wharton's penchant for creating disgusting male characters, this might be a pos-sibility, but *why* would he lie? If to protect another woman, why does she need protection more than the respectable married Margaret Ran-som, and when did he find time to see the other woman while working and visiting Margaret daily? If as an excuse for breaking his engage-ment, he might have thought up a hundred less elaborate lies. Arthur H. Quinn, always a perceptive reader, notes, "The logic of the situa-tion is not quite so inexorable as in Mrs. Wharton's best moments."[28]

Guy's actions would make perfect sense, however, if he were not lying and truly did love Margaret Ransom. The only real objection is the first principle of the English relative, that young men do not fall in love with older, ordinary-looking women. But once the possibility that Guy could be in love with Margaret is admitted, one can observe how Wharton undercuts the relative. She presents Lady Caroline as a very decided person who announces several times her wish "to see Mrs. Ransom" (1: 650–51). She openly scrutinizes Margaret, making one wonder whether she is a lady with a small l, and concludes, "'Oh, I *see*! I ought of course to have asked for Mrs. Robert Ransom *Junior*!'" When informed that only one Mrs. Robert Ransom exists, Lady Caroline concludes, "'Then I simply don't see'. . . . 'I simply don't see,' she repeated" (1: 652–53). Of course she simply doesn't see, and that is the point; Wharton even tells us that "her eyes, divided by a sharp nose like a bill, seemed to be set far enough apart to see at separate angles" (1: 650).

Nor can anyone else in this story about perception and illusion see very well. Certainly not Margaret Ransom, who only too readily accepts Lady Caroline's unflattering edict. If we recall Margaret's self-examination in the mirror at the beginning of the story, we have to question her conclusion at the end that she finally sees her face as others have always viewed it. In fact, her face changes as she steps back or forward, as she lets down her hair. Her husband can even think she looks like a bad woman, but then he is described as "shortsighted" and "unobservant" (1: 635). If eyesight were not fallible enough, people's perceptions may be shaped by the medium. Margaret's mirror, we recall, is a cramped, eagle-topped affair with an "unflattering surface"—a Puritan mirror that cannot properly reflect a sensual woman to whom a young man could be sexually attracted. Margaret's vision is influenced not only by her New England ancestry and community but by her emotions. When strongly affected, she can feel that the light is burning her while she sits in the shade (1: 640) and that the river has suddenly changed into a different one (1: 647).

But Margaret does not misperceive to any greater degree than the other characters in the story or, for that matter, other Wharton reflectors. She does not go wrong by being illusioned in the conventional way of opening herself to the possibility of being fooled; instead, she closes herself off from the possibility of being loved. (Thus, the story probably does comment on Wharton's relationship with Fullerton: *she* would not throw away her opportunity to have something happen.) Margaret's mistake is her desire "to clear her eyes of all illusions," for human beings cannot accomplish that. None of us can see perfectly. Ironically, Margaret Ransom opts for disillusion, the one illusion that dries up her hidden pool of happiness.

It is also ironic that this tale of illusion should be one of Wharton's most misinterpreted stories. One wonders why no one has questioned Margaret's point of view, especially when Wharton pays so much attention, more than I have had space to suggest, to the vagaries of perception (the characters hear as poorly as they see). The main culprit must be the hardening of sexist attitudes among readers; Wharton could hardly be expected to anticipate that Lady Caroline's assumptions about aging women would so easily last the century. But I think the story itself invites misunderstanding because of its structure. The sudden resurgence of plot at the end of such an internally focused story—the stock and obtrusive device of a letter from a friend (who just happens to mention that Guy has broken his engagement) and the melodramatic visit of Lady Caroline—gives too much emphasis to the pretext. Unlike the surprise endings of "Roman Fever" and "The Other Two," which illuminate the stories and make them whole, the conclusion of "The Pretext" allows the reader to forget what has gone before. It seems gimmicky, making the story the kind criticized by one theorist as a mere "device for conveying us to the conclusion with the least interference along the way and the maximum impact at the end."[29]

Although "The Pretext" is thereby flawed, it probably typifies Wharton's practice more than "Roman Fever" and "The Other Two." Many Wharton stories begin very well, only to gradually lose momentum and peter out at the end or be overcome by the complexities of the plot. In "Telling a Short Story" Wharton gives lip service to the need "to end a tale in accordance with its own deepest sense" but stresses the importance of making a good beginning. She again distinguishes between the short story and the novel, arguing that the "inevitableness" of the ending is more crucial to the novel and the brilliance of the beginning to the short story. One can see this emphasis reflected in "The Pretext" and other stories in which the first half surpasses the second.

Wharton's concept of situation as the basis of the short story may engender weak endings. Blake Nevius, her first important critic, says of her stories: "Edith Wharton had a fatal weakness for the anecdote, for the situation capable of taking a surprising turn or of lending itself to an ironic or merely amusing treatment." Such situations might be artfully unfolded in the opening pages yet are "necessarily limited in their power of implication" and thus eventually come to grief (28). In stories like "Roman Fever" and "The Other Two" the central situation's power of implication seems infinite, but Nevius's point applies to "The Pretext" with its skillful exposition of a necessarily limited situation. If "The Pretext" cannot be ranked among Wharton's very best efforts, however, it does belong among her better stories and is more interesting than has previously been thought.

Wharton may have realized some time after completing the story that she had overdone the pretext idea at the end and not assured that Margaret's "theory of the case," as she puts it (1: 649), be given equal weight. In a story published a year later, "The Debt" (1909), she gives a clue to her intent. The protagonist, a young scientist, ignores his professor's beautiful daughter but falls in love with the professor's wife, "poor Mrs. Lanfear, with her tight hair and her loose shape, her blameless brow and earnest eyeglasses, and her perpetual air of mild misapprehension" (2: 63). Uncharacteristically for a writer who usually makes every detail count, Wharton gives the scientist's "blind hopeless passion" no function in the story, which goes on to be about the necessity of independent thinking in science and art. But this loose detail does comment on "The Pretext," constituting as big a hint as the author would furnish.

Wharton would never go very far to make sure her audience got the point. I have tried to show that if her theory of the short story is straightforward, some might say simplistic, her practice is subtle and admits great complexity. She demands a good deal from her readers, and her attitude toward readers is again complex. We have already seen that Wharton considered reading a creative act and expected her audience to meet her halfway and fill in the gaps. But she was unwilling to do a lot to help. For example, she always paid scrupulous attention to adjusting her style to the requirements of the reflector: the maid in "The Lady's Maid's Bell" (1902) thinks in very different language than the Nietzschean "superman" of "The Blond Beast" (1910), who is introduced stepping through "Rhadamanthine portals," recalling "Rastignac's apostrophe to Paris," and comparing his surroundings to Pactolus and Pisgah (2: 131); yet she presumably did not mind that the latter story is barely intelligible and it must have seemed to readers that she had swallowed an atlas.[30] The quotation from *The Writing of Fiction* that begins this chapter shows a certain amount of intellectual arrogance, as Wharton complains of the younger novelists' lack of "general culture" and "cultivated intelligence." We are expected to understand the references and get the jokes. When readers, including publishers, wrote for elucidation, as for instance of the meaning of her story title "Pomegranate Seed," Wharton reacted impatiently.

Wharton's attitude has been criticized by Lawrence Jay Dessner, who complains about her lack of faith in the common reader and castigates her for "refusal to share information with the reader, a central aspect of Mrs. Wharton's work."[31] He thinks that in *The Age of Innocence*, one of her best novels, she extends her lack of respect for the reader to include the novel's central sensibility. Although this criticism concerns a novel, it could just as well be extended to the short stories, for Dessner's essential complaint is Wharton's "ultimate lack of faith in the ability of her central intelligence to reach truth himself, unaided by his author's mechanical and sentimental intervention" (62). But as we have seen propounded in Wharton's theory—for instance, "each witness of a given incident will report it differently"—and illustrated in three short stories, Wharton believed that no one could "reach truth" alone, not even Wharton-y/Waythorn, who is given to satirizing her own limitations. Perhaps one has to accept this basic attitude in order to appreciate her writing.

If Wharton's short-story practice turns out to be more subtle and complex than her theory would suggest, two major criticisms that have been made of her work implicate that theory rather directly. The first charge is that her subjects and messages are inappropriate and the second that her fiction is too cold. In regard to the former, she has been seen as either lacking a message—she "had nothing to say"—or giving the wrong one: she is too refined or too sordid, too reserved or too frank, too old-fashioned or too modern, too male-identified or too feminist.[32] The absurd criticism I discussed in the preface, that she lacked a conception of America as a single culture and was perversely not even trying to "understand America," as if this were the ultimate goal of fiction, has relevance here, as does the related effort to make old versus new New York the overriding theme to which everything Wharton wrote must pertain. In this view "Roman Fever," "The Other Two," and "The Pretext" have to be about the changing mores of New York, as reflected in marriage and divorce and contrasted with New England. But of course Wharton was not a message writer, as "Telling a Short Story" makes clear. It seems unlikely that the Cellinis' salamander could have been American, and the only attribute required of it is significance. If the salamander is rejected, nothing remains to be said.

Wharton's supposed coldness may be a direct result of her theory.

Her stories have occasionally been called "artificial,"[33] and some contemporary theorists of the short story find too much art in the "old way of selection and design" she advocates. Thus, John Bayley criticizes the tradition of the "effective" story, which he sees as French and to which Wharton certainly belongs: "An impression of deadness in the story may arise from too meticulous a control on the part of the writer, and too methodical an awareness of the effects to be achieved."[34] Coldness has also been detected in Wharton's attitude toward her characters.[35] It has always seemed to me that she shows great sympathy for her characters, even making the reader empathize occasionally with repulsive types like Undine Spragg or Andrew Culwin of "The Eyes" (1910), but her theory of point of view admittedly requires distance. She also refuses, as we have seen in "Roman Fever," "The Other Two," and "The Pretext," to take any fixed attitude. While all three stories have their dark aspects, for instance, and from one perspective the characters are caught in appalling situations, Wharton insists that we also see the broadly humorous side of their dilemmas.[36] No story is finally tragic or comic, or finally any one thing, because Wharton really means what she says about "letting it reveal all its potentialities." If this characteristic makes her fiction cold and lacking in important messages, it might also be viewed as her strength, the source of her "original vision" as a short-story writer.

The Early Stories:
Angel at the Grave

The influential Edmund Wilson established the traditional periodization of Wharton's work soon after her death. He thought the significant years in her career were 1905 to 1920, the span between the great novels *The House of Mirth* and *The Age of Innocence*. He found her fiction after 1920 "commonplace," if not downright bad, and dismissed her earliest work as preoccupied with "artificial moral problems" in the manner of her friends Henry James and French novelist Paul Bourget.[37] Although Wilson's evaluation must be questioned, at least as it applies to the short stories, the stories do tend to form three distinct groups. The dates differ a bit from Wilson's because the shorter works anticipate the novels. The short stories that followed the publication in 1901 of Wharton's second collection, *Crucial Instances*, have much in common with *The House of Mirth*, particularly the familiar emphasis on the aristocracy and economic and social institutions. I say "familiar" because readers have learned to associate these features, along with male narrators and the marriage/divorce theme, with Edith Wharton. Yet the twenty-four stories published before 1902 reveal a different Wharton.

In the early stories there are almost as many female narrators and reflectors as male (and in the stories published before 1900 there are actually more female reflectors). Important female characters greatly outnumber the male characters. The upper crust is scarcely more visible than the working and middle classes. Only gradually, in the progression from the uncollected stories to *Crucial Instances*, do aristocratic backgrounds, like male reflectors, begin to dominate. The major themes of the early stories include the responsibilities of the artist, the nature of art and perception, courage versus cowardice, past versus present, and female experience, especially its claustrophobic tendencies. Although these themes would engage Wharton throughout her career, the emphasis changes; for example, in the period Wilson considers the zenith of her career she would stress the institutions that limit women, whereas in the earlier period she focuses on the felt personal experience of restriction. One might also characterize the early

27

stories by what is *not* there—no economics of marriage, no decline of old New York, no obvious ghosts.

Despite the absence of many features for which Wharton has been appreciated, her early stories cannot really be considered apprentice work. As a writer Wharton sprang full grown, as it were, from the head of Zeus. Shock is the dominant tone of the reviews that greeted her first collection, *The Greater Inclination* (1899); the reviewers could hardly conceive of a writer this accomplished being previously unknown to them.[38] Few first books have received such glowing notices. Wharton herself tended to downplay the suddenness of her emergence as an author, pointing out her childhood obsession with "making up" and gradual attraction to writing in adulthood. She notes that *The Greater Inclination* "contained none of my earliest tales, all of which I had rejected as not worth reprinting." The implication is that the first stories had no value except as the means by which she "groped my way through to my vocation" (*BG*, 119).

Wharton's common practice throughout her career, however, was to choose stories to collect on a basis other than quality. She picked her most recently published stories, seldom excluding one unless it had been specifically criticized by someone she respected or unless it related too obviously to her personal life. Thus, she omitted "The Line of Least Resistance" (1900) from *Crucial Instances*, even though she had originally planned to make it the title story, because James found fault with it (Lewis, 125). She rejected "The Fullness of Life" (1893) and some other tales for too openly portraying dissatisfied wives. They were "excesses of youth" not worth reprinting because written at the top of her voice; she describes "The Fullness" as "one long shriek."[39] Although Wharton may have truly considered her initial stories inferior, it is evident she liked the idea of having some youthful excesses to repudiate. At any rate, modern readers have disagreed with her. Her first published story, "Mrs. Manstey's View" (1891), has found favor, along with "The Lamp of Psyche" and "Friends" (1900).[40] These stories eclipse several she chose to collect in *The Greater Inclination*. Wharton's early period must be considered one of significant accomplishment, from the first stories through the two collections. It includes two of her best stories, "Souls Belated" (1899) and "The Angel at the Grave" (1901), and is impressive in quantity as well as quality, the stories constituting between a quarter and a third of her output during her lifetime.

At the same time, Wharton's sophistication as a short-story writer in

the 1890s did not preclude development. The confident pronounce-
ments of *The Writing of Fiction* resulted from experience; and however
distinguished Wharton's early stories may be, they are probably, taken
as a whole, slightly less accomplished than those of her later periods.
Although she could occasionally write brilliant stories like the two
mentioned above, she sometimes fell short from failure of technique
(rather than failure of concentration, as in her later years). A very promising story, "A Cup of Cold Water" (1899), comes to grief because she
cannot overcome the same type of logistical difficulties she later solved
in "The Other Two" with the cognac and the tea. Wharton was also
experimenting with narrative point of view in her early years and moving toward what would become her standard practice. Perhaps most
important, she had to come to terms in this period with her new profession—with literary tradition and the influence of other authors, with
her publishers and readers, with the reflections of her own past and
personal life in her writing. All these issues, which I discuss in the
remainder of this section, would be complicated by her being female
and would in turn affect her writing, sometimes leading to significant
change.

In "Telling a Short Story" Wharton mentions numerous practitioners
of the form who presumably influenced her own work in a general way.
There are the British: Scott, Hardy, Kipling, Stevenson, Quiller-
Couch, and Conrad; the Russians: Tolstoy and Turgenev; the French:
Balzac, Flaubert, and Maupassant; and the Americans: Poe, Hawthorne, and James. Wharton critics have considered most of these writers as models, even drawing some specific parallels between stories in
the case of the most obvious influences, the French and the Americans.[41] Several names have been added to the list, including George
Meredith, William Dean Howells, and Henry Blake Fuller, a Chicago
writer whom Lewis sees as Wharton's "sanction for combining realistic
detail with a melodramatic plot" (85–86). Interestingly, all these writers are male; the only woman Wharton mentions in "Telling a Short
Story" is Jane Austen, although she pays tribute elsewhere in *The Writing of Fiction* to her favorite female novelists, Eliot and Sand.

Wharton's failure to name a female short-story writer would be less
remarkable were her earliest stories not so clearly in a female tradition
and did they not resemble works by the New England local colorists
Sarah Orne Jewett and Mary Wilkins Freeman.[42] "Mrs. Manstey's
View" could have been written by Jewett or Freeman. Although the
title character inhabits a New York boardinghouse and once had a hus-

band, she is at heart a New England nun. She lives a solitary existence, her only friends the animals and plants she can see from her window (there are as many types of flowers named in the story as herbs in Jewett). Mrs. Manstey's neighbors may think her "crazy" (1: 3, 9) but like many a Jewett or Freeman spinster, she stays in tune with an idealized green world. That world is threatened when a neighbor starts to build an extension blocking Mrs. Manstey's view. Wharton's metaphorical description of the threat connects her with a broad range of women's writing, reaching back to the domestic sentimentalists and Emily Dickinson, as well as the local colorists. Not only has Mrs. Manstey's landlady, representing the mass of unobservant humanity, failed to notice the stunning magnolia in the next yard, but the tree is doomed: "One of the [work]men, a coarse fellow with a bloated face, picked a magnolia blossom, and, after smelling it, threw it to the ground; the next man, carrying a load of bricks, trod on the flower in passing" (1: 9).

"Those horrible boots!" as the protagonist of Wharton's next story, "The Fullness of Life," exclaims of the object she associates with her husband (1: 12). Lest these passages be considered "excesses of youth" of the sort Wharton later enjoyed repudiating, it should be pointed out that she uses the same image in her distinguished novel *Summer*, when the heroine's communion with nature is interrupted by a man's muddy boot trampling some frail white flowers. One is reminded of the sylvan child protecting her green world against the hunter in Jewett's "A White Heron" (1886) and the New England nun in Freeman's story sweeping away the tracks of her cloddish fiancé: "She had visions, so startling that she half repudiated them as indelicate, of coarse masculine belongings strewn about in endless litter; of dust and disorder arising necessarily from a coarse masculine presence in the midst of all this delicate harmony."[43]

The theme of the intrusion of the "coarse masculine" into an idyllic female world appears again in Wharton's "Friends," an early story even more reminiscent of Jewett and Freeman than "Mrs. Manstey's View." Penelope Bent quits her teaching job of many years and leaves her New England friends to marry. When she is jilted and returns home, she discovers that her best friend, Vexilla Thurber, has been hired in her place. The friendship survives, as Penelope overcomes her resentment and refuses Vexilla's offer to give up the job—Vexilla needs the money to support her poverty-stricken family. In the end harmony is restored because Penelope has reestablished "her connection with the general scheme of things," becoming "in touch once more with the common troubles of her kind" (1: 214).

Perhaps Wharton thought she was clearly departing from her models; there is even a touch of satire in the names Penelope Bent, Vexilla Thurber, and Euphemia Staples (another teacher), although the hint is not carried through. She emphasizes the seediness of the New England setting (the story begins emphatically, "Sailport is an ugly town"), employing the same technique she would later use in *Ethan Frome* and *Summer*; the description of Vexilla's hovel and shabby dependents—senile grandmother, paralyzed brother, and slatternly sister—anticipates the two novels. In her autobiography Wharton claims she wanted to "draw life as it really was" in New England, "utterly unlike that seen through the rose-coloured spectacles of my predecessors, Mary Wilkins and Sarah Orne Jewett" (*BG*, 293). This contrast is deceptive in that Wharton seems to have the mistaken impression that her predecessors avoided describing poverty; there is actually nothing in "Friends" the local colorists could not have written.

Wharton's failure in "Telling a Short Story" to acknowledge Jewett and Freeman, even if she were ultimately to reject them as too rosy, might be explained by her general disinclination to admit influence, particularly the American variety; she quickly dismisses Poe and Hawthorne, two important models, as outside the "classic tradition" of the short story.[44] There are many possible reasons for Wharton's strong "anxiety of influence," not the least of which is the diminution of her literary reputation that resulted from being falsely categorized as James's imitator.[45] In addition, Amy Kaplan suggests in *The Social Construction of American Realism* (1988) that each generation of female writers "might have to struggle as much against female as male forms of influence."[46] To shape a role for herself, Wharton had to confront "the volubility and commercial success of the domestic tradition of American women novelists" (72). Kaplan goes on to argue that Wharton tried to establish herself as a professional author by disassociating herself from the domestic or sentimental writers.

Two stories about female artists, "The Pelican" (1898) and "April Showers" (1900), are noisy rejections of the sentimentalists. In "The Pelican" Mrs. Amyot takes up lecturing for the same reason many early nineteenth-century women began writing—to support her child after her husband's death. Although she has no particular knowledge or ability, she succeeds, at first because of the "personal accent" she brings to her talks. To her, "art was simply an extension of coquetry: she flirted with her audience" (1: 92). Finally the public grows tired of her silly lectures on Plato and continues to patronize her only out of sympathy. At the end of the story Mrs. Amyot's bearded, self-supporting son is embarrassed to learn that she still gives his education as an excuse for continuing her career.

"April Showers" concerns a budding novelist. The seventeen-year-old Theodora Dace submits a novel to *Home Circle* and somehow or other (the plot is absurd) receives an acceptance meant for the popular author she has imitated, Kathleen Kyd. The pen names (Theodora adopts "Gladys Glyn") suggest the alliterative pseudonyms of nineteenth-century writers like Grace Greenwood and Fanny Fern; Kathleen Kyd's real name is, not surprisingly, Frances G. Wollup. Theodora bears her ultimate rejection with the help of her sympathetic father, who confesses that he once tried a novel. The only parts of this slight story that seem at all real are Wharton's opinion of the novel and her description of Theodora's initial joy at being accepted. The latter is presented in terms of an ecstatic oneness with the green world as Theodora embraces the spring earth and feels that "in her own heart hundreds of germinating hopes had burst into sudden leaf" (1: 193). As for the sentimental novel, Wharton goes to the opposite extreme—it is simply garbage. Theodora's uncle suggests she write a romance about sanitation rather than "the sentimental trash most women wrote" (1: 194). He says, "I don't believe in feeding youngsters on sentimental trash; it's like sewer gas—doesn't smell bad, and infects the system without your knowing it" (1: 190).

Although Wharton thus announces her difference from Grace Greenwood, her rejection of Jewett and Freeman is not thereby explained unless all female writers are being collapsed into a single category. This is the conclusion of Josephine Donovan, who sees Wharton as separating herself from all female writers, not just the sentimentalists. Donovan refers to Wharton's "self-identification as masculine" and need to "distance herself from 'authoresses' in order to establish herself as an 'author'" (45, 48). One may not agree that Wharton reveals "contempt for her own sex" (46) or identifies as masculine, and Susan Goodman's recent book supplies another view. Certainly much of the traditional evidence for Wharton's misogyny, such as her use of male reflectors and the comments of male friends that "she liked to be talked to as a man," is capable of alternative interpretation; for instance, no one explains *why* the saying that she was a self-made man pleased Wharton.[47] Was it because she really wanted to be a man, because she wanted to be taken seriously, or because she appreciated the irony? This intelligent woman probably knew that whatever she accomplished, some excuse would be unearthed to lump her with Grace Greenwood; the ultimate irony is that the reason would be her supposed imitation of a man (that is, Henry James).

Whatever one decides about Wharton's possible male identification or misogyny, Donovan is clearly right when she says Wharton saw herself as inhabiting an entirely different world from the one Jewett and Freeman lived in. It *was* a different world, as young women were leaving the women's culture celebrated by the local colorists and such "friends" as Penelope and Vexilla and for the first time "entering the world of public, patriarchal discourse" (11); unfortunately, as Donovan shows, that discourse was at the same time becoming increasingly social Darwinist and male supremacist. Wharton's Mrs. Manstey might be considered a stand-in for Jewett and Freeman at a loss in the new world. She is an "artist" and even possesses the equivalent of rose-colored spectacles—an "optimistic eye" and "the happy faculty of dwelling on the pleasanter side of the prospect before her" (1: 4). But the loss of her view, when her attempt to burn down the extension fails, kills her. Wharton differs most from her predecessors in her endings: Mrs. Manstey dies; the wife in "The Fullness of Life" cannot escape her husband even in the next world; Penelope must leave Vexilla and move to New York.

In the world of public, patriarchal discourse a woman is an interloper and must tread carefully. If we read "Mrs. Manstey's View" as the story of a female artist, it reveals Wharton's sense of the difficulty, even impossibility, of the role. Mrs. Manstey must have her view, in order to project patterns on the landscape and make up stories about the people, just as Wharton herself needed to "make up" ever since she was a little girl. But to preserve her view Mrs. Manstey has to commit a criminal act—burn down the extension. "Making up" is thus necessary to life but illegal. Although Wharton's trespass eventually succeeded where Mrs. Manstey's failed, it cost her a great struggle and a number of breakdowns, as Cynthia Griffin Wolff details. Wharton even tells us directly in her very reserved autobiography that when her first collection of stories finally appeared, she read the reviews with "mingled guilt and self-satisfaction."

Her transgression was partly against class because aristocrats did not become professional writers, but she also gives some of her own traits to female artist protagonists of the lower classes, who are just as guilty.

Mrs. Amyot of "The Pelican," a woman preternaturally shy like Wharton, needs an excuse to pursue a career and hence embarrasses her son. Theodora of "April Showers," whose novel resembles Wharton's own adolescent novella, actually neglects her domestic duties in order to write, forgetting to sew on her brother's buttons. One looks in vain for satire of this early nineteenth-century rationale for excluding women from authorship; the story clearly implies that women should stop writing and go back to their needlework. Even the artist characters' names—Mrs. Manstey, Mrs. Amyot (toy man?), Theodora—make them lesser versions of men. That Wharton goes to such extremes in dredging up stereotypes of the authoress and then condemning her indicates anxiety over being thought a producer of sewer gas, rather than a reasoned judgment that women shouldn't write. These early stories have the quality of exorcisms, much like Wharton's adolescent reviews; Lewis tells us the teenaged Wharton accompanied her creations with mock reviews harshly condemning them.[48] Imagining the worst might ward it off.

Wharton was extremely sensitive to criticism, as I have already suggested, and she knew the audience that counted was male. Women might read the magazines, but men occupied the critics' and publishers' chairs. Wharton's sense of her audience as male is revealed very directly in the early stories themselves; in the last chapter we saw an example in "The Lamp of Psyche," where the narrator interrupts to reassure the reader about "a heroine whom he would not like his wife to meet." Wharton's eagerness to please shows up in her early letters to her editor, Edward L. Burlingame of *Scribner's Magazine*. She finds his criticisms of the stories he rejected tremendously helpful and fears only that her "cry for help & counsel" might be misinterpreted as (of course) "the wail of the rejected authoress." The unsureness in the early stories and letters and the courting of the male audience are highlighted by contrast with the later Wharton. In *The Writing of Fiction* the established professional makes the following statement about audience: "No writer—especially at the beginning of his [sic] career—can help being influenced by the quality of the audience that awaits him; and the young novelist may ask of what use are experience and meditation, when his readers are so incapable of giving him either. The answer is that he will never do his best till he ceases altogether to think of his readers (and his editor and his publisher)" (*WF*, 21).

Although this passage can be read as sound, if rather conventional, advice to the young writer, it also comments on Wharton's own beginnings. *She* could not help being influenced, especially at the start of her career, by an audience that turned out to be "incapable"; she had to stop thinking of her readers, including editor and publisher, though the extreme word choice in the phrase "ceases altogether" makes one question the possibility. Right after this passage Wharton notes that even for the author least concerned with popularity, "it is difficult, at first, to defend his [sic] personality" (*WF*, 21). She seems to have felt that she did not sufficiently defend hers (the "counsel" she begs from Burlingame becomes in *The Writing of Fiction* a "peril," as "counsellors intervene with contradictory advice"). Wharton indeed claimed that before her first volume of short stories appeared she had no real personality of her own. The counsel Burlingame and other male readers gave must have confirmed her fears as expressed in the female artist stories. The early stories *Scribner's* rejected (and Wharton eventually rewrote) *were* the female artist stories, such as "April Showers" and "Copy" (1900), or to be more precise the stories told from a female point of view and dominated by female characters, such as "Friends" and "The Twilight of the God" (1898).[49] Interestingly, the rejected stories also included those about the lower classes. For instance, Burlingame found the early version of "Friends" too "squalid." Around the same time, he refused to publish the brilliant novella *Bunner Sisters*, which resembles "Friends" in its frank description of poverty; although he gave its length as the main reason, he seems to have found the story "dreary" (Lewis, 66). *Bunner Sisters* only saw print in 1916, after Wharton's reputation had long been established. On the other hand, Burlingame loved "The Pelican" (Lewis, 81), and the fortunes of this story well illustrate the pressures of Wharton's entrance into the world of public discourse.

Reviewers of Wharton's first collection liked "The Pelican" too, one even singling it out as the best in the volume (over a great story like "Souls Belated").[50] In an early assessment of Wharton's work (1903), "The Pelican" is called "one of the best short stories ever written."[51] While no one since has reached that height of enthusiasm, the story has generally been esteemed; it received a big boost from inclusion as one of the five short stories in Louis Auchincloss's *The Edith Wharton Reader* (1965). "The Pelican" thus has greater stature and commands more recognition than other Wharton products of the 1899–1900 period such as "Friends," "A Cup of Cold Water," "The Muse's Tragedy," and "The Line of Least Resistance." The problem is that "The Pelican" is really a middling story about on a level with the works just mentioned. More Jamesian than most Wharton tales, it violates many of the principles of short-story writing she came to consider essential, such as the need for compactness and vividness and the preservation of unity of time. Flaws in the point of view, as I explain in the next section, keep the reader unsure about the narrator, and even the minor characters prove difficult. One of Wharton's most perceptive early readers, Frederic Taber Cooper, complains of Mrs. Amyot's son: "His whole manner is in bad taste—perhaps Mrs. Wharton meant him to be precisely that kind of man, but one doubts it."[52]

All this is not to reduce "The Pelican" to the level of inept stories like "April Showers" or "The Confessional," but to suggest that the story's popularity owes less to its quality than its theme. Auchincloss even explains his choice by observing that the story "inaugurated a lifetime series of satires of ladies."[53] If women controlled the literary establishment, "Friends" might occupy the same position as "The Pelican." As it is, one can understand Wharton's move from working-class women like Penelope and Vexilla to the suave male aristocrat who narrates "The Pelican." In her stories about art, woman increasingly becomes object rather than subject; instead of artist she is muse, as in "The Muse's Tragedy" (1899) or the grisly "The Duchess at Prayer" (1900), in which the Duke poisons his wife and turns her into a statue.

But making the artists male did not improve the quality of the stories. Probably the most solid generalization that can be made about Wharton's short stories is that the artist stories are her least successful.[54] Like Hawthorne and James, she was fascinated by the theme; fully half the early stories concern art in a fairly direct manner (this fact in itself accounts for the slight inferiority of the stories in her first period). Yet unlike her predecessors, Wharton never accomplished much in this subgenre ("Xingu," 1911, is her only real triumph), and she gradually wrote fewer artist stories. The failure of her artist novels, *Hudson River Bracketed* (1929) and *The Gods Arrive* (1932), can no doubt be attributed to the theme rather than diminished talent in old age. Cynthia Griffin Wolff's diagnosis of the novels—"Being unwilling or unable to write a novel that exhibited the *real* connection between an artist's life and work, Wharton filled up her two *Kunstlerromane* with a host of subsidiary 'subjects' "—applies perfectly to the stories.[55]

One finds a good deal of arty conversation, especially about the world of painting, but the real interest lies somewhere else. For instance, the muse's tragedy in the story of that title is the failure of her personal relationship with a deceased poet. Although the world considered her his mistress, he wanted intellectual companionship only; like the young man in "The Valley of Childish Things" (1896), he loved young girls whom he preferred not to talk. In "The Moving Finger" (1901) an artist paints a portrait of his friend's wife and after her death has to confront the friend's insistence that he keep aging the woman in the portrait. Richard Lawson aptly calls this story an "inchoate ghost story" and notes that "the artist situation is the background, perhaps even the catalyst for a personal . . . interaction" (Lawson, 312).

When art provides more than a backdrop, the main issue in the story is usually good art versus bad art. In a continuation of the "sewer gas" theme from "April Showers," an artist must resist the temptation to produce inferior work for money or increased popular reputation. An aspiring poet in "That Good May Come" (1894), a slight early effort, compromises himself to buy a confirmation dress for his sister. The painter in "The Recovery" (1901) becomes complacent when he is lionized in America. After Keniston travels to Europe and views the works of "the masters," he realizes his inferiority. This story has a happy ending, as Keniston's recognition inspires him to start over, thus setting him on the road to recovery.[56] In a later story with the same theme, "The Verdict" (1908), a fashionable painter has to quit in his heyday because he is just no good and it's too late to learn. He considers his one claim to greatness that in spite of his popular success he knew enough to stop painting (1: 622).

Wharton would ring changes on this theme throughout her career. An artist might think he could safely break the rules, as does the painter in "The Potboiler" (1904), who asks, "Why can't a man do two kinds of work—one to please himself and the other to boil the pot?" (1: 671). The man may be a scientist instead of an artist, as in "The Descent of Man" (1904), where a professor gets sidetracked from his serious experiments when he writes a popular book of pseudoscience. Whatever the situation, the creator who does less than his best gets punished. The problem with these stories is that if one does not accept Wharton's view of good art versus bad art, that the difference is obvious and anyone with a brain can instantly detect it, they are much too simple. Even if one does share her view, the stories remain didactic, and where is the salamander in the fire? Wharton usually avoids didacticism, as we saw in Chapter 1, but she often has a message when it comes to art. Although many of the artist stories, such as "Copy" and

"Expiation" (1903), are supposed to be comedies, an occasional ear-
nestness of tone about the quality of art keeps them from being consistently funny.

A more promising theme that appears in some of the artist stories
concerns the blurring of the lines between the artist's personal and
public lives. The protagonist of "That Good May Come" worries about
damaging other people by using them as characters. In "The Portrait"
(1899) a distinguished painter who declines to "wear the portrait painter's conventional blinders" and reveals people as they really are (1:
173) produces one notable failure. He paints an "expurgated" portrait
of a notable villain because he cannot bear to disillusion the man's
worshipful daughter. Interestingly, in this one instance Wharton seems
to approve of an artist deliberately creating a lesser work.

"Copy" treats the other side of the coin: in place of the artist's potential to harm others, the possible invasion of the artist's own personal
life. Helen Dale and Paul Ventnor, former lovers who have become
successful writers, recall the days when they lived instead of writing
about life, "when our emotions weren't worth ten cents a word, and a
signature wasn't an autograph" (1: 285). Helen claims, "I died years
ago. What you see before you is a figment of the reporter's brain—a
monster manufactured out of newspaper paragraphs, with ink in its
veins" (1: 278). The two are now "public property" (1: 278), and indeed they meet because they both secretly want their old love letters
back to use in their memoirs. The threat of becoming public property
and other issues in the relationship between the artist's personal and
public lives are explored at greater length in Wharton's first novella,
The Touchstone (1900). She was obviously preoccupied with this kind of
question as her work became better known, her first collection of
stories having been published in 1899.

As we have seen, Wharton omitted some of her earliest published
stories, like "The Fullness of Life," from the collection because she
feared they reflected her own experience too closely. But other stories
of her first period are more curious, their strangeness suggesting unresolved personal content. "The Portrait," which Lewis gently calls
"somewhat confused" (84), begins with a cogent discussion of realism
in art but in the second half takes on a surreal quality. The arty talk
gives way to the portrait painter's evocation of his subject's daughter,
Miss Vard, who possesses the "guilty secret" of idolizing her father (1:
178–79). If the circumstance of the painter compromising his art to
preserve the daughter's illusions seems a bit forced, it really strains

credibility to have the daughter die when she finally discovers the truth about her father's corrupt business practices. The situation of a woman becoming disillusioned with a man she has previously admired is prevalent in Wharton's early stories, such as "The Lamp of Psyche," "The Valley of Childish Things," and "The Twilight of the God," but the woman's enlightenment does not cause her death. In the case of "The Portrait" we are expected not only to find it logical that the discovery kills Miss Vard but also to approve: the story ends as the painter tells the narrator, "She died last year, thank God" (1: 185).

The characters in "The Portrait" resemble those of "The House of the Dead Hand," a story written in 1898, around the same time as "The Portrait," but not published until 1904. This story, which Lewis frankly labels "inept" (81), is an Italian melodrama filled with Gothic trappings. It makes little sense on the surface, though Wharton does succeed in establishing a creepy atmosphere. Wyant, the reflector, has been asked by an art professor friend to view a painting belonging to Dr. Lombard, an Englishman living in Siena. Dr. Lombard refuses to let anyone photograph, or reproduce in any way, his lost Leonardo, which he bought after its discovery in a farmhouse (Wharton herself had in 1894 discovered lost Giovanni della Robbia terra-cottas in an Italian monastery—see Lewis, 72–73). Wyant duly visits Lombard's home, "the House of the Dead Hand." The ominous name comes from the marble hand above the door, "a dead drooping hand, which hung there convulsed and helpless, as though it had been thrust forth in denunciation of some evil mystery within the house, and had sunk struggling into death" (1: 509).

Inside the house, which is described in terms of cold and decay, Wyant finds an odd trio: Dr. Lombard, an old man who looks and acts like "some art-loving despot of the Renaissance"; his silly, conventional wife, who is too stupid to understand her husband's constant insults; and their "sullen" daughter, Sybilla (1: 509–10). Dr. Lombard seems a kind of vampire, as Wyant contemplates "the contrast between the fierce vitality of the doctor's age and the inanimateness of his daughter's youth" (1: 510). The robotlike daughter actually owns the painting, having purchased it with a legacy from her grandmother. The ritual Sybilla and her father go through to show Wyant the painting is nothing short of bizarre. She has to take a key from a "secret drawer," push aside a hanging tapestry, and fit the key into a concealed door. After the party traverses a narrow passage they come to another door, which is barred with iron and fitted with a "complicated patent lock."

This door is opened with another key and leads to a small dark room wherein a picture is "concealed by a curtain of faded velvet." Lombard instructs Sybilla in a ritualistic reading of verse, whereupon she draws the cord and parts the velvet folds (1: 512). The painting turns out to be a mass of symbols, replete with a crucified Christ, a veiled woman in a red robe, and a human skull holding wine.

Sybilla strikes Wyant as caring little for the painting, and indeed she and her lover, whom Lombard has forbidden her to see, want Wyant to pass letters and help Sybilla run away. The lover claims she lives in horrible fear of her father—"the father is terrible; she is in his power; it is my belief that he would kill her if she resisted him" (1: 521). Wyant, however, one of Wharton's earliest detached men, refuses to help; he reasons that she can simply leave the house and sell the picture: "She isn't walled in; she can get out if she wants to" (1: 526). Several years later Wyant makes a return visit and finds that, in spite of Lombard's death, everything has remained the same. Sybilla has tried many times to sell the painting, which she passionately hates, but her father has prevented her. She claims, "[H]e was always in the room with me. . . . I can't lock him out; I can never lock him out now" (1: 529). In other words, "The House of the Dead Hand" is Wharton's first ghost story.

The situation bears a strong resemblance to that of a much better known ghost tale, "Mr. Jones" (1928). In this story, originally titled "The Parasite,"[57] a female writer much like Wharton herself inherits an old manor house in England. Her attempts to learn about her forebears are thwarted by the "invisible guardian" of the house, Mr. Jones (2: 179). When alive, he had been the jailor of his employer's deaf and dumb wife; as a ghost, he protects the "secret past" (2: 181). Had the invisible guardian been "Mr. Smith," we might not have recognized the father-daughter connection, but Edith Jones Wharton chose to give this ghost her father's name. One does not have to be an analyst to wonder about these daughters with guilty secrets being preyed upon by parasitic fathers who can never be locked out. Nor can one miss the sexual connotations of the keys, lock, secret doors, and velvet folds in "The House of the Dead Hand" (significantly, there is also a long, complicated business with keys and locksmiths in "Mr. Jones").

Wharton's interest in incest as a literary theme has been noted ever since her biographers discovered the pornographic "Beatrice Palmato" fragment among her papers. This piece, which she marked "unpublishable," consists of an outline for a short story and a brief fragment (now published in Lewis, pp. 544–48, and Wolff, pp. 301–305). The fragment is an explicit description of oral sex between the recently married Beatrice and her father, "a rich half-Levantine, half-Portuguese banker living in London." Although Beatrice finds the sex more pleasurable than the "rough advances" of her husband, Wharton indicates that it began in childhood and has made Beatrice "depressed." According to the outline, her older sister mysteriously committed suicide at seventeen and her mother died in an insane asylum after having tried to kill Palmato. Beatrice eventually has children and her father dies. When her daughter reaches the age of five or six, Beatrice becomes disturbed at her husband's innocent displays of affection for the girl. She forbids a simple kiss, and the husband suddenly understands "many mysterious things in their married life—the sense of some hidden power controlling her, and perpetually coming between them." Her secret revealed, Beatrice kills herself.

In some of Wharton's novels the father-daughter incest theme is obvious, if not so explicitly drawn. Charity Royall of *Summer* ends up marrying her foster father; fifteen-year-old Judith Wheater of *The Children* (1928) receives a marriage proposal from her father figure, a middle-aged bachelor friend. The theme has also been traced in other novels, works as various as *Ethan Frome* and *The Mother's Recompense*.[58] Certainly the odd father-daughter stories we have been considering would make more sense if the terrible secret the characters were bent on hiding were incest. In "The House of the Dead Hand" Lombard might be assumed to have symbolically killed Sybilla, accounting, in the traditional Gothic connection between house and female body, for the cold and decay of the house. The painting probably stands for the incest itself, bought with Sybilla's female legacy, kept secret, and protected with keys, locks, and hidden doors; Dr. Lombard, guardian of the secret, understandably refuses to let the picture be photographed and makes Sybilla guardian after his death. The dead hand over the door of the house, in this reading of the story, could be the hand of the mother (or grandmother), too weak to protect the daughter. Or it might be the "third hand" of the Beatrice Palmato fragment, wherein Mr. Palmato and his daughter call his penis his third hand. Cynthia Griffin Wolff makes a convincing association between the third hand and the hand of Wharton's father, which forms a major part of her earliest recollection as recounted in *A Backward Glance*.[59] If the dead hand is the third hand, it practically announces, "This is the house of incest."

Though Wharton's biographers and critics have noted her preoccupation with the incest theme, no one has satisfactorily explained it. The implication seems to be that an attraction to the father or "struggle for the father" between mother and daughter is "natural," especially in a woman who liked men and disliked women (a view of Wharton we have already found too simplistic).[60] Wolff's psychoanalytic explanation is that at age four or five Wharton "conceived an intense and possessive love for her genial, affectionate father" (207). This love somehow got "invaded by the persistent remnants of an earlier, more infantile yearning—a voracious need for comfort and a ravenous, insatiable quality of desire." Confronted "not merely by the crisis of childhood sexuality, but also by the unresolved elements of that earlier crisis of infancy," the child reacted by becoming overdependent on her mother and never resolving her childhood attraction to her father. (252).

Of course, we are left to wonder where all those voracious, ravenous desires came from in the first place. In a very revealing note, Wolff compares Wharton to one of her heroines, Charity Royall of *Summer*: "Both manage the threatening sexual passions of their own natures by interposing an older woman between themselves and the proximate male who is the most immediate object of these feelings. Charity demands a 'hired woman'; Edith Wharton developed a morbid dependency upon her own mother" (433). Interestingly, the psychoanalyst has misremembered *Summer*. In the novel, Charity demands a hired woman only after her foster father has entered her bedroom and tried to seduce her. I am reminded of Sigmund Freud's initial belief in his patients when they confided their childhood sexual abuse by fathers and other men. But because he felt "it was hardly credible that perverted acts against children were so general," especially by prosperous, respectable men, he dismissed his patients' reports as fantasies.[61] In other words, he managed to project the "threatening sexual passions" away from the fathers onto the children's "own natures."

I think Wharton was probably an incest victim in early childhood. Of course, this contention cannot be proved, any more than the psychoanalytic interpretation, but it is certainly suggested by her writings and explains some still unanswered questions about her life. She had many of the same characteristics and life patterns that are now being discovered in survivors of father-daughter incest, as the taboo against talking about incest is broken and an increasing number of survivors speak out in surveys and autobiographical narratives.[62] Like incest survivors who have described the "post-incest syndrome," Wharton experienced the following major difficulties: 1) a miserably unhappy childhood and a troubled relationship with both parents that seems to have no explanation; 2) vexed romantic and sexual relationships in adult life; and 3) occasional to frequent mental breakdowns.[63]

The two adult patterns are detailed by Wharton's biographers, Lewis and Wolff. We know she had problematic romances with Walter Barry and Morton Fullerton and that she avoided a sexual relationship with her husband, whom she eventually divorced. Lewis says, "There is no question that the sexual side of the marriage was a disaster." Apparently the marriage was not consummated for three weeks, and whenever Wharton had to share a bedroom with her husband she suffered asthma attacks.[64] As a young woman, Wharton had several breakdowns, in which she reported the same specific symptoms as incest victims, severe nausea and loss of appetite and choking and breathing difficulties. She later wrote her friend Sara Norton that "for *twelve* years I seldom knew what it was to be, for more than an hour or two of the twenty four, without an intense feeling of nausea." Her illness "consumed the best years of my youth, & left, in some sort, an irreparable shade on my life."[65]

It would seem that Wharton herself traced her adult problems to childhood, for the emphasis on childhood in her autobiographical narratives is striking. "Life and I," an unpublished manuscript, and "A Little Girl's New York," a published article, are both about her childhood, and Wharton's life as a young child plays a prominent part in her autobiography, *A Backward Glance*, both in the amount of attention devoted to it and the intensity with which it is rendered. In her accounts of her life before marriage only 10 to 15 percent of the space is devoted to her adolescence; the memorable images, including the most vivid in *A Backward Glance*, have to do with Wharton as a child rather than a debutante. The unfinished novel, "Literature," which is heavily autobiographical, also emphasizes childhood.[66]

Wharton describes herself as a "morbid" and "unhappy" child plagued by intense fears, including a phobia connected with her father ("Life and I," 40). She says her "external life" (15) seemed normal enough, but her internal life diverged (the splitting into external and internal is mentioned by all sources as characteristic of incest victims). Wharton suffered for seven or eight years from "an intense & unreasoning physical timidity" and lived in a "state of chronic fear." She asks, "Fear of *what*? I cannot say—& even at the time, I was never able to formulate my terror. It was like some dark undefinable menace, forever dogging my steps, lurking, & threatening; I was conscious of it wherever I went by day, & at night it made sleep impossible, unless a light & a nurse-maid were in the room." The daytime fears became associated with thresholds, especially as she returned from walks with her father and sensed that "it" was "behind me, upon me." She felt "a choking agony of terror" if the door did not open immediately (17–18). Wharton says she had a phobia about thresholds, being unable to stand for half a minute on a doorstep, into adulthood.

Cynthia Griffin Wolff, in her biography of Wharton, makes the connection between thresholds and incest, noting Wharton's use of the threshold as motif in her works with an incest theme (see pp. 172–74 and 272–75). Interestingly, the phobias of incest survivors often involve space, as in fear of a certain type of space.[67] Wolff also associates, as I have noted, the hand of Wharton's father, held by her on her walks, with the "third hand" of Mr. Palmato in the incest fragment. It may also be relevant that the vestibule of Wharton's childhood home was painted red (Lewis, 22), for the color red is associated with incest in her works. Siena, the setting of "The House of the Dead Hand," is the red city, and the woman in the mysterious portrait wears red; the home of Charity and her foster father/husband in *Summer* is the red house; Mr. Palmato's third hand is a "crimson flash" (Lewis, 548).

In her autobiographical narratives Wharton portrays her father positively but distantly. Her few references to him have been described as "curiously perfunctory, idyllic, and unreal" (Wilson, 172). She notes that she appreciated his gentleman's library and imagines "there was a time when his rather rudimentary love of verse might have been developed had he had anyone with whom to share it. But my mother's matter-of-factness must have shrivelled up any such buds of fancy. . . . I have wondered since what stifled cravings had once germinated in him, and what manner of man he was really meant to be. That he was a lonely one, haunted by something always unexpressed and unattained, I am sure" (*BG*, 39). This is the only extensive comment Wharton makes about her father, and in the franker "Life and I" George Jones plays even less of a role. Besides his presence on her walks, she mentions only his final illness, referring to him briefly as "my dear kind father" (46). The adjectives "dear" and "kind," one of which Wharton generally uses in speaking of her father, may seem a bit perfunctory and unreal, as in Wilson's complaint; but they have been enough to establish him as a "benevolent presence," in Wolff's terms. However, as Wolff goes on to point out, he seems only a "silent visitor" in the little girl's world: "Never once, in any of her memoirs of childhood, does Wharton quote her father directly; never once do we hear his voice" (34). Goodman concludes that the relationship was problematic because of the father's absence (18).

Wharton spends more time on her "cold" and "disapproving" mother, showing palpable hostility and accentuating her mother's refusal to answer questions about sex. The voice of Lucretia Jones resounds throughout the autobiographical writings, and it always seems to be criticizing, shriveling up any "buds of fancy" in daughter as well as husband.[68] In *A Backward Glance* there is just a glimpse of the mother's reluctance to discuss sex: an older Edith insists on knowing why her cousin George has disappeared from society, forcing her mother to mutter, "Some woman" (*BG*, 24). The same situation is described twice in "Life and I" in much more ominous terms. In the first instance Wharton says that whenever she asked her mother about sex she was told that she was too little to understand or that it was not nice to talk about such things. When at age seven or eight a cousin told her where babies came from, she confessed to her mother and received a severe scolding.

The second instance Wharton describes as follows:

[A] few days before my marriage, I was seized with such a dread of the whole dark mystery, that I summoned up courage to appeal to my mother, & begged her, with a heart beating to suffocation, to tell me "what being married was like." Her handsome face at once took on the look of icy disapproval which I most dreaded. "I never heard such a ridiculous question!" she said impatiently; & I felt at once how vulgar she thought me.

But in the extremity of my need I persisted. "I'm afraid, Mamma—I want to know what will happen to me!"

The coldness of her expression deepened to disgust. She was silent for a dreadful moment; then she said with an effort: "You've seen enough pictures & statues in your life. Haven't you noticed that men are—made differently from women?"

"Yes," I faltered blankly.

"Well, then—?"

I was silent, from sheer inability to follow, & she brought out sharply: "Then for heaven's sake don't ask me any more silly questions. You can't be as stupid as you pretend!"

The dreadful moment was over, & the only result was that I had been convicted of stupidity for not knowing what I had been expressly forbidden to ask about, or even to think of! .... I record this brief conversation, because the training of which it was the beautiful & logical conclusion did more than anything else to falsify & misdirect my whole life . . . And, since, in the end, it did neither, it only strengthens the conclusion that one is what one is, & that education may delay but cannot deflect one's growth. Only, what possibilities of tragedy may lie in the delay! (34–35: ellipses Wharton's)

It is questionable whether Wharton's portrait of Lucretia as a cold and disapproving person who cast a blight on her life should be accepted at face value. While Wolff, in the tradition of psychoanalysis, blames Wharton's mother for most of her ills, Susan Goodman has recently suggested that we consider the dynamics of why Wharton needed to see her mother in a negative light.[69] But the important point here is the vividness of the description and intensity of the language. Although Wharton's account of her mother's refusal to discuss sex is sad, she seems to exaggerate in claiming it did "more than anything" to "falsify and misdirect my whole life" and caused a "tragedy." The passage recalls an earlier one in "Life and I." Before the onset of her fears, Wharton endured what she calls a "moral malady" that seems from her description even worse than the fears. She tells a rather conventional anecdote about confessing a misdeed because of her desire to tell the truth and then being scolded by her mother. She concludes,

Nothing I have suffered since has equaled the darkness of horror that weighed on my childhood in respect to this vexed problem of truth-telling, & the impossibility of reconciling "God's" standard of truthfulness with the conventional obligation to be "polite" & not hurt anyone's feelings. Between these conflicting rules of conduct I suffered an untold anguish of perplexity, & suffered alone, as imaginative children generally do, without daring to tell anyone of my trouble, because I vaguely felt that I *ought* to know what was right, & that it was probably "naughty" not to. (7)

Not only the content but the intensity of the language is similar to Wharton's questioning of her mother about sex. One can sympathize with the child's dilemma, but the language seems overwrought, particularly from a skilled author writing at least fifty years after the event. It is odd that this problem would cause greater "suffering" than any subsequent trouble, and the terms "darkness of horror" and "untold anguish" seem out of proportion to a conflict between truth and politeness, just as "tragedy" does to a lack of information about sex. In general, Wharton's attitude toward her parents appears extreme. Certainly remote parents have always been common among the upper classes, and she provides no evidence that her parents were unusual or that they ever neglected her or intentionally treated her cruelly. What is strange is that her father's supposed kindness should lead to silence and distance and her mother's refusal to discuss sex to virtual rejection. Wharton never gives a satisfactory explanation for the depth of her alienation from either parent or the intensity of the language she uses to describe a seemingly uneventful childhood ("horror," "anguish," "tragedy").

If, however, Wharton was sexually abused by her father when she was a young child, the conflict between truth-telling and politeness could have been a dark horror. Her mother's refusal to provide any explanation that would help her understand the experience might well have poisoned her life and led her to view her mother as a tacit collaborator in male corruption (this last term is used by Donovan [47] to describe mothers in many Wharton stories). It would be no wonder, then, that Wharton seemed to feel she was an orphan, a "homeless waif" (*BG*, 119), and created so many orphaned heroines.[70] Wharton's phobias and fears, such as her fear of being alone in the dark (she slept with the light on until she was 25), her nausea, depression, and feeling of being an outsider, are all routinely described by incest survivors. Her family also fits the pattern so far established through surveys of victims: a financially stable, even high-income, family that stresses appearances—"conventional to a fault," as one researcher puts it.[71] Although the fathers in such families tend to impress outsiders as "sympathetic" and occasionally even passive, sex roles are firmly adhered to in the family; for instance, sons are privileged and daughters isolated and heavily supervised.[72]

We might expect that Wharton's attitude toward her parents would differ from that commonly expressed by incest survivors, for the victim would presumably feel hostile toward the perpetrator. But, although nearly all survivors hated and tried to escape the abuse, the majority make excuses for their fathers. Even through their wariness, they tend to pity the fathers and view them as especially intelligent and gifted.[73] The common attitude toward the mother is ambivalent at best. Most survivors see her as "cold," blaming her for not coming to their aid. A researcher notes, "The personal accounts of incest victims are replete with descriptions of distant, unavailable mothers and with expressions of longing for maternal nurturance."[74] This whole scenario fits Wharton completely.

It was a consecutive reading of Wharton's short stories, however, rather than her biography or "Beatrice Palmato," that first led me to the belief that she may have been an incest victim. This might be because, as Candace Waid suggests, "the short stories provide the most intimate record of Wharton's fears and desires as she negotiated the boundaries between art and life."[75] Critics sensed some mystery about Wharton's life, something that her art fed on, even before her papers were opened and "Beatrice Palmato" discovered. In discussing "Mrs. Wharton's Mask" back in 1964 Marius Bewley noted that the dearth of information about Wharton had not been fortunate for her critical reputation. Bewley continued,

> She belongs among those writers whose work, however obliquely, is an extension of their personal tensions and their intimate personal ties, a knowledge of which may do more to illuminate their creative motives and the particular effects their art achieves than anything else can. The quality that so many of her heroines and heroes have of being hopelessly trapped . . . seems projected from some deep center in herself, from some concealed hopelessness, frustration, or private rage that we are never allowed to see except at several removes in the disguising medium of her art.[76]

More recently, Jean Gooder uses the comment by an acquaintance of Wharton's that "I think she's never been really unlocked, and that most of her emotions have gone into her books" for the article title "Unlocking Edith Wharton" (35). This is an interesting metaphor, considering the importance of keys and unlocking in "The House of the Dead Hand" and other stories. Lev Raphael has written several essays on the theme of shame in Wharton's longer fiction; although he has not explained its significance to Wharton, shame is central to incest victims, who tend to blame themselves for the abuse.[77]

The repressed memory of childhood sexual abuse might be the hidden "deep center in herself" that critics have sensed in Wharton. I think there are two reasons why no one has put forth this theory,[78] even after the discovery of "Beatrice Palmato" and increased discussion of the incest theme in Wharton's work: first, the incest taboo—that is, the taboo against talking about it, and the resulting ignorance about the characteristics and life patterns of incest victims; and second, Wharton's hostility toward her mother and compassion for her father in the autobiographical narratives, attitudes that fit perfectly with the general tendency of society to excuse the father and blame the mother. Without the knowledge that incest survivors frequently portray their fathers as gifted and deserving of pity and their mothers as cold and distant, critics have been misled. Thus, for instance, Lewis assumes that the source of Wharton's threshold terrors has to be her mother. Wharton's statement that the menace lay *behind* her as she hovered on the doorstep must therefore be wrong: "For surely the threat lay *inside* the house. And who was waiting there . . . but her own mother?"[79] But surely one does not make this big a mistake in describing one's own phobias. Lewis's instincts are right, as usual, because when he goes on to develop Wharton's supposed fear of her mother, he adds that "nobody, not even her good looking father, could protect her" (645). Why "good looking," an odd and seemingly irrelevant choice of adjective, unless the father is being eroticized?

It was not only the strange father-daughter stories that led me to the incest theory but also the obsessive themes of hidden male corruption and revelation of past crimes and secrets. (Survivors of childhood sexual abuse, having been almost universally threatened not to tell, are usually preoccupied with secrets.) In Wharton's second collection, *Crucial Instances,* all the stories have to do with the past, and many of the early stories already discussed deal specifically with past crimes and secrets, including "The Lamp of Psyche," "A Cup of Cold Water," "The House of the Dead Hand," and "The Portrait." In addition, the slight tale "A Coward" (1899) concerns a man's past moment of cowardice that has overshadowed his life, and "The Confessional" treats the secret past of two Italian-Americans. The theme of past secrets becomes even more central in Wharton's later period, as does the related situation of a man's hidden corruption, which is often accompanied by a woman's complicity. This related theme can be traced in all the short stories mentioned above, as well as "That Good May Come," "The Duchess at Prayer," "The Rembrandt" (1900), and even "The Journey."

The latter story, which I mentioned previously as an effective portrait of a woman who conceals her husband's death during a train ride, is generally interpreted as a death wish fantasy in which Wharton succeeded in getting rid of her husband.[80] However, it quite literally fits the incest paradigm—a man's hidden corruption accompanied by a woman's complicity. Wharton based one of her last stories, "Confession" (1936), titled in the magazine version "Unconfessed Crime," on the Lizzie Borden case; interestingly, she departs from history and has the Lizzie character kill only her father and not her mother. While acknowledging that the story, and the play version she also wrote, stemmed from a real case, Wharton told a correspondent that the young woman could just as well have murdered an intolerable husband.[81] One might apply this clue in looking at some of Wharton's early stories and ask whether the familiar claustrophobic wife in stories like "The Journey," "The Duchess at Prayer," "The Moving Finger," and "The Lady's Maid's Bell" could just as well be seen as a walled-in daughter/incest victim.

Part of the feeling of claustrophobia seems to lie in having to protect the terrible secret from oneself even more than from others. The ghost of the father, Dr. Lombard or Mr. Jones, with his admonitions not to tell, may be less threatening than the remembering itself. A very common characteristic of incest survivors is their tendency to repress incidents of abuse, resulting sometimes in occasional memory gaps and sometimes in almost total amnesia, even into middle age.[82] Amnesia would, of course, be very likely if the sexual abuse occurred before the child's memory was firmly established (Wharton's walks with her father, which are clearly connected with her childhood phobias, began before she was four). The stories indicate that Wharton probably had no consistent memory of abuse, although she may have had flashbacks or partial recall at various periods in her life. The heroine of "The Quicksand" (1902), who is shattered by the discovery of her husband's moral corruption, cannot forget, even after his death: "But something persists—remember that—a single point, an aching nerve of truth. Now and then you may drug it—but a touch wakes it again" (1: 410).

In other stories also it is the simple revelation of the secret, and not particularly its nature or ill effects, that destroys the protagonist. The oddities of "The Portrait," for example, cannot be explained merely by reference to an "incest theme." There is no indication in the story that Miss Vard and her father have had an incestuous relationship or that his corruption involves anything more than dishonesty in business; but the story does shriek at the top of its voice that the revelation of a father's evil might well kill the daughter. In later short stories, as we shall see, the discovery of a secret or of hidden corruption leads to immediate mental breakdown, as in "The Triumph of Night" (1914), or to suicide, as in "The Young Gentlemen" (1926).

If the secret must be guarded even from consciousness, the daughter has to be rendered mute, and so Miss Vard is "monosyllabic" (1: 178) and Mr. Jones's first victim deaf and dumb. The latter, whose only name is that on a monument, "Also His Wife," looks out from her portrait "dumbly, inexpressively, in a stare of frozen beauty" (2: 606). Also His Wife reminds the reflector of generations of silenced women, piled up like dead leaves around the house; she thinks of "the unchronicled lives of the great-aunts and great-grandmothers buried there so completely that they must hardly have known when they passed from their beds to their graves" (2: 599). But the reflector herself happens to be a writer, an independent, tweedy travel writer who loves gardens. This most Wharton-y character, although afraid of Mr. Jones, succeeds in challenging him. Even Sybilla is named after the sibyl, female prophet or fortune teller; she may seem more dead than alive but she finally does "tell." The attention Wharton gives to the communicative ability or inability of the women in the incest-related stories underscores its importance for her. This writer begins her autobiography expressing her "long ache of pity for animals, and for all inarticulate beings" (*BG*, 4). According to Wolff, the horrors of Wharton's childhood (interpreted by Wolff as "insatiable oral longing," 206, and by me as sexual abuse) became at an early age "inextricably bound in Wharton's mind with the ability to communicate. Nothing is worse than to be 'mute'" (25).

Significantly, this conclusion dominates the literature about incest. Although one might expect therapists and their clients to stress the importance of talk, they place a surprisingly heavy emphasis on writing; book after book describes its healing effects.[83] Wharton seems to have made this discovery in childhood when she became obsessed with "making up."[84] She learned early to "tell" but tell it slant; her mother, her first audience, would not listen to agonized questions about sex but would pay attention to made-up stories. Of course, to publish the stories as an adult was something else again. Wharton portrays female artists as lawbreakers, as we have already seen, and the artist who reveals secrets is doubly criminal. On top of Mrs. Manstey's dilemma—I must create, but it's illegal—she adds Sybilla's dilemma—I must tell, but Father might kill me. No wonder Wharton had such a difficult time, as is well documented by Wolff, coming to her vocation as writer. Wolff notes that the greatest strength of writing, that she could use the process to come to terms with the "hidden elements in her nature," lay close to its greatest danger, that access to these elements would overwhelm her (87). Wolff thus explains Wharton's bad breakdown in 1899, *after* she had managed to let go of her first short-story collection, as the "flooding into consciousness of hitherto-repressed infantile feelings," her childhood beasts. If writing "summoned the beasts to consciousness" (86), we have seen their shadows in the early stories.

For Edith Wharton, then, writing was in many ways an act of courage. That fact may explain the prevalence in her stories of the theme of courage versus cowardice. Several of her early stories, like "The Coward" and "The Line of Least Resistance," debate such questions as "What is a coward?" and "How could one act bravely in this situation?" This concern is at least secondary in such stories as "The Lamp of Psyche," "Friends," and "A Cup of Cold Water," and Wharton would never lose interest in the subject. She connects it with art in stories like "That Good Might Come" and "The Recovery" and with the courage she thinks artists must have to avoid selling their souls. The "sewer gas" theme that dominates the artist stories discussed earlier seems to have personal relevance. The strength the artist needs to produce serious work instead of trash, and most Wharton artists do weaken and pander to the public at some point, could be interpreted as a disguised form of the courage Wharton felt she had to summon to write at all.

Wharton's attitude toward writing and its relation to incest and other issues discussed in this chapter is effectively revealed in "The Angel at the Grave," one of the best stories of her early period. Indeed, it is one of her finest short stories and reminds us that Wharton, like all great writers, could one day project her personal conflicts into a queer, half-jelled sketch like "The House of the Dead Hand" and the next day transmute them into a perfectly cohering work of art. Wharton is in total control in "The Angel at the Grave." She departs somewhat from her usual practice by making the point of view so distanced from the reflector, Paulina Anson, that it often seems omniscient narration. In this story the voice of the author-narrator comes through very strongly, colored throughout by Wharton's most sparkling and epigrammatic wit.

Paulina is the granddaughter of Orestes Anson, the famous philosopher (the name recalls Orestes Brownson, a minor transcendentalist friend of Emerson). Because Anson had no sons or intellectual daughters, Paulina devotes her life to keeping up the Anson House and the great man's memory. Or, as Wharton puts it, when "nature" denied the Anson daughters the gift of intellect, "fate" directly fitted the granddaughter for her role as custodian (1: 246). The controlling metaphor of the story is, appropriately, transcendentalism, and Wharton plays throughout with terms like "necessity," "destiny," and "predestination." She gets in as many titles of Emerson essays as possible, not only "Nature" and "Fate" but even "Compensation"—Paulina's existence is viewed as such by her grandmother, who considers her "designed to act as the guardian of the family temple" (1: 247). The House, always capitalized, even has a central "fane" and an "altar," where the priestess Paul-ina memorializes the divine Anson by writing his biography. It is funny but not merely a joke, as we shall see, since the working of fate turns out to be a serious theme.

The first ominous note strikes when Paulina rejects a suitor because he refuses to live in the House, and the author-narrator tells us directly that she did not leave to marry him because of "an emanation from the walls of the House, from the bare desk, the faded portraits, the dozen yellowing tomes that no hand but hers ever lifted from the shelf" (1: 249). Then her remaining relatives die and "the House possessed her"; Paulina can hardly leave it for a day, as she loses herself in "filial pantheism" (1: 249). The Anson House seems to be turning into the House of the Dead Hand with its paternal ghost. After tourists stop coming to see the house and the publisher rejects Paulina's biography, explaining that Anson is no longer a big name, Paulina joins Sybilla, the duchess at prayer, and Wharton's other claustrophobic ladies: "[I]t seemed to her that she had been walled alive into a tomb hung with the effigies of dead ideas. She felt a desperate longing to escape into the outer air, where people toiled and loved, and living sympathies went hand in hand. It was the sense of wasted labor that oppressed her . . . There was a dreary parallel between her grandfather's fruitless toil and her own unprofitable sacrifice. Each in turn had kept vigil by a corpse" (1: 253).

Like Sybilla, Paulina has a potential rescuer. One day the doorbell rings (for some reason, probably connected with Wharton's threshold phobia, there is much ado about the bell in this story, as in "The House of the Dead Hand").[85] A young man appears, asking to see an Anson pamphlet, and Paulina "drew a key from her old-fashioned reticule and unlocked a drawer beneath one of the book-cases" (1: 256). But here the resemblance to the earlier story ends, for this man is a true savior bringing welcome news. It turns out that before Anson became a transcendentalist he had made a major scientific discovery, identifying a species of fish that formed an evolutionary link. Thus his reputation will be revived, and Paulina can share in the work; as the story ends, she feels touched by youth.

Although the story is generally considered one of Wharton's best, this sudden "happy ending" has been criticized. Lewis finds it "at once unexpected and not quite persuasive" (99). Donovan thinks it shows Wharton's growing acceptance of patriarchy. She notes parallels with Mary Wilkins Freeman's "A New England Nun" but observes that the local colorists would never have ended the story with Paulina feeling useful and vindicated: "It should be pointed out . . . (and Wharton does not) that in the end Paulina has served as a vehicle for the transmission of a patriarchal tradition; her own work remains unpublished and therefore on the margins, silent" (53). Lest we suspect the critic is trying to impose contemporary standards on Wharton, it should be noted that Wharton was perfectly capable of this kind of feminist thought. In a comic story about authorship, "Expiation," she even sets up an analogous situation: the plot of *Through a Glass Brightly*, a novel she satirizes, involves a poor consumptive girl with two sisters to support who manages "to collect money enough to put up a beautiful memorial window to her grandfather, whom she had never seen" (1: 443). It would be hard to find a better description of the maintenance of patriarchy. Why, then, are we supposed to believe that Paulina has *not* wasted her life memorializing her grandfather when the consumptive girl obviously has? We might also ask, from our knowledge of the parallels to Wharton's incest stories, how does Paulina manage to escape so easily from being "walled in"? Isn't the ending a lapse?

I would suggest that just as Wharton makes the coincidence of meeting ex-husbands part of the situation in "The Other Two," she presents us with a deus ex machina as part of the theme of destiny. A writer might quite realistically end up being remembered for something altogether different from the work that acquired a contemporary reputation (Wharton herself considered Herman Melville an author of sea adventures for boys). It is a quirk of fate much like the "accident" of Paulina's having been born an Anson or "designed" to guard the family heritage (1: 245). Moreover, this type of quirk is one of the few trump cards of the powerless; the powerful do not have complete control from beyond the grave. To quote Ralph Waldo Emerson, speaking of the "landlords" from the perspective of the earth,

> They called me theirs,
> Who so controlled me;
> Yet every one
> Wished to stay, and is gone,
> How am I theirs,
> If they cannot hold me,
> But I hold them?
> ("Hamatreya," ll. 53–59)

Fate finally allows Paulina to hold her grandfather and the House of Anson. Although it is true she will be transmitting a patriarchal tradition (the pendulum has simply swung from transcendentalism to Darwinism), she is not really silenced. Clearly, with the reversal in her grandfather's reputation, her biography will become a hot item; Paulina will have work, will be published—and she controls the House of Anson.

It is very important in the story that Paulina has not always found the House a prison. The first description emphasizes its nearness to the street: it "opened on the universe" (1: 245), for the street "led to all the capitals of Europe; and over the roads of intercommunication unseen caravans bore back to the elm-shaded House the tribute of an admiring world" (1: 246). This is the opposite of claustrophobia, and Paulina loves the House, finding it "full of floating nourishment" (1: 247) and absorbing from the atmosphere "warmth, brightness, and variety" (1: 248). She loves her work and, like the New England nun, has no trouble giving up her suitor to preserve it. The event that changes the House into a tomb is not the loss of her beau but the *rejection of her manuscript.* Only when Paulina is denied communication with the world through being published, and secondarily through showing the House to visitors, does she begin to feel walled in. Thus the restoration of communication at the end of the story immediately lifts the walls, and the promise that she can resume her work makes Paulina feel that she has not wasted her life. Writing or, more precisely, being published gets you out of the House of the Dead Hand.

The working out of Wharton's personal dilemmas can easily be recognized in "The Angel at the Grave." She seems to have succeeded in playing angel at the grave of her own past; as this favorite metaphor is explicated in another story, "It's as if an angel had gone about lifting gravestones, and the buried people walked again, and the living didn't shrink from them" ("Autres Temps . . . ," 2: 264). But Wharton also gets beyond her own situation in a way she could not in "The House of the Dead Hand" and other stories. With the help of a very distanced narrative point of view and the controlling metaphor of transcendentalism, she creates a story that coheres on several levels and can be read in terms of different themes, including art, fate, and the past. Moreover, as is often the case in her best work, she maintains a double perspective toward all these issues. The story may be read as a Hawthornesque satire of transcendentalism with its "cloudy rhetoric" (1: 252) that doesn't deserve to survive, or of past doctrines in general; why waste one's time at the grave keeping watch over dead ideas, especially when they cannot be trusted and a prehistoric fish may suddenly gain precedence over an elegant exposition of nature? On the other hand, only the angel's vigilance permits any continuity in individual consciousness or public tradition. The past must be come to terms with.

In its particular incarnation as the Anson heritage, the past both buries Paulina and keeps her alive. Donovan's interpretation of the story, which forms part of her treatment of the Demeter-Persephone myth in Wharton, makes Paulina a Persephone figure, kidnapped from the sphere of the mothers by the god of the underworld to serve the fathers. The tradition Paulina transmits is patriarchal, as we have seen. If we read "The Angel at the Grave" as a female artist story, we can add that the protagonist is merely another lesser artist—"Paulina," like Theodora, Mrs. Amyot (toy man), and Mrs. Manstey in earlier tales. The tradition she will transmit, as represented by Anson, is moribund besides. But on the other hand, Wharton does not let us forget that Paulina has escaped muteness. Hers is not to be one of the "unchronicled lives of the great-aunts and great-grandmothers" piled up like leaves. A turn of the wheel of fortune gives her the opportunity to rewrite the dead tradition and in fact inscribe herself. The author-narrator tells us, "It was not so much her grandfather's life as her own that she had written" (1: 250). In the last female artist story of Wharton's early period, a woman finally gets to be a professional writer.[86]

Young Gentlemen Narrators, Ghosts, and Married Couples in the Middle Stories

Between 1902 and the beginning of World War I in 1914, Edith Wharton established her reputation as a novelist. She also wrote thirty-five short stories and brought out her two best collections, *The Descent of Man* (1904) and *Xingu*; the latter was not published until 1916 but consists almost entirely of stories written before the war. Many critics have followed Edmund Wilson in calling the prewar period Wharton's greatest. In terms of short stories, however, her middle years are pretty much on par with the others. If she produced her best story collections, she also came up with one of her worst, *Tales of Men and Ghosts* (1910). Reviewers found these tales "of strangely unequal merit" and for the first time accused Wharton of writing "magazine fiction."[87] The unevenness in quality was characteristic of her early stories too, and there is a strong continuity in theme between the early and middle periods. Wharton would continue to write about good art versus sewer gas, courage versus cowardice, and marriage versus divorce.

The difference is one of emphasis and can be seen in a story already considered at length, "The Other Two." Like the early "The Lamp of Psyche," the story depicts a newly married person's disillusionment with an initially admired spouse. But "The Other Two" has more to do than "The Lamp of Psyche" with the institutions of marriage and divorce and their economic ramifications. Wharton stresses the system that helps create the personal dilemmas of the characters. Similarly, the concern with individual honesty in tales like "A Cup of Cold Water" and the early artist stories broadens in the middle period to touch the dishonesty of the economic system; the projection of the incest situation, which I have described as "a man's hidden corruption accompanied by a woman's complicity," is extended to a wider social sphere.

In this section I consider Wharton's economic emphasis in her ghost stories and marriage-divorce stories, but first I want to discuss another important development. "The Other Two" also differs from "The Lamp of Psyche" in having a male reflector. I have noted that Wharton began her career with as many female reflectors as male and with middle- and lower-class, as well as upper-class, characters. But in the stories of the middle period fully two-thirds of the reflectors and first-person narrators are male and almost all of them upper class. Even the characters in the stories tend to be male and we encounter increasingly the "old boy" atmosphere many readers associate with Wharton: the stories come to us wafted through a cloud of smoke as gentlemen relax with their cigars in the leather armchairs of a private library. No wonder critics exaggerate and claim "the narrators . . . are *always* men."[88]

Why did Penelope and Vexilla gradually give way to the Waythorns and other storytelling gentlemen? We saw in the last section that the young Wharton wanted to please her male editors and this audience preferred "The Pelican" to "Friends." If the author could not surmount the crime of being female, she could at least make amends and legitimate her fictions by adopting male points of view. The use of male reflectors and first-person narrators also gave her the opportunity to characterize men in more detail. It did not take reviewers long to realize that Wharton had more success creating female characters than she did male. Among the chorus of praise that greeted her first two short-story collections were complaints about her depiction of men.[89] Of course, macho readers would continue to label her fiction "manless,"[90] because the leisured chaps do not fulfill their definition of "real men," but the gentlemen narrators and reflectors lent a stronger male presence than the stories had initially shown.

Wharton also discovered what many of her female predecessors, even the despised sentimentalists, knew—that it is often more effective to make feminist points through a male narrator.[91] He might be a basically sympathetic man like Ralph Gannett, the reflector in the last section of one of Wharton's best early stories, "Souls Belated." The first part of the story is told from the point of view of Lydia, the woman who has "run away" to Europe with Gannett. Symbolically, Lydia lacks a last name: she has just received the final papers divorcing her from her husband but has not yet married Gannett. In fact, she prefers not to marry, arguing, "It may be necessary that the world should be ruled by conventions—but if we believed in them, why did we break through them? And if we don't believe in them, is it honest to take advantage of the protection they afford?" (1: 111). It seems to Lydia that in the "vast horizon of their leisure," a continent away from the mansion where she was shut up for years, she should finally be "free" (1: 104, 106). But ironically their life as "outlaws" who try to "live everywhere" becomes just as claustrophobic (1: 108).

Wharton's switch to Gannett's point of view for the last section of the story is very effective, although she may not have done it later in her career when she came to adhere more rigidly to her rule that the action "be seen through only one pair of eyes."[92] Gannett watches Lydia from his window as she tries to leave him—buys a steamboat ticket, awaits the boat, and then changes her mind. His point of view creates more sympathy for Lydia and her predicament than hers could have done, as the reader is allowed to infer her thoughts and feelings as she eventually realizes she has nowhere to go. Gannett can speak of Lydia's return to her "cell," as she herself could not without seeming melodramatic and self-absorbed (1: 125). The sudden switch to Gannett also creates a chopped-off effect, as though the previous center of consciousness had died—and so in a sense she has.

Gannett is one of Wharton's most attractive male reflectors. She tends more often to score her feminist points through unsympathetic, or at least highly fallible, narrators. "The Other Two" comes to mind, and in a story written around the same time, "The Dilettante" (1903), Wharton creates a reflector who makes Waythorn look good. Thursdale is an extremely detached type, a dilettante in matters of the heart. He has recently surprised Mrs. Vervain, the woman he has kept company with for years, by announcing his engagement to a younger woman. He feels authorized to bring his new fiancée for a visit, since he needs someone to discuss her with, and he needn't fear a scene because of the training he has provided Mrs. Vervain over the years in suppressing her emotions: "He had taught a good many women not to betray their feelings" (1: 412). Thursdale's cruelty to Vervain, which is based clearly on his sense of male entitlement—he even thinks of her as "a work of art that was passing out of his possession" (1: 411)—is effectively presented through his own thoughts. The feelings, perceptions, and reactions of the "reflecting mind," as Wharton calls it in "Telling a Short Story," characterize it more tellingly than an outside view. If Thursdale were revealed through Mrs. Vervain or Waythorn through Alice, Wharton might be thought to have stacked the deck.

"The Dilettante" has been interpreted as a feminist revenge story in which Mrs. Vervain gains the upper hand as she nearly tricks Thursdale into breaking his engagement.[93] Actually the second half of the story is so confused it is hard to make out what happens, but a late work with a similar situation has a clear revenge scenario. In "Diagnosis" (1930) the reflector, Paul Dorrance, has tired of his mistress, Eleanor Welwood, who has sacrificed everything for him. He plans to ditch her but receives a medical diagnosis meant for someone else (not even Wharton can make this absurdity credible) and thinks he is dying. He realizes that no one will care except Eleanor; if she were his widow, she could "proclaim her love and anguish, could abandon herself to open mourning on his grave" (2: 728). So he marries her and eventually finds out he is not suffering from a fatal disease. However, Paul does not discover until many years later, after Eleanor's death, that she had known all along about the mistaken diagnosis, had been informed by the doctor and never told him. "Woman's revenge" might be a more accurate term than "feminist revenge" in that it scarcely seems the height of feminism to trick a man into marriage.[94]

Furthermore, in both "Diagnosis" and "The Dilettante," the feminist analysis sometimes veers into misandry. Wharton very skillfully makes the reflecting minds reveal their own narcissism, and she connects Thursdale's and Paul Dorrance's selfish detachment to their certainty, which is supported by social institutions, that women exist to serve them—to provide aesthetic enjoyment; listen, even to praise of their rivals; comfort as death approaches; and, finally, become angels mourning at the grave. But she gives Thursdale and Dorrance no redeeming qualities. Compared to them, Waythorn, who at least has an easy-going nature and a sense of humor, and the much-criticized suitors of the heroines in *The House of Mirth*, *The Reef* (1912), and *Summer* are princes among men. Significantly, Wharton's female reflectors are often fallible, like Mrs. Slade of "Roman Fever" and Margaret Ransom of "The Pretext," but seldom repugnant. As Elizabeth Ammons has pointed out, Wharton's contempt for men "plagued her work from the beginning."[95] If the use of male reflectors and first-person narrators gave Wharton greater ease in making feminist points, it also allowed her to exercise her misandry but mask it at the same time.

In her early period Wharton experimented a good deal with narrative point of view. Occasionally she even violated what would come to be her first principle, as when she steps in to address the putative male reader in "The Lamp of Psyche." A manuscript of this story shows that before she settled on the third person, Wharton had tried using a first-person narrator.[96] She imagined him an interested observer who would put forth his discoveries about Delia Corbett's past. Wharton may have dropped this approach because, even while it allowed her to address the reader without awkwardness, the use of first-person narrators tended to give her trouble in other ways. Of all the different points of view she tried in her early stories, including the third-person limited and the less familiar omniscient and purely dramatic, as in the dialogues "Twilight of the God" and "Copy," the first person caused her the most difficulty. Either she strictly preserved the narrator's observer stance, as in "The Portrait," "The Moving Finger," and "The Confessional," but created too much distance from the characters, as I will discuss shortly, or she let the narrator escape from her control and become an ambiguous actor in the story.

The latter is the case in the celebrated attack on nineteenth-century sentimentalists, "The Pelican." Everything we learn about Mrs. Amyot comes to us through the first-person narrator, whose sole function seems to be to tell her story. We never learn his name or even his exact profession, only that he is very learned—especially in contrast to Mrs. Amyot, of whom he says, "I don't think nature had meant her to be 'intellectual'" (1: 88). Indeed, he begins the story by informing us that she is "very pretty" and praising her dimples. Only her unfortunate family background prompts the lovely widow to take up lecturing to support her son: "Her mother, the celebrated Irene Astarte Pratt, had written a poem in blank verse on 'The Fall of Man;' one of her aunts was dean of a girls' college; another had translated Euripides—with such a family, the poor child's fate was sealed in advance" (1: 88). The critics who promote "The Pelican" take this sort of comment as Wharton's opinion, making no distinction between author and narrator.[97] However, it should be noted that this statement, along with others in the story, is clearly misogynist; it is not only an individual, the foolish Mrs. Amyot, who is being patronized but any woman aspiring to intellectual achievement.

Considering that the conjunction of female and intellectual, as well as female and artist, was always vexed for Wharton, she may not be criticizing the narrator here; yet almost immediately his character is called into question again. At his first encounter with Mrs. Amyot he engages to meet her the next day but, as he says laconically, "On the morrow, I left too early to redeem my promise" (1:90). He thus joins a gallery of detached Wharton men who break their promises to women and flee to the other side of the ocean. Typically, the only time he actually pursues Mrs. Amyot is the one instance when she withdraws from him, out of shame at her impoverished circumstances: "It was perhaps because she so obviously avoided me that I felt for the first time that I might be of use to her" (1: 94). One can point out so many examples of the narrator's bad faith that he must be considered eminently fallible, if not unreliable. The problem with the story is that we are not given enough information about the narrator to sustain our interest in him as more than a mere observer of events. Because the focus remains securely on Mrs. Amyot, the reader questions the point of the narrator's negative characterization. Amy Kaplan suggests that he maintains his self-image by patronizing Mrs. Amyot but is really as dilettantish as she; thus the story might be about "the collusion between the genteel man of letters and the sentimental and domestic woman artist." Such an ingenious interpretation makes for a more unified story, though it might be considered a late twentieth-century projection.[98]

In another artist story with a first-person narrator, "The Rembrandt," the narrator is also the protagonist. His social-worker cousin persuades him to take time from his duties as museum curator to evaluate a destitute old woman's supposed Rembrandt. He cannot bring himself to tell the woman her picture is worthless and ends up buying it for the museum. The story closes as the narrator's enemy on the museum board, instead of demanding the money back, praises him for his charity and gives him the picture as a reward. We might conclude that the narrator has been caught in a difficult situation, between the Scylla of professional ethics and the Charybdis of generous impulse; he acts rightly, or at least reasonably, and ironically ends up with a painting he abominates. On the other hand, the narrator could be viewed as a cowardly liar found out by his enemy who exacts a cute revenge. Evidence can be collected for either interpretation. Wharton introduces the narrator in a way by now familiar as he makes supposedly humorous but insulting remarks about a woman and contemplates flight; yet he also has some benevolent motives and does not actually take off for Europe. As with "The Pelican," the reader is given just enough information to distrust the narrator but not enough to understand him. Although in both cases there is more than one possible interpretation, the possibilities are mutually exclusive.

Wharton's difficulty with first-person narrators seems to be connected with their gender. The critics' impression that all her narrators are male is no exaggeration when it comes to first-person narration. Of the many first-person narrators in her eighty-five stories, only two are female. The observation made earlier that a male point of view legitimates a narrative applies even more strongly to first-person narration:

here the uncertain tones of the "authoress" can be concealed in the "authoritative" voice of a man. This situation produces eerie effects when the story is about an authoress; whereas we expect the author to be safely behind the curtain pulling the narrator's strings, it sometimes appears in "The Pelican" that the narrator has broken loose to pass judgment on his author. In her early stories especially, Wharton's male narrators reflect her belief that men are the only legal inhabitants of the public sphere, but at the same time they take on other elements of her attitude toward men, such as her resentment of their tendency to patronize women and detach themselves from human responsibility and connection. Thus the legitimate observer easily turns into the tainted male character. After "The Pelican" and "The Rembrandt," in the stories of her middle and later periods, Wharton moved toward restricting the first-person narrator to his role as observer. When she does involve him heavily in the story, as in "The Young Gentlemen" or "Miss Mary Pask" (1925), she tries to make his character clearer and more closely related to the story's theme.

The use of a first-person narrator, especially one who functions solely as observer, increases the distance between the author and her material. The narrator's belonging to the other sex also makes for greater distance, and this is the most common explanation for Wharton's preference for male narrators.[99] But despite the ease of invoking distance as a panacea, it does not solve all problems. I suggested in the last section that a more distanced point of view in "The Angel at the Grave" may have helped Wharton translate her personal preoccupations more effectively than in other stories of the period. Yet the same strategy in "The House of the Dead Hand" and "The Portrait" failed to produce an intelligible story. Wharton did not try to present the experience of Sybilla and Miss Vard from their own points of view. The first tale has a male reflector who is a definite outsider and the second a first-person narrator who relates the story as told him by the artist acquainted with Miss Vard. In each case the ultimate effect of all the distancing was merely to generate an odd story seen through the wrong end of the telescope rather than an odd story seen close up.

Distance can prove a mixed blessing. Wharton's occasional use of narrative points of view that create too much distance may be responsible for the impression of some readers that her fiction is cold. "The Daunt Diana" (1909), a story about an art collector, might have been an intriguing study of the acquisitive instinct were it not for the over-elaborate point of view. The collector's story comes to us through the reminiscences of a first-person narrator, who is introduced by still another first-person narrator. While the narrators are scarcely characterized and have no part in the story themselves, their intervening presence makes the protagonist seem so far away that we can hardly get interested in him. The same holds true in "The Moving Finger," another artist tale that fails to make us care. Here there are also two first-person narrators, plus various confidantes who share their recollections. The story is so fragmented and overwhelmed by the manner of its telling that the title seems a self-parody. If in Wharton's source, *The Rubaiyat of Omar Khayyam*, "The Moving Finger writes; and, having writ, Moves on," Wharton's moving finger reproduces itself uncontrollably as it writes, and the story recedes as the storytelling gentlemen proliferate at an alarming rate.[100]

In some cases, of course, the proliferation of storytellers is perfectly appropriate. We expect stories about the distant past, for instance, to seem remote. Both "The Duchess at Prayer," an early story, and "Kerfol" (1916), a later but similar effort, have first-person narrators who piece together a story about a husband's cruelty to his wife in the 1600s. Wharton took the plot from Balzac's "La Grande Breteche" and perhaps the narrative framework as well;[101] she notes in *The Writing of Fiction* that "Balzac showed what depth, mystery, and verisimilitude may be given to a tale by causing it to be reflected, in fractions, in the minds of a series of accidental participants or mere lookers-on" (*WF*, 92). The looker-on in "The Duchess at Prayer" gets the story from an aged caretaker who heard it from his grandmother who was the Duchess's maid. The narrator of "Kerfol," made an "accidental participant" by encountering ghosts, eventually learns the story from friends and old judicial records. In both cases, Wharton's method—reflection in fractions, as she puts it—assures that the reader remain distanced from the characters and their terrible fates. However, the distance suits the subject, as it does not in the artist stories, and the remoteness of the events narrated adds to the eerie atmosphere in both tales.

Reflection in fractions can be very effective when the manner of narration is essential to the story instead of being a mere artificial device. In "The Eyes," one of Wharton's most admired ghost stories, she gives the narrative frame considerable attention and much more space than usual, over a third of the story. The unnamed first-person narrator depicts the ultimate in old-boy atmospheres: eight gentlemen have dined luxuriously with their friend Andrew Culwin and then lit their cigars and told ghost stories in Culwin's library. After most of the men leave, the youngest guest, Phil Frenham, who has been newly introduced to the group by Culwin, asks his revered host to describe a personal encounter with a ghost; Culwin obliges with a first-person account. In the introductory section the narrator characterizes Culwin at some length. He is older than the other men and looks like a "phosphorescent log" with "the red blink of the eyes in a face like mottled bark" (2: 116). He has used his leisure to cultivate a natural intelligence and acts as mentor to young intellectuals; he so appreciates the "lyric qualities in youth" that one friend claims he "liked 'em juicy" (2: 116). It seems unlikely that Culwin would have had experience with ghosts because he is a confirmed rationalist who has banished all disturbing emotions. He remains "essentially a spectator, a humorous detached observer" (2: 115).

Although the narrator says nothing in itself too terrible, the general description reminds us of like types in earlier stories, such as Thursdale and the narrators of "The Pelican" and "The Rembrandt." Culwin even has the requisite misogynist world-view: he thinks "women necessary only because someone had to do the cooking" (2: 116). Our initial suspicions are more than confirmed when Culwin's narrative shows him to be one of the most reptilian of Wharton's men. Not only is he detached, but he destroys other people for his momentary pleasure. His ghostly visitation takes the form of a disgusting pair of eyes that appears to him in the dark after he has used another person and rationalized his motives as benevolent. The first time he saw the eyes, Culwin tells us, was the night he proposed to his cousin, Alice, whom he did not love but had encouraged out of curiosity. He claims to have proposed marriage, which he considers "being good," so as not to hurt Alice, but the eyes appear: "The orbits were sunk, and the thick red-lined lids hung over the eyeballs like blinds of which the cords are broken. One lid drooped a little lower than the other, with the effect of a crooked leer" (2: 120). The eyes seem ancient and express a "vicious security," the security of "someone much too clever to take risks," a man who "had done a lot of harm in his life, but had always kept just inside the danger lines" (2: 120–21).

Culwin flees to Europe but is bothered by the eyes again years later when Alice sends him her young cousin, Gilbert, an aspiring writer. Gilbert is described as though he were female. Culwin finds him lacking in talent but beautiful, charming, slender, smooth, enchanting, and so on. The reader cannot but recognize that Culwin likes them male and juicy in more than an intellectual sense; no wonder he thought making a conventional proposal of marriage "being good," and perhaps his unstated motive in pursuing Alice was to try heterosexuality. The eyes appear again when Culwin lies to Gilbert about his writing talent, ostensibly to avoid hurting him but really to keep him at his side. The intervening years have made the eyes even more hideous until they seem like "vampires with a taste for young flesh" (2: 126). Culwin weighs telling Gilbert the truth in order to get rid of the eyes: "The temptation was insidious, and I had to stiffen myself against it [an unintended pun?]; but really, dear boy! he was too charming to be sacrificed to such demons. And so, after all, I never found out what they wanted" (2: 127).

At this point Culwin breaks off his story, and the narrator has to cross-question him to find out whatever happened to Gilbert (he soon left Culwin and ended up an alcoholic). Because it does not directly concern him, Culwin is not really interested in Gilbert's fate (and we never hear more about Alice). Nor does Culwin yet understand the meaning of the eyes. As he invites the narrator and Phil Frenham to explicate, it becomes clear that Phil is shaken by the story. Ironically, Culwin worries that his evocation has made Phil see and fear the eyes, as indeed it has: Phil realizes he is Culwin's latest victim. The narrator and Culwin also identify the hideous eyes as Culwin's own when Culwin looks in a mirror and "he and the image in the glass confronted each other with a glare of slowly gathering hate" (2: 130). The frame is thus a crucial part of the story and our sense of immediacy increased by the fact that Phil Frenham and the narrator are not "mere lookers-on" but involved participants. "The Eyes," no doubt because of its narrative framework, qualifies as one of the few Wharton short stories that ends more vividly than it begins.

Something about the portrait of Andrew Culwin has evoked considerable speculation as to the existence of a real-life model. Perhaps critics have seen Culwin as the exemplar of Wharton's detached, self-centered dilettante, though he would seem to be the evil extreme of the type, and have thought that identifying him would reveal the original of the most recurrent male character type in her fiction. Until recently, the favorite candidate was Wharton's close friend, Walter Berry, who had the aloof and dilettantish personality. Lewis suggests her lover, Morton Fullerton; not only did Fullerton once get engaged to his cousin, but he was bisexual and communicated a "sense of unrealized literary gifts" (288). The Wharton intimate best known for his extraordinary eyes, however, was Henry James, and Adeline R. Tintner finds in Culwin and his circle "the figure of the homoerotic James with his devotees."[102] Probably Wharton drew on her ambivalent feelings toward all three friends, but it must be remembered that Culwin is a truly evil man who preys on youth, offering himself to young men as a literary patron in order to disguise his real motives. Although the story could be read as antihomosexual,[103] Wharton consistently emphasizes the discrepancy between Culwin and his protégés in terms of age, power, and worldly experience. Culwin's problem is not his homosexuality but his "taste for young flesh" (2: 126).

Why, then, introduce the issue in the first place by making Culwin homosexual rather than heterosexual? For an answer to this question we must consider Wharton's need for disguise and distance as explored earlier in this chapter. I suspect the portrait of Andrew Culwin, and thus perhaps Wharton's detached male character type, owes less to Berry, Fullerton, or James than to her father, George Frederic Jones. Mr. Jones is the "parasite" (the original title of the story "Mr. Jones") with the taste for flesh much younger than his and related to him by blood. In her brief account of her father in *A Backward Glance*, Wharton depicts a man similar to Culwin in both a broad sense and in specific details. The wealthy, dilettantish Mr. Jones prefers to lead a leisurely life in Europe and has "unrealized literary gifts." He possesses a comfortable library appointed in oak and filled with books with dark bindings (*BG*, 64). Also like Culwin, he enjoys giving dinner parties because of his "gastronomic enthusiasm" (*BG*, 58); ("gastronomy" is the only science Culwin reveres [29]). Most important, in her physical descriptions of her father Wharton always emphasizes his "intensely blue eyes" (*BG*, 2). When she describes his death fifty years after the event, she says she is "still haunted" by the look in his eyes (*BG*, 88).[104]

It is thus not surprising to have "the eyes" appear in a ghost story. Unlike Culwin's cousin Gilbert, who has no writing talent and is thus doomed to fade away in an alcoholic stupor, Edith Wharton succeeded in becoming an author and airing her ghosts. Perhaps she did not have total control; if, as we have seen, the incest situation tends to obtrude on stories ostensibly about art or some other topic, we might also speculate that Mr. Jones threatens to take over as narrator—thus the proliferation of Culwin-type narrators and their tendency to turn into tainted characters. Just so, Wharton's first ghost, Dr. Lombard of "The House of the Dead Hand," a man with "large prominent eyes" (1: 509), came back from the dead in an attempt to keep his daughter Sybilla from telling her story.

Nearly everyone who has written about the subject observes that the Wharton ghost story "secretes a sizable proportion of the erotic," as Lewis puts it.[105] He thinks Wharton distanced sexual feelings by projecting them into various forms of fantasy. The context of the ghost story "permits a more direct acknowledgment of sexual experience than we normally find in the dramas of manners and the social life" (1: xvii). In other words, it legitimates material that in stories like "The House of the Dead Hand" seems odd and vaguely distasteful. Thus we should expect to find, as we do, frequent echoes of the incest situation in Wharton's ghostly tales. The presence of Mr. Jones and other shadows from her childhood is seldom hard to detect.

In "The Lady's Maid's Bell," for instance, Mr. Jones surfaces as the handsome but villainous husband. Mr. Brympton possesses not only the blue eyes but the "ruddy complexion" of Wharton's description of her father (*BG*, 2; 1: 461). He even drinks "the old Brympton port and madeira" (1: 462), reminding us of the celebrated Jones Madeira Wharton's father drank (*BG*, 58). Although the story has a contemporary setting, it resembles "The Duchess at Prayer" and "Kerfol" in its plot: a sensitive wife is kept at home by a brutal, woman-chasing husband; she seeks solace in his absence with a more understanding man but is discovered by her husband, who then destroys her.

Wharton portrays Mr. Brympton as more of a sexual libertine than the other husbands, who are also promiscuous but more remarkable for their cruel authoritarianism. The female first-person narrator, Hartley the lady's maid, can make the situation clearer than the male observers in the other stories. When Mr. Brympton looks Hartley over, she knows from experience what the look means and how to interpret his turning his back on her—"I was not the kind of morsel he was after" (1: 461). One night as she meets him coming upstairs drunk on his way to Mrs. Brympton's bedroom, she feels "sick to think of what some ladies have to endure and hold their tongues about" (1: 462). The "other man" part of the plot seems an afterthought, as the danger Hartley wants to protect her mistress from seems less the discovery of the other man than rape by the "coarse" Mr. Brympton (1: 462).

In her attempts to aid her mistress, Hartley finds other people useless: the other man, Mr. Ranford, is too "cheerful" to heed warnings (1: 471)[106]; the butler spends his time reading the Bible and thus ignores reality; the head female servant, Mrs. Blinder, lives up to her name. In her refusal to answer any of the narrator's questions she suggests Wharton's mother. Mrs. Blinder replies to Hartley as to a child ("now do run along, Miss Hartley, dear" [1: 468]) and closes her door before the trouble starts. Hartley is assisted only by the ghost of the former lady's maid, who materializes in Mrs. Brympton's bedroom when "the lady's maid's bell" rings (a bell, we recall, signals the arrival of the protectors of the walled-up daughters in "The House of the Dead Hand" and "The Angel at the Grave"). It can hardly be accidental that the main protector in Wharton's childhood was her nursemaid, whose presence established "the warm cocoon in which my infancy lived safe and sheltered; the atmosphere without which I could not have breathed" (*BG*, 26). Wharton's other defenders, her dogs (*BG*, 3–4), show up in "Kerfol" as the ghosts that shield the wife from her husband's attack and end up killing him.

The ghosts in Wharton's middle stories are basically protective. They either challenge the villain directly or try to warn the observer or protagonist of impending danger. In "The Triumph of Night," an underrated story, the ghost warns the reflector, George Faxon, that his new friend's uncle plans to kill his nephew for his money. As the smiling uncle gets his young nephew to sign his will, a ghostly double appears to George; the ghost regards the nephew with "eyes of deadly menace" (2: 336) and tries to keep George from witnessing the will. Even in "The Eyes" the young Culwin might have been saved by the apparition had he been able to interpret it. Despite ghostly intervention, however, the victims always seem to perish. Culwin becomes a vampire, and Mrs. Brympton and the rich nephew die, having been weakened in health by the villains. The wife in "Kerfol" is tried for murder and goes mad. In all cases the power of the "father" surpasses that of the ghost: Culwin's wealth and position allow him to act as he pleases; similarly, the evil uncle is a powerful businessman who can easily neutralize George, and lady's maids are no match for Mr. Brympton.

Wharton presents the situation most elegantly in "Kerfol," where she reveals the extent of the patriarchs' power and the nature of their mentality. At her trial the wife, Anne de Cornault, tells the judges the following story. Her father had married her as a young woman to Yves de Cornault, the sixty-year-old lord of Kerfol. Her husband forbade her to leave home but brought her a little dog for company when he was away on his frequent trips. After Anne had some innocent meetings with a young neighbor and gave him her necklace, she found the dog on her pillow strangled with the necklace. Each subsequent dog she was given would appear on her pillow strangled to death. One night when about to escape to the neighbor she discovered her husband dead with dog bites all over him. The judges have Anne shut up in the keep of Kerfol. Of course, they do not believe that canine ghosts killed Yves de Cornault, nor are they impressed by the story of the strangled dogs: "What did it prove? That Yves de Cornault disliked dogs, and that his wife, to gratify her own fancy, persistently ignored this dislike" (2: 296).

The narrator of the story can conjure up the ghost dogs of Kerfol three hundred years later because of his sensitivity to the "long accumulation of history" (2: 283) connected with the place. He opens himself to "be penetrated by the weight of its silence"; instead of trying to "see more" and "know more," he seeks to "feel more: feel all the place had to communicate" (2: 283). The possession of this unusual facility, called by Mary Boyne of "Afterward" (1910) the "ghost-seeing faculty," might have allowed some of the victims just discussed to work with the ghosts in challenging the power of the patriarchs. Mary Boyne unfortunately lacks the ghost-seeing faculty. When she and her husband move into an English country house, she romantically thinks she wants to see a ghost. But she is the kind of person who feels at home only in the "bright outer light" (2: 162). Mary seeks "the dispersal of shadows" and needs constant reassurance that everything is "all right" (2: 159–60). So when the ghost comes to reveal her husband's business dishonesty and demand restitution, she does not want to know the truth and fails to heed the ghost.[107] Ghosts are ignored at one's peril, and the second time it appears it takes Mary's husband. Perhaps if the young Andrew Culwin had been less of a rationalist, if he had not "belonged to the stout Positivist tradition" and possessed a "light, spacious and orderly mind" (1: 115–16), he could have heeded the first admonition of the eyes.

The ghost stories of Wharton's middle period bear a close relation to other stories of the time about reason versus intuition. There is a dialogue between the two, a "strange duel" (2: 317), in a marriage/divorce story called "The Long Run" (1912). The married Paulina Trant tries to convince Halston Merrick to run away with her because their love should not be concealed and denied (Paulina has the same name as the angel at the grave, Paulina Anson). Merrick responds with rational arguments against an impulsive act. He thinks she lacks "logic and understanding" and invites her to the "dissecting table." She claims that his logical demonstration is "a dead body, like all the instances and examples and hypothetical cases that ever were!" (2: 319). Although Merrick eventually wins the argument and the two separate, in the long run they lead miserably impoverished lives and realize they made a mistake. Possibly Wharton shares Merrick's belief that reason and intuition cannot be balanced; she has her character conclude that one cannot serve two masters, "theory and instinct. The gray tree and the green. You've got to choose which fruit you'll try; and you don't know till afterward which of the two has the dead core" (2: 306). (Similarly, Mary Boyne does not see the ghost until "afterward," or too late.)

In "The Hermit and the Wild Woman" (1906), however, Wharton tries to reconcile theory and instinct. The story is an allegory set in medieval times. Although it might well strike the general reader as "tedious and contrived," in Lewis's words (1: xviii), it has fascinated Wharton scholars because of the biographical implications. Also, Wharton shines verbally, the story being packed with metaphor and epigram; for instance, the hermit becomes a hermit because "his desire was to be perfectly good, and to live in love and charity with his fellows; and how could one do this without fleeing from them?" (1: 572). After his family is killed by marauders, the hermit accepts Christianity and lives quietly like the "scholar" he is (1: 571). He writes beautiful lauds that he hides because they might be sinful.

The wild woman enters the story when the hermit returns from a pilgrimage and finds that a woman has watered his dying garden. She had escaped from a convent and been chased through the woods like an animal by a band of drunken men. When the hermit cannot persuade her to return to the cloister, because the nuns forbid her taking cool nightly baths in their marble tank, the hermit and the wild woman live next to each other and the wild woman becomes a healer. At the end of the story the hermit finds her in a nearby stream, dead but with the aureole of a saint. He dies too and in the remarkable last paragraph of the story "hears a peal of voices that seemed to come down from the sky and mingle with the singing of the throng; and the words of the chant were the words of his own lauds, so long hidden in the secret of his breast, and now rejoicing above him through the spheres. And his soul rose on the chant, and soared with it to the seat of mercy" (1: 589).

As Andrew Culwin says to his listeners, "Put two and two together if you can" (2: 129). Of course, both Walter Berry and Henry James have been identified as playing hermit to Wharton's wild woman, and Lewis quite reasonably thinks the story concerns religion versus sensuality, though it is hard to see what this contrast has to do with Berry or James.[108] It seems more likely that the hermit and the wild woman represent two sides of Wharton herself, and the conflict should be construed more broadly. The hermit suggests Edith Wharton more than anyone else: he is a solitary person, his family having been dead to him since childhood, and both a gardener and an artist; he feels so guilty about his writing that he hides it. I think the hermit represents something larger than religion, what one might call theory. Living according to the conventions of theory (and thus believing the wild woman should return to the convent), he embraces the externals of life. He feels happiest with "space and brightness," being "not naturally given to the contemplation of evil"; he actually composes his lauds to drown out the howl of wolves and calm his night fears (1: 573).

On the other hand, the wild woman possesses the "ghost-seeing faculty." She can become a healer when the hermit cannot because of her intuitive powers and her ability to sense evil and "cast out devils" (1: 586). She is completely at home in nature, having lived with wild animals and learned to communicate with them. Like some of the characters in Wharton's ghost stories, where ghost sight is connected with intuition, openness to feeling, and sensuality, the wild woman does not deny the erotic. If there is any doubt about the sexual connotations of her need to bathe in cool water, we can recall Margaret Ransom of "The Pretext," which was written around the same time as "The Hermit and the Wild Woman." Margaret's hour of love gives her "a secret life of incommunicable joys, as if all the wasted springs of her youth had been stored in some hidden pool, and she could return there now to bathe in them" (1: 645–46).

The wild woman reminds the hermit of his little sister, who had her throat slit on the altar steps; significantly, the wild woman has also been hunted and endured sexual abuse. It seems when the wild woman waters the hermit's garden, restoring it to life, and the two live side by side in peace, that the sister has been reincarnated and united with the hermit. The split between "theory and instinct," as Wharton designates it in "The Long Run," has been reconciled. But only temporarily, for Wharton kills off the hermit and the wild woman after two years. His secret writing can be released only with death and she actually drowns in the erotic pool.[109]

As in the ghost stories, the trick would be to gain the ghost-seeing faculty but not be overwhelmed by the ghosts, and Wharton cannot envision this happening. The seers occupy the same position as incest victims with limited recall, who are described as struggling between "needing to know and being afraid to see."[110] Wharton can only imagine the characters being destroyed by their insight. When Mary Boyne finally realizes "long afterward" that she saw the ghost, she feels her insides crumble, "like inward falling ruins," through which she cannot communicate (2: 176). George Faxon misses saving his friend from the evil uncle because he flees from the ghost in terror, thereby assuring "the triumph of night" in the story's title. Several months later, as he tries to recuperate from his "nervous collapse," he imagines blood on his hands; if he had not run away, "he might have broken the spell of iniquity, the powers of darkness might not have prevailed" (2: 344).

One of the best opportunities for breaking the spell of iniquity should belong to young Phil Frenham in "The Eyes." Frenham has some ghost sight, as he quickly perceives the meaning of the eyes when the rationalist Culwin does not. However, the recognition seems to immobilize him. He drops his head on his arms and stays that way for the entire last scene of the story. The concluding sentence is: "Frenham, his face still hidden, did not stir" (2: 130). Fortunately for the sake of the story Wharton does not say he is dead; his death would be as hard to account for as the lady's maid's lady's or the daughter's in the early story "The Portrait." But ghost sense tells us Frenham is dead, at least in Wharton's imagination, and the situation in fact duplicates that of "The Portrait": the exposure of an older man's evil kills the youth who had previously venerated him. If revelation of the ghost shatters so completely yet ghosts cannot be ignored—exactly the circumstance in "Afterward" and many other stories—the result must be death or some kind of stasis. The only alternatives Wharton can suggest are illusion or madness.

In comic stories written around the same time as "The Eyes," young people live by fantasy. A son cherishes the illusion that he has been fathered by a romantic stranger ("His Father's Son," 1909),[111] or he has a protector ("The Blond Beast," 1910). Draper Spence of the latter story is shielded by his father's secretary, Hugh Millner. Conceiving of himself as a Nietzschean superman, Hugh plans to get rich by blackmailing the corrupt elder Spence. His well-laid plot is foiled by his own humanity when he becomes fond of Draper and realizes that divulging the father's evil would ruin his new friend. Stories that are not comic, such as the Poe-esque "The Bolted Door" (1909), tend to have protagonists who go crazy like the mad wife in "Kerfol." Hubert Granice's ghost is not a material one but rather his own secret past. He cannot forget that many years ago, in order to obtain the money and leisure to write, he murdered his rich cousin, fashioning a clever alibi for himself. When he confesses and no one will believe him, he becomes a "prisoner of consciousness" (2: 24). He takes to writing the newspapers and accosting strangers with his story and eventually ends up in a mental institution babbling about his hidden crime. Thus all doors—to death, life, success, the past—are bolted. Unfortunately, "The Bolted Door" sounds better than it reads; the story bores instead of chilling, as Wharton concentrates on Granice's efforts to make lawyers and reporters believe him. The main interest of the story lies in its reflection of Wharton's own preoccupations and fears. One telling detail left unexplained is Granice's original motive for confessing: he feels less guilty about the crime than depressed over his failure as a playwright. We need only recall Paulina Anson of "The Angel at the Grave," who only became "walled in" when her manuscript was rejected.

Shortly after "The Bolted Door" Wharton wrote a much better story about a prisoner of the past. In "Autres Temps . . . ," one of her greatest successes, she in fact refers to an angel at the grave. Mrs. Lidcote, a social outcast since her youth, rushes to New York to support her daughter when she hears that Leila has followed her example and left her husband for another man. But Leila needs no help. Mrs. Lidcote is stunned to learn that social mores have changed to the extent that divorce no longer carries a stigma: "It's as if an angel had gone about lifting gravestones, and the buried people walked again, and the living didn't shrink from them" (2: 264). Mrs. Lidcote has been virtually entombed by her past; she cannot even try to forget it because it is the central fact of her existence. The past forms a giant obstruction in her mind, the connection between "prisoner of consciousness" and prisoner of the past being better made in this story than in "The Bolted Door." During her long exile in Europe Mrs. Lidcote has accepted the fact that "it was always the past that occupied her. She couldn't get away from it, and she didn't any longer care to. . . . it would always be there, huge, obstructing, encumbering, bigger and more dominant than anything the future could ever conjure up. . . . she had learned to screen and manage and protect it as one does an afflicted member of one's family" (2: 257).[112]

Spatial metaphors dominate the story. Wharton's descriptions make the past seem like a material presence in Mrs. Lidcote's consciousness;

for instance, there is one part of her history, the decline of her second husband who could not deal with social ostracism, that "she had not trusted herself to think of for a long time past: she always took a big turn about that haunted corner" (2: 268). But the obstruction of the past is not just in Mrs. Lidcote's mind, as cuts by former acquaintances and whispered conversations show. Her space has also been constricted in the real world, where the past forms "a great concrete fact in her path that she had to walk around every time she moved in any direction" (2: 257). This leaves little room for Mrs. Lidcote. In the first sentence of the story she is introduced as shrinking back into her corner; when she visits Leila's "spacious home" she is "squeezed" into the smallest bedroom (2: 268); at the end, after she realizes that the new dispensation does not apply to her, she finds herself "moving again among the grim edges of reality" (2: 281). The angel does not really lift the gravestone, and Mrs. Lidcote remains in her "prison," explaining, "I've lost any illusions I may have had as to an angel's opening the door" (2: 279).

Here is another bolted door, and we recognize in the story Wharton's personal situation as a "prisoner of consciousness" who conceives herself at the margins tiptoeing around her huge obstructing secret past. But "Autres Temps . . ." makes sense on another level as Wharton successfully connects the personal to the social, as she does not in "The Bolted Door," and the story illuminates the workings of social convention. Although it has been suggested that "Autres Temps . . ." might be outdated now that divorce has become socially acceptable,[113] the subject is not really divorce but the violation of social mores. The first people to break with convention will be stigmatized forever, even after the convention has been discarded. It does not matter whether they divorced, had a child out of wedlock, or married someone of a different race or religion; they might be social radicals or, as Mrs. Lidcote describes herself, "middling people" who just want to be happy (2: 279). In this story Wharton has it right in every little touch. The generations that come after cannot appreciate the social struggles of "Other Times, Other Manners," as the story was first titled. Leila loves her mother but does not understand her, as shown by her reduction of her mother's social unease to a personal quirk: "I know how you've always hated people." Mrs. Lidcote thinks, "*Hated people*! Had Leila forgotten why?" (2: 270).

Most of the stories Wharton wrote from 1902 to 1914 concern not only social conventions and institutions but their specifically economic aspects. Even the ghost stories, traditionally the repository of the personal, take on such strong economic overtones that one critic has dubbed them "business gothic."[114] The man looming in the creepy Gothic house has cheated his business partner ("Afterward"), stolen millions ("The Triumph of Night"), or made a killing by exploiting South American workers ("The Blond Beast"). The tycoon who dominates the stories often disguises himself as a philanthropist, like the uncle in "The Triumph of Night" and the father in "The Blond Beast." In the latter story the millionaire father publicly denounces peonage abuses but privately transfers his stock to a dummy corporation instead of selling it. The figure of the hypocritical businessman, charitable and ethical on the outside but corrupt on the inside, seems an obvious projection onto the social realm of the abusive father, and in some stories he is joined by a complicit wife. The husband in "Afterward" is aided in cheating his partner and driving him to suicide by the wife's detachment from business matters. She chooses to know little "of the material foundation on which her happiness was built" (2: 161); her willful "continued ignorance," even after several hints, helps lead to catastrophe (1: 172).

"The Quicksand" (1902) is a revealing, though insufficiently dramatic, story about female complicity. It is essentially a debate between the widowed Mrs. Quentin and Hope Fenno, who wants to marry her son Alan but has qualms about the newspaper he inherited from his father; the newspaper, an unprincipled scandal sheet, has harmed many people. At first Mrs. Quentin, urged on by Alan, argues that Hope should learn to compromise. Hope obediently changes her mind, proclaiming the woman's influence theory: she will gradually reform Alan by loving him and not "preaching" or "interfering" with his work (1: 407). Mrs. Quentin then tells Hope the truth. She had thought she could persuade her husband to sell or modify the scandal sheet, but a delicate son was born and they needed the money to care for his health. Then she caught "the habit of luxury" and decided to ignore the source of her money, vainly trying to purify it through charitable contributions (1: 409).

Thus Wharton shows how Mrs. Quentin herself became contaminated, but in line with her social emphasis in this period she concentrates on the way economic corruption is *institutionalized* and passed on. Mrs. Quentin's punishment is that she has no way to educate her son in moral principles without condemning her own way of life; she can only "disguise the inner ugliness" by building a "wall of beauty" (1:

409). So when Alan grows up and inherits the newspaper, he has no basis on which to renounce it, as Mrs. Quentin had planned, because "he loved power, and meant to have all he could get" (1: 410). Alan's love for Hope, the proposed new Mrs. Quentin, will not change him. As his mother explains to Hope, "It is you who would have to change—to die gradually, as I have died" (1: 410).

Mrs. Quentin's gradual moral decline, motivated at first by the need for money for her son, recalls the early artist story "The Pelican." It is also relevant that the Quentin family business is a newspaper, a form of popular culture. The stories I have just examined bear a relation to the good art/bad art tales in that Wharton seems to have viewed popular art as actually immoral and contaminated by the economic motive. Not counting the artist tales, fully a third of Wharton's middle-period stories deal directly with economic corruption. But if the definition of economic corruption were extended to cover prostitution of artistic talent, the percentage would be half. If the definition included marriage for money, another preoccupation of the middle period, the figure would be even higher.

The marriage-for-money stories were written between 1905 and 1910. As Lewis notes of Wharton's marriage stories, the "chief cluster" of her accounts of marriage, adultery, and divorce preceded her own divorce in 1913. I have already discussed several of the middle-period marriage stories, including "The Other Two" and "The Pretext," and they often differ from those of the early period ("The Fullness of Life," "The Lamp of Psyche," "A Journey," and so on) in bearing a stronger economic emphasis. Even when financial dishonesty does not play the crucial part it does in "Afterward" and "The Quicksand," the marriage system is explored and found corrupt. A character from "The Introducers" (1905) concludes rather baldly, after he has been disappointed by the woman he loves, "Bah,—there's something rotten in our social system; but it isn't her fault" (1: 543). "The Introducers" and its slightly improved French version, "Les Metteurs en Scène" (1908), are about young people who introduce their rich employers to high society and arrange marriages for them. The "awful power of money" (1: 560) in both stories makes a mockery of marriage, and individuals are contaminated by having to disguise the fact that marriage is a "business partnership" (1: 548).

As the "something rotten" quotation indicates, Wharton develops her point in these stories with less than her usual subtlety. A much better marriage-for-money story is "The Last Asset" (1904), the most

Jamesian of Wharton's first-rate tales. Mrs. Newell, a status-seeking American divorcée, who "used up everything too quickly—friends, credit, influence, forbearance" (1: 593), plots to establish herself in society by marrying her mousy daughter to a French count. James is suggested by both the international theme and the characters, such as Mrs. Newell's boyfriend, the vaguely villainous Baron; the Baron has been cast out of society for financial misdealings and has seized on Mrs. Newell as his "last asset." In a story that rings changes on the theme of use there are actually several last assets. Mrs. Newell regards her ex-husband, whom the French family requires to attend the wedding, as the "last stake in her game" (1: 615). And, of course, there is the bride: Hermione Newell gets moved around like "a piece of furniture" and a financial "investment" (1: 596).

"The Last Asset" has a somewhat unexpected ending in which Wharton incorporates the double view of experience typical of her. The reflector, who has helped produce Mr. Newell for the wedding, watches the ceremony "with a deep disgust for what the scene signified, and for his own share in it" (1: 615). On the other hand, as he contemplates Hermione's "illuminated presence," he realizes that the bride and groom are well suited and that its foundation on "base connivances" does not necessarily "unsanctify" Hermione's marriage: "It was more testimony to life's indefatigable renewals, to nature's secret of drawing fragrance from corruption" (1: 615).[115]

Also drawing fragrance from the corruption of her marriage is Lizzie West, the protagonist of a story published in 1910, "The Letters" (not to be confused with the Italian melodrama "The Letter," perhaps Wharton's worst effort). Lizzie discovers after three years of marriage that her husband probably married her for her money—at the least he lied about the love letters she sent him before their engagement. He claimed he had failed to answer them because he felt unworthy of her, but she now finds the letters unopened and realizes that he sought her only after she received an inheritance. One wonders why the husband bothered to keep the unopened letters, especially when they prove his misdeeds; although letters are a frequent device in Wharton's stories, their centrality often signals an overcomplicated plot riddled by coincidence. But if "The Letters" is vastly inferior to "The Other Two" and even the earlier "The Lamp of Psyche," it develops the same theme. Lizzie feels disillusioned with the mate she formerly idolized but decides to stick with him: "He was not the hero of her dreams, but he was the man she loved, and who had loved her" (2: 206). The ending of the story is uncharacteristically didactic, as Lizzie forcefully argues her position with the unmarried friend who serves as her double.

Is Wharton saying in these stories that no matter how contaminated its roots might be, marriage is somehow "sanctified" and the partners should stay together and draw fragrance from corruption? Allen F. Stein, in his three chapters on Wharton's marriage stories in *After the Vows Were Spoken: Marriage in American Literary Realism* (1984), argues that she is. He claims Wharton never departed from the view of marriage presented in the early stories "The Fullness of Life" and "The Lamp of Psyche." Although marriage might be suffocating or disillusioning, it allows for social stability and individual moral growth. At any rate, divorce is out; one might "incur disastrous results" in leaving a marriage and so must stay and endure it (221).

Certainly the stories furnish abundant evidence for this view. Characters like Lizzie, Waythorn, and Delia Corbett of "The Lamp of Psyche" do better to accept the flaws in their spouses than to divorce. Their loss of illusions and adjustment to reality will presumably lead to personal growth. In one comic story, "The Mission of Jane" (1902), a man's endurance of a mediocre marriage actually leads to happiness when parenthood brings the couple together. Divorce, on the other hand, reduces characters to the margins of life, as in "Souls Belated" and "Autres Temps . . . ," or destroys their identity, as in "The Other Two." "The Reckoning" (1902) concludes with a very strong antidivorce statement. Julia Westall's belief in "the new ethics" collapses when her second husband leaves her. Now she understands how her first husband felt when she divorced him. She decides that people must recognize an "inner law," the obligation created by love, as opposed to the outer law of divorce, in order to avoid "spreading ruin unhindered" (1: 436).

Once we have noted Wharton's view of the potential of marriage and her reservations about divorce, however, we are left with a raft of stubborn stories that refuse to fit in. What about two works considered earlier in this chapter, "The Long Run" and "The Quicksand," in which a woman realizes in middle age that she was *wrong* not to divorce in her youth? Not only has the woman been miserable, but in "The "Quicksand" the marriage has spread corruption and in both cases other people (the lover, the son, the fiancée) have been harmed. In "The Line of Least Resistance" a man's decision to remain with his unfaithful wife is the easiest choice but not necessarily the best one.

Surely the wife in "Kerfol" was right to flee her strangler husband? One could go on listing counterexamples to Stein's theory.

Moreover, it is easy enough to find contradictory statements in the same story. If "The Long Run" is one of Wharton's most vigorous prodivorce stories, it also offers a devastating criticism of extramarital affairs (2: 316). If "The Reckoning" contains Wharton's strongest antidivorce statement, it also includes a powerful indictment of marriage. To quote just a small part, Julia's first marriage was a "bondage of body and soul." She thinks, "Her husband's personality seemed to be closing gradually in on her, obscuring the sky and cutting off the air, till she felt herself shut up among the decaying bodies of her starved hopes. . . . If marriage was the slow lifelong acquittal of a debt contracted in ignorance, then marriage was a crime against human nature" (1: 427).

The author of this statement could hardly believe, as Stein claims, that "it is people who fail, not the darkly demanding institution of marriage itself" (243). Wharton was far too intelligent for this view, which reminds me of the argument of the gun lobby: people kill, not guns. When people fail in large numbers, there must be something wrong with the institution, as Wharton suggests with her "there's something rotten in our social system, but it isn't her fault." Of course, she could not completely accept the converse either, for an attempt to found a "new ethics," as in "The Reckoning," might be based on personal selfishness. The two positions coexist in "Souls Belated." Lewis says Gannett speaks for Wharton in presenting the latter view; I agree but suggest that Lydia speaks for Wharton at the same time. Stein's project of illuminating the central ideas about marriage of several realist writers may work for some of the writers but is doomed to failure with Wharton because her "ideas" on marriage and divorce (and most other topics) cannot be codified.

For Wharton, morality is contextual—everything depends on the particular situation. As Paulina Trant says in "The Long Run": "Remember, I'm not attempting to lay down any general rule . . . ; I'm not theorizing about Man and Woman, I'm talking about you and me. How do I know what's best for the woman in the next house?" (2: 317). In this respect Wharton strongly resembles the female predecessors she sometimes disparages, and her approach fits in with women's morality as described by Carol Gilligan in *In a Different Voice* (1982). The coexistence of two opposing views in the same Wharton story registers something more than the author's own ambivalence, such as her uncertainty about divorce. The presence of two views often signals the necessity of weighing alternatives. As Marilyn Jones Lyde notes, the essence of moral action for Wharton is whether one follows or rejects convention "blindly or with full consciousness of the alternatives."[116] Lyde illuminated Wharton's contextual morality long before Gilligan and contemporary feminism in her *Edith Wharton: Convention and Morality in the Work of a Novelist* (1959).

The only central ideas about marriage that Wharton puts forth consistently in all her stories are those of "The Other Two": that the woman is an object of exchange in marriage, and divorce is not the answer to the marriage problem. The latter may be seen as a corollary of the first. Wharton does not criticize divorce because she is conservative or has "faith in matrimony" (Stein, 276) but because it fails to provide a solution to the use of women as exchange objects. The divorced woman remains a commodity whether she remarries or not. If she does not remarry, she loses her worth and is relegated to life as a discarded object on the fringes of society, like Lydia of "Souls Belated" or Mrs. Lidgate of "Autres Temps . . ." (note the similarity of the characters' names). If she does marry again, she just gets stretched, like Alice Haskell/Varick/Waythorn, until she wears out. This is not the same as saying, I hope it is clear, that a person should never get divorced, or that Wharton is "against divorce," but merely that divorce does not solve the marriage problem. Interestingly, one of the only two claims I have found for Wharton as an innovator in the short story specifies her "concern about the role of woman as commodity." In "The American Short Story: 1900–1920," Ellen Kimbel argues that the "importance [of this concern] for the short story is incontestable. Until Wharton's work, we have no record in this form of the haplessness of the female in American culture."[117]

The other claim is also based on Wharton's marriage-divorce stories. Lewis says that marriage was the "one area of experience which she was perhaps the first *American* writer to make almost exclusively her own: even more, I dare say, than Henry James, who would in any event be her only rival in this respect." But the era of the marriage stories was ending. James died in 1916 and Wharton had already written most of her stories on the marriage question before the war. In fact, she would publish only four new stories during the next ten years. She devoted the World War I years to refugee work in France and immediately after the war concentrated on novels. By the time she returned to short stories in the 1920s, the world had changed and Wharton herself had entered her sixties. In the stories of her last period marriage is no longer a central concern and the strong economic emphasis has all but disappeared. The tales we will encounter in the next section bear a stronger resemblance to the early Wharton.

The Refugees:
The Revenge of the Dispossessed
in the Late Stories

Critics from Elizabeth Ammons to Edmund Wilson have found Wharton's late work inferior. Ammons claims that her fiction deteriorated because the war, age, and expatriation made her too conservative. Wilson introduced the view I discussed in the Preface, that once Wharton's "emotional strain" passed (apparently he means her marriage) she settled down and lost her talent. As a recent critic updates the Wilson theory, the "dowager in pearls triumphed over the frightened child."[118] But Ammons and Wilson are really talking about the novels, and the verdict on the short stories is more mixed. One can find opinions at opposite extremes, from the view that Wharton wrote her best stories in the twenties and thirties to the idea that she produced only "slick magazine treatments."[119] This opposition has a simple explanation: some of the late stories are excellent and some terrible (just like their predecessors); one can support one's thesis with brilliant successes like "After Holbein" and "Roman Fever" or with tired parodies of early work. In "Permanent Wave" (1936), for instance, a married woman's "imprisonment" turns out to be four hours at her hairdresser's (2: 791). In "A Glimpse" (1932) Wharton burlesques her own style when the reflector searches his soul about his rental car: "And to begin with, why had he hired it? Why hadn't the train been good enough for him? What was the matter with him, anyhow?" (2: 687).

The bad stories lend themselves to the belittling generalizations made about the late novels because they are bad in a new way. They tend to be comedies of manners instead of smug artist tales or plot-ridden adventures, the bad stories of the prewar period. "Charm Incorporated" (1934) provides a good example. A farce about a conservative American businessman who marries a Russian refugee and her family, it is not funny enough to compensate for the shallowness in characterization and lack of import. The explanation given by Marilyn Lyde for the failure of Wharton's novels applies also to the comedic stories: that comedies of manners depend on the "connotative rich-ness" of social convention, and conventions so fragmented after the war that they could not easily be invested with meaning (172). "Charm Incorporated" met with some popular success, however, as Hearst's paid $5,000 for the story and Hollywood made a film version. These developments lend some credence to the complaint that Wharton went commercial. If F. Scott Fitzgerald could earn big bucks with "Berenice Bobs Her Hair," why not Edith Wharton with "Permanent Wave"? I think we have to believe Wharton when she tells her publisher she "cannot write down to the present standard of the American picture magazines" because she has no idea what they want. Yet the hope of making money may have influenced her to essay more light comedies than she normally would have done.

It is understandable that the *Woman's Home Companion* did not want the story Wharton mentions to her publisher. "Duration" (1936) con-cerns a spinster who celebrates her hundredth birthday and becomes through "duration" the center of a snobbish family that formerly re-jected her. The comedy falls flat because Martha Little's revenge is just as unpleasant as her relatives' earlier treatment of her. Wharton's humor is often problematic in the late stories, even the better ones. Though I earlier dismissed critics' attempts to deny Wharton a sense of humor, it is true that her humor can take on a ruthless quality readers may find offensive. One can sympathize with Blake Nevius's horror-stricken reaction to "After Holbein," a story in which two senile so-cialites mistake a mashed potato supper for a grand occasion. Although everyone else considers this portrayal of old age and approaching death a marvelous tour de force, it struck Nevius as a "heartlessly bad and rather theatrical joke" (193). Another story in which death plays a prominent part, "The Day of the Funeral" (1933), begins with the following lines: "His wife had said, 'If you don't give her up I'll throw myself from the roof.' He had not given her up, and his wife had thrown herself from the roof." Wolff finds this curtain raiser scream-ingly funny (396), as Wharton herself probably did, but it seems like a bad joke to me.

"The Day of the Funeral" illustrates both the strengths and weak-nesses of Wharton's late stories. After his wife's funeral the reflector, Professor Ambrose Trenham, visits his mistress, symbolically named Barbara Wake. At first he wants to return her letters because he blames her for "tempting" him into the affair; then his anger subsides and he seeks her pity. But Barbara shrinks from him once she discovers his wife had known about the affair and her death was not an accident. "'Pity?' she repeated slowly. 'The only pity I feel is for *her*'" (2: 683). The story ends brilliantly as the rejected Trenham returns home and finds the maid waiting to admit him. Although he had previously thought her sour and lazy, his "dreadful sense of loneliness melted a little" under her new solicitousness, and we know who the next Mrs. Trenham will be (2: 686). It's clever and the story is flawlessly written, but the misandry, or perhaps misanthropy, gives it a bitter flavor. Not only does Trenham outdo Andrew Culwin of "The Eyes" in selfishness and cruelty, but all the characters and even the basic situation are repellent.

This criticism recalls Henry James's comment about Wharton's "The Line of Least Resistance," an early story: "a little *hard*, a little purely derisive" (Lewis, 125). James went on to excuse her: "But that's because you're so young, and with it so clever," and his remark reminds us that Wharton's "hardness" (a more accurate descriptor, I think, than "coldness") intruded at the beginning of her career and cannot be blamed on the war, life in Paris, or women's magazines. Nor can the repellent givens and slightly off humor be attributed to a new stodginess or conservatism in Wharton. To some extent she was always socially and politically conservative in that she never showed any inclination to renounce her class and race privileges and never could imagine any institutions to replace the ones she criticized in her writings.[120] And in the 1920s she loudly stated her preference for certain of the "old ways" over postwar developments like experimental fiction. Nevertheless, as we shall see, the late short stories are less conservative than her earlier work. Maybe the dowager in pearls composed *The Writing of Fiction*, but the frightened child wrote the stories.

Wharton presents the contrast metaphorically in her three war stories, which reveal how she felt about herself and her writing at the start of her last period. "Coming Home" (1915) is an adventure with a female hero. Yvonne Malo, the fiancée of the soldier-narrator's friend, Jean de Rechamp, had been visiting Jean in eastern France when war broke out. At the front Jean worries not only about his family's safety in an area taken by the Germans but about his grandmother's dislike of Yvonne; his family disapproved of her bohemianism—her living alone in Paris as a musician and her upbringing by a foster father with whom it was rumored she had a sexual relationship. But when Jean and the narrator finally make their way east through a ruined landscape, they find his home still standing. The family now adores Yvonne, who has saved them from the depradations of the sadistic German officer, Scharlach. The grandmother tells the narrator: "My grandson Jean's fiancée is a very clever young woman: in my time no young girl would have been so sure of herself, so cool and quick. After all, there is something to be said for the new way of bringing up girls. My poor daughter-in-law, at Yvonne's age, was a bleating baby" (2: 247). We guess what the grandmother doesn't, that some old ways never change and Yvonne has had to propitiate Scharlach with sex, but her sacrifice has saved the family.

"Coming Home" suffers from some typical Wharton failings. It has an unnecessary proliferation of narrators, an overcomplicated plot, and a confused ending (Jean may or may not deliberately kill a man who may or may not be Scharlach). But the story offers us an interesting heroine: a solitary, independent, and clever Parisian who has an incest secret in her past but during the war saves a part of France—in other words, Wharton herself. All three war stories include self-portraits. In the second story, "The Refugees," which was written in 1914–15 but not published until 1919, the Wharton figure is a middle-aged English spinster. Audrey Rushworth mistakes the reflector, Charlie Durand, for a Belgian refugee and drags him to the English countryside (the premise of this comedy is that the gentry compete for refugees). Audrey's niece persuades Charlie to keep up the charade because it is "literally the first thing that's ever happened to her. . . . nothing much ever happened to the unmarried women of her time. Most of them were just put away in cottages covered with clematis and forgotten. Aunt Audrey has always been forgotten" (2: 589). But by the time Charlie meets her again at the end of the war Aunt Audrey has become Colonel Audrey Rushworth, an administrator of Y.M.C.A. war work in France. Although Charlie fears being taken up by her again, she does not even recognize him. The niece explains that she "has a lot of other things to think about nowadays. . . . it's she who does the forgetting now" (2: 593). Colonel Audrey has just been promoted and is engaged to a bishop.

Typically for Wharton, having something happen requires a man; yet Audrey's and Yvonne's lovers are always off somewhere, giving them the opportunity for heroic action. Wharton thus locates herself within another women's literary tradition as she portrays war broadening women's horizons, becoming a source of liberation as well as suffering.[121] The war does not, however, improve the situation of the woman writer. In her last war story, entitled "Writing a War Story" (1919), Wharton introduces Miss Ivy Spang, a young clinging vine at the opposite pole from Yvonne and Audrey. Having published a "little volume of verses" before the war (2: 359), Ivy is asked to contribute a short story to a journal for wounded soldiers. The "puzzled authoress" has no idea how to write a story—Wharton devotes several pages to her attempts to begin—and only completes it with the aid of her former governess (2: 362). When the journal appears, the soldiers in the hospital where Ivy works praise the photo that accompanies her story. The only invalid who actually reads Ivy's attempt is a famous novelist, Harold Harbard; this Jamesian figure ridicules the story and asks for a photograph instead. As Ivy starts to cry, Harbard complains, "You were angry just now because I didn't admire your story; and now you're angrier still because I do admire your photograph. Do you wonder that we novelists find such an inexhaustible field in Woman?" (2: 370).

So much for the aspiring authoress, as the story ends in midair with the novelist's put-down. One wonders whether this story qualifies as slick magazine fiction; it did appear in *Woman's Home Companion*, ironically accompanied by a photograph of the author. Wharton probably chose not to collect "Writing a War Story" because of its obvious personal relevance. The photo of Wharton shows a matron in her fifties rather than a beautiful ingenue, but if we hesitate to detect Miss Ivy Spang underneath, we are given unmistakable clues. Ivy entitles her story "His Letter Home" and names her hero Emile Durand; Wharton's first war story is titled "Coming Home" and the hero of her second is Charles Durand. We have to conclude that the weak and passive Ivy, the "bleating baby" the grandmother contrasts with the new woman, represents Wharton as much as the strong Yvonne and Audrey.

Ivy differs as much from the female writers portrayed by Wharton in her middle stories as she does from the war heroines. Once her career was solidly established Wharton seldom wrote stories about female artists, but the few she does present are competent, no-nonsense figures who could never be reduced to tears by the likes of Harold Harbard. This is not to say that they do not meet with discriminatory treatment or that Wharton totally approves of them. She usually subjects her artists to mild satire, comparing them to someone with more common sense. In "Xingu," a funny story based on wordplay, an arrogant novelist is brought down a peg by the shrewd Mrs. Roby. The novelist, Osric Dane, seems to be a mixture of Henry James and Wharton herself. She has just written *The Wings of Death*, a novel as rarefied as James's *The Wings of the Dove*: "Osric Dane, overcome by the awful significance of her own meaning, has mercifully veiled it—perhaps even from herself" (2: 212). But like Wharton, Dane has a superior air and is known primarily for her pessimism ("the dark hopelessness of it all—the wonderful tone-scheme of black on black" [2: 212]).[122]

The writer in "Expiation" is also a Wharton figure. Paula Fetherel's first novel has the same title as Wharton's adolescent effort, *Fast and Loose*, and her Teddy-like husband busies himself collecting reviews. Paula errs in trying to turn her novel into a best-seller. Her double, a nature writer, pays no attention to sales and thus does not have to endure the final result of Paula's machinations, that part of the credit for her success goes to a man (an interesting comeuppance in light of the sexist treatment of Ivy Spang). But the criticism of Paula remains good-natured, like the satire of Osric Dane. All these characters, whatever their flaws, are sophisticated and self-aware, solid and confident in a way very different from the vulnerable heroine of "Writing a War Story." To find the prototype of Ivy Spang one has to reach back to the beginning of Wharton's career, to the "puzzled authoress" of "April Showers." Although Ivy is treated more sympathetically than Theodora, the producer of "sewer gas," she feels crushed by rejection in the same way as Theodora and Paulina Anson of "An Angel at the Grave."[123]

Wharton must have been anxious about resuming her career after the war (Spang is an anagram of "pangs"). As a short-story writer she seems to have returned in a sense to her early years and started anew. If "Writing a War Story" resembles "April Showers," her next artist story, "The Temperate Zone" (1924), expresses the same uncertainty about women and art as her early novella, *The Touchstone*. The Osric Dane type would not reestablish herself until the late twenties with "Mr. Jones" and its sensible travel writer and "A Glimpse," which introduces a musician who openly competes with men. But it is not only the artist stories that indicate a reversal in direction. Wharton essentially abandons the economic emphasis and characteristic marriage-divorce theme of her middle period and takes up the dominant concerns of the early stories: the past, especially the impossibility of burying it; perception and the prison of consciousness; and the need for courage. She also reverses the trend toward male and aristocratic characters and narrators. The characters in the late stories are overwhelmingly female and include more lower-class types than ever before. Although male narrators and reflectors still predominate when the late stories are taken as a whole, Wharton was gradually using more female and more lower-class reflectors. Of her last fifteen stories, nine have female reflectors; of the last five, four have female reflectors.

The characters and reflectors tend to be older now, Ivy Spang's youth being a notable exception. If Wharton may be thought of as beginning anew, she starts out in her fifties and adds to her early themes a new concern with old age, illness, and death. The emphasis on old age can be confused with conservatism and may have reinforced the mistaken impression that Wharton's late work is conservative.[124] Actually the elderly characters in the short stories form another category of the dispossessed; as Wharton's movement toward female and lower-class reflectors also suggests, her horizons were broadening to incorporate people excluded from the mainstream. Rather than leisured men or pretty young women on the make, they tend to be exploited servants, as in "A Bottle of Perrier" (1926), or ugly women, particularly "old maids" like Miss Mary Pask in the story of that title or the 100-year-old woman in "Duration."

This change of outlook is signaled in one of the first stories Wharton wrote after the war, "The Young Gentlemen."[125] The action takes place in Harpledon, a coastal New England artist's colony that has once been a thriving seaport. The protagonist, the aloof widower Waldo Cranch, hails from a family of merchants and sea captains, one of whom brought back a Spanish bride; her portrait hangs in the seventeenth-century Cranch house. When the house becomes the subject of a magazine article on early architecture, Waldo's secret comes out: he is not really the last of the Cranches but has twin sons, dwarfs, whom he has hidden away for thirty years in a wing of the house. The discovery of the "young gentlemen," as the housekeeper calls them, drives Waldo to suicide: "He rushed out and died sooner than have them seen" (2: 398).

Much about this story is familiar. The Spanish ancestor recalls the sea captain's lonely bride in Sarah Orne Jewett's fine ghost story, "The Foreigner" (1900), and suggests the influence of Jewett even more than "Friends" and "Mrs. Manstey's View," reinforcing our sense of Wharton's having returned to her beginnings. We recognize the incest connection of the basic situation and thus are not surprised at Waldo's suicide; the revelation of the guilty secret inevitably leads to death. The story also has a typical male narrator, an artist friend of Waldo's who pieces together Waldo's past with the help of another friend, the widowed Mrs. Durant. The narrator and Mrs. Durant become guardians of the dwarfs after Waldo's suicide. Mrs. Durant visits them daily, while the narrator flees to Boston, explaining that he has "never yet had the courage to go down to Harpledon and see them" (2: 402). Geographically, it should be "up," for Harpledon is supposed to be north of Boston. Psychologically, the narrator represents a side of Wharton with which we are acquainted—the non-ghost-seeing self that refuses to "go down to . . . see them."

But if the situation, characters, and narrative mode of "The Young Gentlemen" are everyday Wharton, the theme of the story, which turns out to be racism, represents a departure. Wharton is not a writer one expects to concern herself with racism. The plight of 10 million African-Americans does not seem to have come within her purview (the only such character in her stories is a stereotyped servant, Cyrus, in "The Lamp of Psyche," who appears briefly to deepen the contrast between Boston and Paris as he is compared to the French valet). And Wharton was openly anti-Semitic. Like such contemporaries as Cather, Hemingway, and Fitzgerald, she portrays Jews as greasy and money-grubbing (to Wharton the stereotyped Wolfsheim in *The Great Gatsby* was Fitzgerald's "*perfect* Jew").[126] The depiction of Jews makes some stories almost unreadable; in the early "The Potboiler," for instance, the Jewish Mr. Shepson has "the squat figure of a middle-aged man in an expensive fur coat, who looked as if his face secreted the oil which he used on his hair" (1: 664); Mr. Shepson speaks the same broken English as Cyrus. There is some evidence that Wharton also shared Nietzsche's prejudice against what he called "Latinate, southern weakness" since it can hardly be accidental that Wharton planned to make her archvillain, Mr. Palmato, "a rich half-Levantine, half-Portuguese banker living in London" (Lewis, 545).[127] Perhaps she had a change of heart, for in the published versions Mr. Palmato is entirely British, like both the real and the fictional Mr. Jones.

In "The Young Gentlemen," at least, the idea of "Latinate, southern weakness" is mocked. The narrator learns from the housekeeper that Waldo Cranch was a secret racist who abominated "the Spanish blood in him, and all that went with it" (2: 401). Because the portrait of his Spanish great-grandmother shows a very short woman with one shoulder higher than the other, he blames her for his sons' deformity: she "put her poisoned blood in us" (2: 401). But Wharton suggests at least two other possibilities—the renowned beauty for whom Waldo was named, Euphemia Waldo (the name suggesting "euphemism"), and the Englishwoman he married. Although she was "the loveliest soundest young creature you ever set eyes on" (2: 401), her soundness did not prevent an early death.

At the same time that Wharton deflates Waldo's racist theory she connects it with sexism through her characterization of the narrator, a milder version of Waldo. He too is proud, aloof, and given to racist explanations; ironically, he attributes Waldo's remoteness from human connection to his "Spanish blood" (2: 389). At the end of the story the narrator separates himself from Mrs. Durant, who is "other" because of her female nature. He seems angry at her care for the dwarfs even addressing the putative male reader, "Would you have believed it? She wanted it—the horror, the responsibility and all," and concludes with the sort of free-floating misogynist comment that brings so many Wharton stories to an abrupt end, "Women are strange" (2: 402).

"The Young Gentlemen" is not Wharton's only antiracist tale of the postwar period. A story about white Christian missionaries, "The Seed of the Faith," takes place in Morocco, which Wharton had recently visited. As is usually the case when a Wharton setting is either very cold or very hot, the atmosphere is beautifully done. From the beginning of the story "the blinding June sky of Africa" plays a major role, as it keeps the reflector, Willard Bent, and his supervisor, the head missionary, asleep (2: 421). Willard finally awakes to the fact that his 10 years (and Mr. Blandhorn's twenty-five) of trying to convert the heathen have been pointless. They had some success before Mrs. Blandhorn's recent death because she possessed medical skills useful to the Moroccans. Now Mr. Blandhorn preaches to an empty room and Willard begins to doubt their own superiority. He thinks, "They talked, he and Mr. Blandhorn, of the poor ignorant heathen—but were not they themselves equally ignorant in everything that concerned the heathen? What did they know of these people, of their antecedents, the origin of their beliefs and superstitions, the meaning of their habits and passions and precautions?" (2: 441–42).

Ultimately Willard has to face the most disturbing question of all: Who are "the heathen" anyway? Mr. Blandhorn earns our admiration when he throws off his torpor and decides to "witness for Christ" (2: 442). But without his civilized half (Mrs. Blandhorn) he reveals "the seed of the faith," anger and hatred. His courageous gesture turns out to be throwing the Koran in the dust in a mad frenzy: "'Spit—spit! Trample—trample! . . . Christ! I see the heavens opened!' shrieked the old missionary, covering his eyes with his hands." As Mr. Bland-

horn stands "black and immense" against the flaming sky, the boundaries between blind and sighted, heathen and civilized, black and
white, are blurred (2: 446–47).

Willard's survival at the end of the story, as opposed to his supervisor's death from a "weak heart," implies that his experience may provide the seed of a new faith, one based more on Mrs. Blandhorn's
healing than Mr. Blandhorn's racist egotism. The Blandhorns in fact
recall the hermit and the wild woman, and the too-obvious names,
"Blandhorn" and "Bent," also suggest allegory. Both "The Seed of the
Faith" and "The Young Gentlemen" are a bit more didactic than the
typical Wharton story but are also above average in quality.[128] If Wharton's departure from the characteristic themes and settings of her middle period can be viewed as a falling-off, it might also be seen as a
source of new strength. In the same way one can emphasize Wharton's
failure to be "an historian of the American society of her time" or appreciate the new diversity of settings. At any rate, "The Seed of the
Faith," along with such successes as "A Bottle of Perrier" and "Roman
Fever," belie Edmund Wilson's contention that "the intensity dies
from her work as the American background fades"(26).

Perhaps the most significant new direction in the late stories is the
emphasis on the lower classes. These characters and reflectors range
from middle-class artists and professors to characters like Willard Bent
and the Blandhorns, who are no more aristocrats than the rural types,
the French family in "Coming Home" or the Americans in the *Ethan
Frome*–like ghost story "Bewitched" (1925). But most evident is the
stronger presence of servants. In Wharton's prewar stories, servants
remain in the background as part of the furniture.[129] They may accen-
tuate a thematic contrast, as in "The Lamp of Psyche," or signal a
change of scene, as in " Autres Temps. . . ." Whenever Mrs. Lidcote
travels to a new place her maid appears; thus the last line of the story—
"She opened her bedroom door and called out 'Annette!'"—announces Mrs. Lidcote's decision to return to exile (2: 281). But the call
"Annette!" also has an effect Wharton may not have intended. It
comes close to spoiling the story for me because it dampens my sympathy for Mrs. Lidcote's plight. How hard can life be when your maid
takes care of the luggage? I also find myself perversely wondering
about Annette and *her* story, which has not been told. One of Louis
Auchincloss's anecdotes about Wharton illuminates this issue. He says
the novelist and short-story writer Jean Stafford was thinking of writing

a biography of Wharton; when he told Stafford the rumor that Wharton had been fathered by her brothers' tutor, she quipped, "I'll do the tutor instead."[130]

In her late stories Wharton does the tutor to a much greater extent than she did in her earlier work. Annette's counterparts become more than names. We can compare Lavinia, the maid in one of Wharton's most frequently anthologized stories, "After Holbein." As we will shortly see, the servants play a large part in this brilliant tale. The title alludes to Hans Holbein's *Dance of Death* woodcuts,[131] and Lavinia and her mistress, indeed most of the characters, are old and ill, on the brink of death. Evelina Jaspar, once New York's leading hostess, has become senile and gives imaginary dinner parties. One evening her contemporary, Anson Warley, also an inveterate socialite, forgets where he was supposed to dine and shows up for the grotesque banquet that disturbed critic Blake Nevius. Mrs. Jaspar in purple velvet and Mr. Warley in formal attire eat their mashed potatoes and spinach and drink the soda water they mistake for wine. The strain of conversation with imaginary guests leads Mrs. Jaspar to retire early: " 'Tired,' she said suddenly, in a whimper like a child's" (2: 549). For his part, Mr. Warley praises the excellent talk as he leaves for "another engagement," stepping off the stoop into nothingness (2: 550).

The satire of the lives of the grand perhaps deserves Nevius's epithets, "chilling" and "bitter" (194). Richard Lawson adds, "The society represented by Jaspar and Warley was long dead, Wharton seems to be saying, even when it affected to be alive still. Perhaps nowhere else is her retrospective quite so astringent, so pitiless" (Lawson, 320). A distinction should be made, however, between the society Mrs. Jaspar and Mr. Warley represent and the characters themselves, for Wharton does show sympathy for them as individuals: Mrs. Jaspar's reversion to childhood is pitiable, as is Mr. Warley's losing struggle to remain lucid. Mr. Warley even had a better self when he was a young man, a literary and artistic side that lost out to the attractions of society, especially haute cuisine and "young beauty" (2: 534). The socialite lesser self gradually "murdered" the better self, leaving "a small poor creature, chattering with cold inside, in spite of his agreeable and even distinguished exterior" (2: 532, 534). We would recognize Mr. Jones even if Warley's first name were not Anson ("The Angel at the Grave") and Mrs. Jaspar were not based on Mrs. William Astor, George Frederic Jones's cousin (Lewis, 13).

If the emptiness of the aristocrats' lives has turned them into "small

poor creatures," Wharton is most critical of their treatment of their servants. Mr. Warley, who prides himself on his agreeability as a dinner
guest, continually loses his temper with his valet, Filmore: "No; *not*
those studs, confound it. The black onyx ones—haven't I told you a
hundred times? Lost them, I suppose? Sent them to the wash again in
a soiled shirt?" (2: 543). Filmore, aware of the precarious state of Warley's mental and physical health, tries to protect him. In return, Warley
treats Filmore as an extension of himself, projecting onto him his frus-
tration with old age. Thus he accuses Filmore of being forgetful and
deaf and thinks of replacing him with a younger valet. Similarly, Mrs.
Jaspar lacks the ability to see her servants as separate individuals; she
even calls all the nurses by the same name as her first one, unaware of
the changes in staff. She has no appreciation of her maid's devotion,
which is symbolized by Lavinia's daily purchase of fresh flowers out of
her own pocket (the Jaspar daughters have shut down the country
hothouses and supplied their mother with artificial orchids). In an exact
parallel to Warley, Mrs. Jaspar becomes irritated with the faithful Lavinia. Her words echo Warley's: "Quick, Lavinia! My fan, my gloves,
my handkerchief . . . how often have I got to tell you? I used to have
a *perfect* maid—" (2: 540; Wharton's ellipses).

This cruelty reduces Lavinia to tears as she replies, "That was me,
madam" (2: 540). Lavinia is as diminished as Mrs. Jaspar from her
former self. She trembles continually and cannot walk without hob-
bling, tottering, or stumbling. As the nurses realize, Lavinia is "a very
old woman, so old as to make Mrs. Jaspar appear almost young," and
is sicker physically than Mrs. Jaspar (2: 539). Her mind has begun to
fail, so that she too has trouble remembering, but she is not senile.
Wharton shows, in fact, that servants cannot afford senility. The kind
of rationalizing that dominates Anson Warley's consciousness, so that
he can imagine himself still young and alert, can only be maintained
because his social position shields him from the criticisms to which he
subjects Filmore. Mrs. Jaspar's dinner party fantasy is sustained by the
servants' need to keep their jobs. In the lives of the servants the in-
firmities of age have much grimmer results, so that the servants provide
an entirely different view of the imaginary dinners.

From Lavinia's perspective the dinner parties are "killing" her with
their extra work (2: 541). Moreover, Munson, the elderly butler, has
been losing his memory and keeps forgetting to show up on dinner
nights. What if Mrs. Jaspar should notice Munson's absence or the
lapses of his stand-in, George the footman, who sets the table with the

servants' plates and crumples up old newspapers as flowers? Lavinia fears the Jaspar family will blame the servants. If they send Munson off "and they will—where's he going to, old and deaf as he is, and all his people dead? Oh, if only he can hold on till she dies, and get his pension" (2: 546).

Wharton reinforces the point that the lower-class characters can never disregard their economic situation in her contrast of Mrs. Jaspar's two nurses. The day nurse, Miss Dunn, is nice; she seems to care about her patient and even offers to stay late to help with the dinner problem. The night nurse, Miss Cress, is mean. Not only does she avoid work to daydream about her boyfriend and new fur scarf, but she purposely torments Mrs. Jaspar. Even though she has been warned against it by the day nurse, it amuses her to administer "little jolts," like telling Mrs. Jaspar she is wearing her jewels when she really isn't— "it was irresistible to get a rise out of the old lady," for she is "better than any circus" (2: 540–41). The negative characterization of Miss Cress, who is a lower-class version of Mrs. Jaspar, helps Wharton avoid sentimentalizing the class issue. But in one sense the question of whether the nurses are nice or not nice is irrelevant. Wharton subtly reveals that the sweet Miss Dunn has a selfish economic motive for wanting Miss Cress to stop fretting their mistress. She has to support a large family and thus pleads, "We're very well off here, take it as a whole, and I don't want her pressure rushed up for nothing" (2: 537).

Thus there is less difference between the two nurses than at first appears. Ultimately they tend to blur into each other, just as the older characters in the story do. Warley, Jaspar, Filmore, Lavinia, Munson— they are all old and forgetful. If not totally senile, they are isolated in their own perceptions, having, like Lavinia, "purblind eyes bedewed with memories" (2: 543). As Warley puts it, the light has flagged in their minds, and they all have to face "the dizzy plunge of the sands in the hourglass, the everlasting plunge that emptied one of heart and bowels, like the drop of an elevator from the top floor of a skyscraper" (2: 537). In the Holbein woodcuts, Death dances with figures from every station, from Pope and Empress to Ploughman and Serving Maid. Wharton's story can be interpreted as a brilliant evocation of the universal feelings and problems of old age or as a "paradigm of the human condition."[132]

The two young characters, especially Miss Cress with her totally un-deserved sense of superiority, make us question whether their view of reality is any less suspect than the old people's. For instance, Mrs.

Jaspar replies to Miss Cress's assurance that she is wearing her jewels, "You must be mistaken, my dear. Don't you think you ought to have your eyes examined?" (2: 539). The joke is partly on Miss Cress and partly on the reader because we too enjoy the circus, smiling at the ludicrous dinner and the characters' distance from "reality." Ironically, the foggy Anson Warley, who can't tell wine from soda water, experiences earlier in the day a "sudden insight of age" that is not available to anyone else. He realizes he cannot tell his younger companions that "he had arrived at the turn in the path from which mountains look as transient as flowers—and that one after another they would all arrive there too" (2: 537).

On the other hand, and there is usually an other hand in Wharton's best stories, the very similarity of the elderly characters, regardless of class, and the constant reminders of our common end serve to point up the arbitrariness of the class system. Because Wharton has portrayed the downstairs as well as the upstairs in "After Holbein," we are aware of the extra burdens in the lives of the servants—Lavinia's reduction to "a mere feather, a straw," Miss Dunn's need to please, Munson's lack of a place to go (2: 539). With the example in mind of the devoted Lavinia, who has sacrificed her life for her ungrateful mistress and still wants only "to live long enough to wait on Mrs. Jaspar to the last" (2: 541), it is easier to notice that the mean Miss Cress is considerably nicer to the servants than to Mrs. Jaspar and to ask ourselves why Miss Cress shouldn't be preoccupied with her own life and feel hostile toward her rich employers. Class antagonism is obvious throughout "After Holbein," not only in Miss Cress's behavior but in the relationship between Mr. Warley and Filmore and Mrs. Jaspar and Lavinia (though Lavinia displaces her negative feelings onto the Jaspar daughters). Wharton's choice of two reflectors for the story, each from a different class, underlines this antagonism. Miss Cress airs her contempt for "the old lady," while Mr. Warley imagines that Filmore would like to make himself superior, would like to be pushing a paralyzed Warley around in a wheelchair.

Miss Cress's little torments and Warley's guilty projections suggest some of Wharton's late ghost stories, in which servants actually take their revenge. In "All Souls'" (1937), Wharton's last story and a tale that resembles "After Holbein," Sara Clayburn's servants abandon her country estate on All Souls' Eve during a snowstorm. Mrs. Clayburn has just broken her ankle, so her dance with Death consists of stumbling about the cold, empty house, where the electricity and telephone have been cut off, terrified by the total silence. The servants later deny that they disappeared, but Mrs. Clayburn and her cousin, the reflector, think these "old-stand-bys" who were "inherited" long ago (2: 880) belong to a local coven that holds orgiastic rites. Allan Gardner Smith makes the perceptive point that the story "dramatizes the psychic deformations entailed by Mrs. Claymore's [*sic*] inheritance of an authoritarian male position in relation to the house and servants." Beneath her commonsense acceptance lies her sense of "the irrationality and instability of her financial and class-determined position" (91). The servants, Smith concludes, are as much a threat as a comfort.

The servants' actions and point of view remain a mystery in "All Souls'," but the reflector in the comic "The Looking Glass" (1935) is a retired Irish masseuse who used to serve the rich and has definite opinions about them. Cora Attlee both "pities" and "resents" her wealthy clients (2: 855). She repeats the old saying that they don't know what real trouble is but have manufactured something almost as bad. Her comments on the sickly aristocrat Mrs. Clingsland are masterpieces of ambivalence: "There was nothing she wouldn't do for you, if ever for a minute you could get her to stop thinking of herself . . . and that's saying a good deal for a rich lady. Money's an armor, you see; and there's few cracks in it. But Mrs. Clingsland was a loving nature, if only anybody'd shown her how to love" (2: 849; Wharton's ellipses). Cora extorts money from the vain Mrs. Clingsland in return for acting as a "medium" in her affair with a ghost. The extorted funds provide her with what the butler in "After Holbein" lacks—a "little house" for retirement in old age (2: 845).

An even more errant servant appears in "A Bottle of Perrier," a story set in a Middle Eastern desert. The reflector, Medford, arrives to visit an archaeologist colleague but finds his host absent. He is well looked after by the colleague's friendly servant, Gosling, and only gradually discovers that Gosling has drowned his master in the well. The reason? The master had canceled his first vacation in twelve years. One can easily detect in "A Bottle of Perrier," "A Looking Glass," or any of the servant stories the aristocratic writer's guilt and fear. Although Wharton was known for treating servants well in her personal life, she also recognized at some level the arbitrariness of her having servants at all, and especially as she aged and became more dependent, she may have feared that they could torment or abandon or rob or even kill her. But it must be remembered that all the stories except "All Souls'" articulate the perspective of the servants as well as the fears of the aristocrats.

Both Cora Attlee and Gosling are, in fact, presented sympathetically. Cora takes no more than she needs, and Gosling's murder of his master has been provoked; his tyrannical master is characterized as wholly evil, even in some respects resembling Culwin.[133]

It is thus hard to find support for Elizabeth Ammons's "hunch," based on Wharton's novels, that age, life in Europe, and postwar conservatism triggered "class-bias" in the later work. Ammons continues, "I now wonder to what extent age, fears about *big* change happening (Marxist revolutions, ordinary women refusing motherhood), and the visible destruction of ancient European monuments, many of the formidable symbols of rank and hierarchy, actually activated deep class prejudices instilled in Wharton all of her life."[134] To be sure, Wharton never completely shed her "deep class prejudices," any more than she did her uneasiness about women entering the public sphere. Yet the late short stories show a relaxation of those prejudices to the point where there is a greater lower-class presence with the perspectives of lower-class characters, especially servants, being presented more strongly and sympathetically. What seems to have been triggered in Wharton was increased thinking about class and a willingness to look beneath the surface of the class system. In "A Bottle of Perrier" Medford first considers his colleague's "desert fortress" (read class system) an oasis—"in the heart of the wilderness green leafage, water, comfort" (2: 512). But the well is poisoned. Below the surface of the fortress's "beauty" and "peace" (2: 514) is Wharton's familiar underside—violence and corruption.

Gosling's revenge, along with the revenge of the servants in "The Looking Glass" and "All Souls'," bears a relationship to the most frequently discussed pattern in Wharton's short stories, female vengeance in the late ghost tales. The selection from Gilbert and Gubar in Part 3 provides a good summary of this recurrent theme, the "fantasy of supernatural or quasi-supernatural vengeance." Miss Mary Pask in the story of that title masquerades as a ghost and drives the detached narrator to a nervous breakdown, proving her departure from his patronizing stereotype; she is not really "like hundreds of other dowdy old maids, cheerful derelicts content with the innumerable little substitutes for living" (2: 534). Our old acquaintance Also His Wife finally bests Mr. Jones when the Wharton-y Jane Lynke (link between past and future) uncovers her letter and allows her to speak. Gilbert and Gubar also discuss "Pomegranate Seed" (1931), in which a dead wife sends her husband letters that summon him to join her (we know the significance to Wharton of publishing one's writing). The critics conclude about the last two stories: "If not in life, Wharton here implies, then in death, beyond the boundaries of logic and the logic of boundaries, a kind of female victory becomes possible."

In a ghost tale that Gilbert and Gubar do not mention, "Bewitched," a woman achieves a partial victory even in life. The story takes place near the isolated Starkfield of *Ethan Frome* and is permeated with the same cold and snow imagery Wharton uses to such creepy effect in "The Triumph of Night" and "All Souls'"; the snow falls steadily and the characters feel "as if a winding sheet were descending from the sky to envelop them all in a common grave" (2: 410).[135] As in many of Wharton's ghost stories, it is hard to distinguish the living from the dead. Prudence Rutledge's husband Saul has been turned into a "haggard wretch" (2: 408) by the ghost of an old girlfriend, Ora Brand. Mrs. Rutledge herself looks like a graveyard carving and has leaden white skin and bulging gray eyes like Mary Pask's. Mrs. Rutledge summons the local patriarchs, including Ora's father, to get rid of the ghost. When they break into the cabin where the ghost of Ora supposedly seduces Saul Rutledge, Sylvester Brand shoots something. The identity of the victim is left ambiguous and the reader offered alternative explanations—the supernatural (the ghost of Ora) or the natural (Ora's wild younger sister, Venny, who is said to die the next day of pneumonia).

The witchlike Mrs. Rutledge is not the most pleasant of avengers—she reminds the reflector of his mad aunt who once strangled a canary in its cage. Elizabeth Ammons's fine analysis of *Ethan Frome* as a fairy tale in which women's terrible isolation turns them into witches applies just as well to "Bewitched." But at the end of the story Mrs. Rutledge gets her husband back and, however the reflector views her, wears her best bonnet to Venny Brand's funeral, "lording it above the group" (2: 420); she at least feels she has achieved a certain "female victory." Indeed, she has been called an "avenging fury," a "rural Clytemnestra."[136]

The revenge fantasies that play themselves out in Wharton's late work are not solely female, however, as the stories about servants show. It would be more accurate to speak of the revenge of the dispossessed, those in society, female or male, who have the least power. The preoccupation with vengeance also applies to *all* Wharton's late stories, not just the seven ghost tales. If Also His Wife pays back Mr. Jones, the

Spanish ancestor in "The Young Gentlemen" triumphs over her racist great-grandson. If the dead wife in "Pomegranate Seed" reclaims her husband, the suicide in "The Day of the Funeral" posthumously breaks up her husband's affair—and through letters too, as the husband's return of letters to his mistress initiates the split (and in this tale a female servant may get the last laugh). Of the 26 stories, only a handful of comedies do not portray the revenge of the dispossessed. We have only to look at a familiar story from a different point of view, like the view of the servants in "After Holbein" or Mrs. Slade's friend in "Roman Fever" or the wife in "Diagnosis," for the avenger is almost never the reflector.

In "Atrophy" (1927), for instance, the reflector, Nora Frenway, is a young, beautiful wife and mother who tries to visit the sickbed of her secret lover. The lover's sister, Jane Aldis, a "dowdy self-effacing old maid," prevents Nora from seeing him, cleverly controlling the interaction (2: 503). She refers continually to a conversation she once had with Mr. Frenway, in what seems to Nora a veiled threat to expose the affair. The reader's first sympathies tend to go with the reflector, but we gradually realize from Miss Aldis's comments that Nora has always ignored her; Miss Aldis might naturally focus on Mr. Frenway because he bothered to converse with her. Usually the avenger is a woman disadvantaged by or in relation to a man (or a servant by an aristocrat), but in this case Nora plays the oppressor role. She uses the same words, "dowdy old maid," to describe Miss Aldis as were applied to Miss Mary Pask. Wharton treats Nora more gently than she does the narrator of "Miss Mary Pask," perhaps because Nora is in some ways as powerless as Miss Aldis. But while Nora is given insight she must still endure the old maid's revenge for not having been thought of. Forgotten "old maids" enjoy similar victories in "The Refugees," where the war widens her sphere, and "Duration," where advanced age puts her in the limelight.

The old maid, or the single woman who has been widowed or divorced, is the prototype of the avenger in the late stories because she represents for Wharton what the revenge is truly for—exclusion. All the dispossessed characters have been barred to some extent from power and money, but the old maid is also cut off from sex. Considering the men Wharton portrays, this exclusion might be thought a stroke of luck, but I believe more than heterosexual sex is at issue. Perhaps Miss Aldis is "insignificant" for the conventional reason that she lacks a man, but the spinster in "The Refugees" needed work and the hundred-year-old woman's biggest trauma was her ostracism at a large party in her youth. In "All Souls'" most of the servants Sara Clayburn imagines as having an orgy while she is confined to an empty house are female. As Annette Zilversmit notes of the story, "[T]he menace of the occult is its failure to include, to want, the heroine. The harrowing thirty-six hours at the center of the tale is the confabulation of the fears of exclusion, not only from the desired man, but from the other women, from the human community itself."[137]

The heroine with nightmarish fears of exclusion from the human community suggests another category of the dispossessed, the incest victim. In fact, the most common complaint of women who have survived incestuous abuse is a feeling of being set apart from other people and marked as different; one researcher uses the suggestive phrase "cut off from human intercourse."[138] Although I have not emphasized incest in this chapter, in order to consider other issues, I trust the reader has noticed the frequent reflections of the incest situation in the late stories, along with the accompanying themes of hidden male corruption and inability to escape the past. These themes are even more prevalent in the late stories than in the earlier ones; one has only to consider the terrible secrets that cannot stay buried in "The Young Gentlemen," "Mr. Jones," and "Roman Fever." Many of the "revenge of the dispossessed" stories combine the several elements. In one common pattern, the avenger, often a dead or half-dead woman or her living champion, brings to light past corruption, battling a man who is trying to rationalize and hide the truth.

It seems likely that some event in the 1910s triggered Wharton's memory and made her write more explicitly about incest. "Coming Home," where the French heroine has incest in her past, was published in 1915 and the novella *Summer*, where Charity marries her foster father, in 1917. Wolff dates the writing of "Beatrice Palmato," the most explicit treatment, and "Life and I," the revealing autobiographical fragment, to around 1919 (407–415, 417). Wharton would continue to fictionalize the incest secret until her death. In her last short story, "All Souls'," she creates a powerful metaphor for sexual abuse. As we have seen, Sara Clayburn is left alone in her cold, empty house (read body), wounded and in pain. She feels "she must find out what was happening belowstairs—or had happened" and thus limps around the house hesitating at thresholds (2: 886). As she approaches the kitchen, which might be considered the female center of the house, she hears a low, emphatic male voice (which turns out to be coming from a portable radio) and fears she has betrayed her presence.

> But to her astonishment the voice went on speaking. It was as though neither the speaker nor his listeners had heard her. The invisible stranger spoke so low that she could not make out what he was saying, but the tone was passionately earnest, almost threatening. The next moment she realized that he was speaking in a foreign language, a language unknown to her. Once more her terror was surmounted by the urgent desire to know what was going on, so close to her yet unseen. (2: 889–90)

I submit that one-way communication, low and secretive, passionate and threatening, and in a language foreign to the victim, is a perfect paradigm for child sexual abuse. Sara Clayburn may seem a dowager in pearls but she is really, as her cousin calls her, "a frightened child." As she finds the radio, Mrs. Clayburn enacts the incest victim's typical struggle between needing to know and being afraid to see, and reacts like most Wharton characters who see ghosts—she faints in terror and though "her memory of what next happened remained indistinct," drags herself from the ground floor up to her own room where "apparently, she fell across the threshold, again unconscious" (2: 890). Thus, while other people are off at a coven having enjoyable sex, Sara Clayburn's only human intercourse has been violation at her center by a male foreigner who can speak only his own needs and cannot hear hers.[139]

The aftermath is also much like child sexual abuse, as Mrs. Clayburn feels that a "tissue of lies was being woven about her." The other members of the household claim her experience never took place, and the doctor feels "embarrassed at being drawn into an unintelligible controversy with which he had no time to deal" (2: 892). Mrs. Clayburn is expected to be silent about the lost 36 hours. The outer manifestation of the "tissue of lies" to be wrapped around her life is the snowstorm that covers the house, "muffling the outer world in layers on layers of thick white velvet, and intensifying the silence within. . . . Silence—more silence! It seemed to be piling itself up like the snow of the roof and in the gutters. Silence. How many people that she knew had any idea what silence was—and how loud it sounded when you really listened to it?" (2: 885). Wharton intended to give the title "Silences" to a short-story collection she planned in the twenties but never completed.[140] Silence, or breaking silence, is the major theme of survivors of incest and other forms of sexual abuse. The editors of the anthology *Voices in the Night: Women Speaking about Incest* (1982) introduce the volume in a typical manner: "This book is about breaking silence. . . . the most eloquent silence of all . . . has been the history of most incest survivors—eyes averted, voices unheard." Each woman who writes about her experience "gives increased permission to others still frozen in their terrorized silence."[141]

In Wharton's late stories this frozen silence or tissue of lies is almost always part of the atmosphere in some way. It may be fog, as in "Miss Mary Pask," or snow, as in "All Souls'" and "Bewitched," or even white velvet earpads in a comic tale.[142] The farce with this title has a protagonist who wears earpads to cushion himself from "noise and promiscuous human intercourse" (2: 474). Stories that are more socially oriented than the ghost tales tend to represent the web of lies as a social attitude. For instance, Christine Ansley of "Joy in the House" (1932) is trapped in a "stifling atmosphere of tolerance and benevolence, of smoothing over and ignoring and dissembling" (2: 721). She has just returned to her husband after a trial relationship with her lover, who proved too poor and unstable. The husband is a father figure who calls her "my child" and looks after her with "paternal vigilance" (2: 708, 713). He forbids any suffering in his house; when Christine asks how he will keep it out, he replies, "By ignoring it, denying it" (2: 715). He tries to convince Christine that "any return to the past would only stir up evil sediments, that the 'nothing has happened' attitude was the safest, the wisest—and the easiest" (2: 717). We know that the past cannot be buried, and sure enough a ghost pops up in the form of the lover's discarded wife, who informs Christine of his suicide. Christine knows she will forever after be haunted by this avenger, "a blot on the threshold, a black restless ghost in the pretty drawing room" (2: 721).[143]

Another martyred Christine, enmeshed forever with her father in a tissue of lies, appears in an unpublished work written around the same time as "Joy in the House"; Wharton left an incomplete 60-page typescript and a detailed outline of "Tradition."[144] Christine Grayson lives with her parents and older sister on the French Mediterranean in an exclusive colony of "conservative" and "old-fashioned" English and American families. Her father heads the Old Respectables, as the families are called, but when Christine wants to marry, her fiancé discovers that Mr. Grayson is really a dishonest businessman and the colony composed of people who "have been obliged to exile themselves for financial or moral reasons, but have succeeded in concealing their past."[145] Wharton planned that the story would end as Christine, her engagement broken, overhears her father and the Old Respectables "exchanging the same edifying views about the deterioration of society . . . and congratulating themselves on the fact that they at least have . . . kept up the old fashioned traditions" (2). So much, one feels, for Wharton's conservatism in old age. In the outline of "Tradition," Mr. Grayson's guilty secret appears solely financial, but the manuscript presents him as a man with red hair and red mustache who becomes furiously angry at his daughter's engagement and tries to sequester her. Interestingly, the Graysons have the same family configuration as the Palmatos: an authoritarian father; a passive mother; a knowing older sister who hates the father (she points out the true motives under his benevolent appearance); and a naive younger sister who initially adores the father.

The Palmato family structure also appears in a published story, the ghost tale "Bewitched." Here the perfectly named Brand family has been founded on incest or near incest: the community feels that Sylvester Brand should not have married his cousin "because of the blood" (2: 414). But they have two "handsome" daughters (2: 419) and all seems well until the Brand women mysteriously begin dying like the Palmato women in Wharton's outline. Mrs. Brand simply "pined away and died," and Ora, after a conflict with her father when he refuses to let her marry Mr. Rutledge, "wasted away" (2: 419). The younger daughter, Venny, who is "wild and ignorant," either dies of pneumonia or, more likely, is shot by her father (2: 414). Wharton portrays Sylvester Brand as violent and alcoholic. He is "animal and primitive," "savage and morose," and has a "rough bullying power" (2: 408, 414). The only character strong enough to deal with him is the avenging Mrs. Rutledge, and indeed these two are the story's real antagonists. Mrs. Rutledge avenges not only her husband's bewitching but the crime of incest. Sadly, the revenge destroys the victim rather than the perpetrator, recalling Mary Wilkins Freeman's "Old Woman Magoun" (1909); in this story the supposed "rose-coloured spectacles" of Wharton's predecessor envision a woman who has to kill her beloved granddaughter to prevent her incestuous abuse.[146]

In the stories of Wharton's last decade the incest victim more frequently survives to enjoy some living advantage. She kills her father in "Confession," and although her experience has split her in two, one half gets to be happily married to a man who "forgives" her past.[147] In

"Dieu d'Amour" the potential victim escapes her evil parents, who are trying to marry her to her uncle. In "The Glimpse" she has become a successful musician while the socialite Mr. Jones character looks on with envy, regretting his wasted life. Even Sara Clayburn, Wharton's last short-story heroine, survives the terrifying experience of sexual abuse. Although she ends in some ways a "frightened child," unable to return to her home, she does break through the tissue of lies. Her greatest fear was that "no one will ever know what has happened here. Even I shan't know" (2: 889). But Mrs. Clayburn breaks the silence and tells her cousin, who believes her and narrates the story.

Significantly, "All Souls'" is the only Wharton short story in which the gender of the narrator is not specified; we infer the narrator is a woman because she has a live-in maid in her New York apartment and nurses Mrs. Clayburn. But if the narrator is female, she is not an "authoress"—we receive no picture of her, like the soldiers' photo of Ivy Spang. In contrast to Wharton's first heroine, Mrs. Manstey, who is estranged from her only female relative and ends up silenced, Sara Clayburn has a champion, a modern angel at the grave who is a truly independent woman to boot. The story to be passed on is not a man's story, like the essays of Orestes Anson, but a woman's. It is "confused and fragmentary," as the narrator admits, and full of "half-avowals and nervous reticences" (2: 881).[148] But if Wharton could not say the unsayable very directly even in her ghost stories, she foresaw that something would eventually surface, like the prehistoric fish (in this case the feminist movement), to help piece together the fragments. She had managed to say just enough, "enough to cry out . . . the unuttered loneliness of a lifetime, to express at last what the living woman had always had to keep dumb and hidden" ("Miss Mary Pask," 2: 382).

In some of her incest-related tales, like "All Souls'," Wharton creates a situation that makes sense on the literal level and is still broadly allusive. Other stories, like "Confession," "Dieu d'Amour," and "The Glimpse," include bizarre unexplained details. It is no wonder a magazine rejected "Joy in the House," for how could readers understand a scene like the one in which a wife leaves her husband for another man, and the husband obligingly drives her to the station and settles her in the train with a newspaper and box of chocolates? (The husband represents the abusive father; he can afford paternal benevolence because he's a parasite and knows she cannot get rid of him for good.) But "All Souls'" has both social significance in its treatment of class and universal overtones. The empty house that represents the abused body and the snowy pall that surrounds it like the tissue of lies imposed on the victim also suggest the tomb and the silence of death. Thus Leon Edel can argue that Wharton was foreseeing her own end and that her sense of impending death provided "the acute and eerie sense of absence, separation, desertion, [and] panic" that permeates the story.[149]

This is not to say that sexual abuse is a limited subject, for its high incidence suggests the opposite, but to recall that Wharton's best stories succeed in achieving the goal she sets in "Telling a Short Story" of being jewels that simultaneously give out many fires. Certainly the form of the ghost tale helped Wharton achieve the organic wholes she sought. The form legitimates the death-in-life atmosphere and unexplained mysteries that often jar in the realistic tales. No wonder she became so partial to the genre that in "Telling a Short Story" she hurries to discuss it before introducing the basic elements of the story. But the often made point that the ghost tale gave Wharton a "literature apart" can also be overworked. We have seen that she actually speaks the unspeakable in stories of many different types, and if the ghost tales are sometimes better, there are clear exceptions. I have to agree with Lewis's assessment of "Bewitched," for instance, as "an artificial yarn which strives for effect by converting the figurative into the literal" (1: xvii). Moreover, the two best stories of Wharton's late period, "After Holbein" and "Roman Fever," are not ghost stories.

Or are they? "Roman Fever" concerns a past ghost, and "After Holbein" has been called a ghost story.[150] On the other hand, the narrator of "All Souls'" says "This isn't exactly a ghost story" (2: 880), and "The Looking Glass" lacks a real ghost (in the first collection of Wharton ghost stories it was replaced by "A Bottle of Perrier"). But if "A Bottle of Perrier" is to be included, when there is no apparition and only a hidden corpse, why not "The Journey"? Why not "The House of the Dead Hand," in which the dead father controls the daughter from the grave? The collecting of Wharton ghost stories would seem to be a perilous enterprise, for all her stories deal with the same themes and situations. Recent criticism of the short stories has focused almost entirely on the ghost tales, as defined by inclusion in *The Ghost Stories of Edith Wharton*. I hope this interest will broaden in the future to include a wider range.

Almost everyone who has written about Wharton's short stories concludes that they are good enough to deserve much more attention than they have so far received. Lewis estimates that Wharton wrote eighteen or twenty stories that are "very good indeed," and Lawson places her "among the most brilliant American short-story writers," declaring that she "can lay just claim to first rank."[151] Perhaps even more significant are the evaluations of the critics of the fifties and sixties, who are obviously influenced in their assessments by Wharton's waning reputation. Thus Plante, after accenting the negative in her summary of Wharton's reviews, ends with a plea that the tales continue to be read in spite of their flaws (379). Nevius argues that most of Wharton's stories are "slight in subject and execution" but then lets slip that "she wrote perhaps a dozen short stories good enough for any anthology" (29). So he essentially agrees with Lewis and Lawson; at least in my view, anyone who writes a dozen stories that would grace any anthology should be considered an important practitioner of the form. Wharton wrote well in several genres, but she never lost her special affinity for the tale, in her words "the sense of authority with which I take hold of a short story." It is time to recognize her achievement.

Notes to Part 1

1. Edith Wharton, *The Writing of Fiction* (New York: Charles Scribner's Sons, 1925), 154; hereafter cited in the text as *WF*.

2. Edith Wharton, *A Backward Glance* (New York: D. Appleton-Century Co., 1934), 126; hereafter cited in the text as *BG*. For Wharton's wish to disassociate herself from old-fashioned standards of "decency" in fiction, see her biographer's account of her relationships with Sinclair Lewis and F. Scott Fitzgerald in Lewis, 433–35 and 467–68. See also a letter to Zona Gale quoted in Eric La Guardia, "Edith Wharton on Critics and Criticism," *Modern Language Notes* 73 (December 1958): 587–89. The two short stories referred to are "The Seed of the Faith" (1919) and "Bewitched" (1925).

3. "Telling a Short Story" appears in its entirety in Part 2 of this volume. Hereafter I will note in the text only those references to *The Writing of Fiction* that are not in "Telling a Short Story."

4. Edith Wharton, "Character and Situation in the Novel," *Scribner's Magazine* 78 (October 1925): 396.

5. When I refer to Wharton's "best" stories, I mean the dozen stories that have been chosen for collections intended to represent her finest work, such as *The Best Short Stories of Edith Wharton*, ed. Wayne Andrews (1958) and Charles Scribner's Sons' *Roman Fever and Other Stories* (1964), or rated highly by the two leading critics of Wharton's short stories, Richard H. Lawson and R. W. B. Lewis. These stories are the following (in order of publication): "Souls Belated" (1899); "The Angel at the Grave" (1901); "The Other Two" (1904); "The Last Asset" (1904); "The Eyes" (1910); "Autres Temps . . ." (1911); "Xingu" (1911); "A Bottle of Perrier" (1926); "After Holbein" (1928); "Pomegranate Seed" (1931); "Roman Fever" (1934), and "All Souls'" (1937). I could tinker with this list, starting with replacing "A Bottle of Perrier" and "Pomegranate Seed" with other ghost stories, but I have no serious quarrel with it.

6. For Wharton's Gothic, a neglected topic, see Kathy Fedorko, "Edith Wharton's Haunted House," Ph.D. diss., Rutgers University, 1987. Susan Goodman quotes Virginia Woolf in characterizing Wharton as a writer quintessentially "neither this nor that." See her *Friends and Rivals: Edith Wharton's Women* (Hanover, N.H.: University Press of New England, 1990), 5.

7. See Edgar Allan Poe, review of *Twice-Told Tales*, by Nathaniel Hawthorne (1842), in *The Complete Works of Edgar Allan Poe*, ed. James A. Harrison (New York: Thomas Y. Crowell and Co., 1902), 11: 106–13.

8. Edith Wharton to R. W. Gilder [editor of *Century*], 26 May 1909, Edith Wharton Papers, Beinecke Library, Yale University.

9. Geoffrey Walton, *Edith Wharton: A Critical Interpretation*, rev. ed. (Rutherford, N.J.: Fairleigh Dickinson University Press, 1982), 167; Josephine Donovan, *After the Fall: The Demeter–Persephone Myth in Wharton, Cather, and Glasgow* (University Park: Pennsylvania State University Press, 1989), 82. For a perceptive discussion of critics' tendency to come to opposite conclusions about Wharton's works, see the first chapter of Marilyn Jones Lyde, *Edith Wharton: Convention and Morality in the Work of a Novelist* (Norman: University of Oklahoma Press, 1959), 3–24. Hereafter cited in the text.

10. Edith Wharton, *The Collected Short Stories*, ed. R. W. B. Lewis, vol. 2 (New York: Charles Scribner's Sons, 1968), 833; hereafter cited in the text with the volume number preceding the page number. I refer to the characters as Wharton herself does, instead of to "Slade" and "Ansley," because titles reflect social reality and are often symbolic in Wharton. Thus the reader will sometimes find a male character referred to by his last name and a female character by her first. I choose the form of name that I think best represents the character.

11. But not entirely, as is characteristic of her best work. There is one paragraph (2: 836) from the point of view of Mrs. Ansley.

12. When the point of view is what has traditionally been called "selective omniscience," I use Wharton's own term, "reflector," instead of "narrator" for the character from whose point of view the action is seen.

13. Jean Frantz Blackall, "Edith Wharton's Art of Ellipsis," *Journal of Narrative Technique* 17 (Spring 1987): 146; hereafter cited in the text. Wharton told her friend, French novelist Paul Bourget, that he "underestimated the intelligence of his readers in supposing that it was necessary to analyze in advance the motive of every act, almost of every word, instead of letting these be revealed by the speech and action of the characters." Quoted in Jean Gooder, "Unlocking Edith Wharton: An Introduction to *The Reef*," *Cambridge Quarterly* 15, no. 1 (1986): 34.

14. Alice Hall Petry, "A Twist of Crimson Silk: Edith Wharton's 'Roman Fever,'" *Studies in Short Fiction* 24 (Spring 1987): 163–66.

15. For a discussion of the "collaborative" and "interdependent" identities of Mrs. Slade and Mrs. Ansley, see Goodman, 154–55.

16. John Gerlach, *Toward the End: Closure and Structure in the American Short Story* (University: University of Alabama Press, 1985), 60.

17. Michael J. O'Neal, "Point of View and Narrative Technique in the Fiction of Edith Wharton," *Style* 17 (Spring 1983): 270; hereafter cited in the text.

18. See, for the most detailed criticism, Frances T. Russell, "Melodramatic Mrs. Wharton," *Sewanee Review* 40 (October–December 1932): 425–37.

19. Consider, for instance, this passage from Wharton's second pub-

lished story, "The Fullness of Life": "But I have sometimes thought that a woman's nature is like a great house full of rooms: there is the hall, through which everyone passes in going in and out; the drawing room,where one receives formal visits; the sitting room, where the members of the family come and go as they list; but beyond that, far beyond, are other rooms,the handles of whose doors perhaps are never turned; no one knows the way to them, no one knows whither they lead; and in the innermost room, the holy of holies, the soul sits alone and waits for a footstep that never comes" (1: 14).

20. Although she does not mention Undine Spragg, Mary Gordon gives this interpretation in her introduction to *Ethan Frome and Other Short Fiction by Edith Wharton* (New York: Bantam Books, 1987), xv. She finds Alice possessed of "ambitiousness" and "the strength of being able to invent herself in the image of whatever man is the next step on her steadily upward climb." Blake Nevius was the first to put forward a totally negative view of Alice, referring to "the known fact of Alice Waythorn's callous treatment of her first two husbands" and "the boundless extent of her ambitions." See *Edith Wharton: A Study of Her Fiction* (Berkeley: University of California Press, 1953), 71. Hereafter cited in the text.

21. Richard H. Lawson, "Edith Wharton," in *American Short-Story Writers, 1880–1910*, ed. Bobby Ellen Kimbel (Detroit: Gale Research, 1989), 322.

22. Edith Wharton, *The House of Mirth* (New York: Charles Scribner's Sons, 1905), 5.

23. Richard H. Lawson, *Edith Wharton* (New York: Frederick Ungar Publishing Co., 1977), 81; Plante, "Edith Wharton as Short Story Writer," 367. On the other hand, Cynthia Griffin Wolff notes that Waythorn is the perpetrator, not the victim. See her introduction to Edith Wharton, *Roman Fever and Other Stories* (New York: Collier Books, 1987), xiv.

24. The reference could be, of course, to her husband, Teddy Wharton. There is not much resemblance, but Teddy did like his comfort and occasionally became obsessed with money.

25. Henry James to Edith Wharton, January 1908, in *Henry James and Edith Wharton Letters: 1900–1915*, ed. Lyall H. Powers (New York: Charles Scribner's Sons, 1990), 87–88. The letter is discussed and the relevant part reproduced in Millicent Bell, "A James 'Gift' to Edith Wharton," *Modern Language Notes* 72 (March 1957): 183, and in Millicent Bell, *Edith Wharton & Henry James: The Story of Their Friendship* (New York: George Braziller, 1965), 261–63.

26. Bell, "A James 'Gift' to Edith Wharton," p. 184.

27. Ibid. The critics who think Guy named Margaret to protect another woman are Lawson, "Edith Wharton," 315; Lewis, 201; and Allen F. Stein, *After the Vows Were Spoken: Marriage in American Literary Realism* (Columbus: Ohio State University Press, 1984), 225; references to Stein hereafter cited in the text.

28. Arthur Hobson Quinn, *American Fiction* (New York: D. Appleton-Century Co., 1936), 560.

29. Susan Lohafer, *Coming to Terms with the Short Story* (Baton Rouge: Louisiana State University Press, 1983), 96.

30. I stole this phrasing from *St. Twel'mo*, a nineteenth-century parody of Augusta Evans Wilson's best-selling *St. Elmo* (1866); Wilson's scholarly vocabulary, replete with classical allusions and obscure quotations, prompted the parodist to claim that the heroine had swallowed an unabridged dictionary. Although Wharton would have scorned completely the popular "sentimental" Wilson, their language is not the only link between the two writers. See my "Edith Wharton's *Summer* and 'Woman's Fiction,'" *Essays in Literature* 11 (Fall 1984): 223–35. Wharton once stated that "a narrative should be clothed in a style so born of the subject that it varies with each subject." See "A Cycle of Reviewing," *Spectator* (London), 3 November 1928, supplement.

31. Lawrence Jay Dessner, "Edith Wharton and the Problem of Form," *Ball State University Forum* 24 (Summer 1983): 60; hereafter cited in the text.

32. Springer, *Edith Wharton and Kate Chopin*, 128. One way to get a sense of the extent to which Wharton has been dismissed for her subject matter is to read left-wing male critics, who resent her writing about the upper classes. See, for instance, Robert Herrick, "Mrs. Wharton's World," *New Republic*, 13 February 1915, 40–42; Parrington, 151–54; and Ludwig Lewisohn, *Expression in America* (New York: Harper & Brothers, 1932), 465–68. James W. Tuttleton suggests that "there may be regional bias, as well as an ideological one, involved in some of the critics' judgments." See "Edith Wharton: An Essay in Bibliography," *Resources for American Literary Study* 3 (Autumn 1973): 177. For various criticisms of Wharton's subject matter and message, skim the following: Plante, "Edith Wharton as Short Story Writer"; Springer and its update—Marlene Springer and Joan Gilson, "Edith Wharton: A Reference Guide Updated," *Resources for American Literary Study* 14, no. 1–2 (1984): 85–111; Tuttleton and its update—James W. Tuttleton, "Edith Wharton," in *American Women Writers: Bibliographical Essays*, ed. Maurice Duke, Jackson R. Bryer, and M. Thomas Inge (Westport, Conn.: Greenwood Press, 1983), 71–107; and Katherine Joslin, "Edith Wharton at 125," *College Literature* 14, no.3 (1987): 193–206.

33. For example, by Nevius, 30; Howe, 2; Louis Kronenberger, "Mrs. Wharton's Literary Museum," *Atlantic Monthly* 222 (September 1968): 99. Regarding Wharton's supposed coldness, see especially Plante, 363, 366, 372, and 379. Edward O'Brien speaks of the "arctic frigidity" of her stories in *The Advance of the American Short Story* (New York: Dodd, Mead & Co., 1923), 202. Distinguished story writers have also complained of Wharton's coldness: see Graham Greene, "Fiction," *Spectator* (London), 5 May 1933, 654; and Katherine Mansfield, "Family Portraits," *Athenaeum* (London), 10 December 1920, 810–11.

34. John Bagley, *The Short Story: Henry James to Elizabeth Bowen* (New York: St. Martin's, 1988), 35. Gerlach, *Toward the End*, 58, thinks "Roman Fever" may be "too mechanically perfect for modern taste."

35. Russell, "Melodramatic Mrs. Wharton," 431, says, "She gives little impression of feeling with or for the sufferers she creates."

36. I mean humorous, not just ironic. For a valuable discussion of humor in Wharton's stories, see Plante, 366–68. As she points out, many reviewers tried to deny Wharton a sense of humor (see Springer, 27 and 146, for instance); or, recognizing the impossibility of defending that position, critics have tried to make a sharp distinction between irony and humor, so that Wharton's irony becomes "remote from humor," as argued by Agnes Repplier, "A Sheaf of Autumn Fiction," *Outlook*, 28 November 1908, 698. Russell, 433, claims that Wharton belongs to the category of wits who have no real sense of humor.

37. Wilson, "Justice to Edith Wharton," 19. Wilson also complained that the early stories "take place either in a social void or against a background of Italy or France." Only with *The House of Mirth* did Wharton emerge "as an historian of the American society of her time." Here again is the attitude I discussed in my preface; actually, fewer than a third of the early stories take place outside the United States.

38. See Springer, 2–5.

39. Edith Wharton to Edward L. Burlingame, 10 July 1898, in *The Letters of Edith Wharton*, ed. R. W. B. Lewis and Nancy Lewis (New York: Charles Scribner's Sons, 1988), 36.

40. See, for instance, Goodman, 7–8; Lawson, "Edith Wharton," 309–10; Walton, 78.

41. For a comparison of Poe's "The Cask of Amontillado," Balzac's "La Grande Breteche," and Wharton's "The Duchess at Prayer," see June E. Downey, *Creative Imagination: Studies in the Psychology of Literature* (New York: Harcourt, Brace & Co., 1929), 202–208. Eleanor Dwight compares "The Cask of Amontillado" and "The Duchess at Prayer" in "Edith Wharton and 'The Cask of Amontillado,'" in *Poe and Our Times: Influences and Affinities*, ed. Benjamin Franklin Fisher IV (Baltimore: Edgar Allan Poe Society, 1986), 49–57. Wharton's "The Dilettante" and James's "The Two Faces" are discussed as "related stories" in Stanley J. Kozikowski, "Unreliable Narration in Henry James's 'The Two Faces' and Edith Wharton's 'The Dilettante,'" *Arizona Quarterly* 35 (Winter 1979): 357–72. For further echoes of James in Wharton and vice versa, consult works by Bell and Tintner listed in the bibliography. The possible influence of Washington Irving on Wharton's short stories could be explored. Wharton was certainly familiar with Irving's work, having used *The Alhambra* (1832), a collection of tales about Moorish Spain, for her childhood "making up." Wharton resembles him in her fondness for exotic settings, penchant for melodrama, and pictorial and satirical bents.

42. In addition, one could argue that Wharton's comments on the short story versus the novel in her letter to Robert Grant (see Part 2) imply that the short-story tradition is basically female.

43. Mary E. Wilkins Freeman, *The Revolt of Mother and Other Stories* (New York: Feminist Press, 1974), 89. For a general discussion of the "green-world archetype" in women's fiction, see Annis Pratt and Barbara A. White, "The Novel of Development," chap. 2 in Pratt, *Archetypal Patterns in Women's Fiction* (Bloomington: Indiana University Press, 1981), 16–24. For treatment of this theme in Emily Dickinson and other writers, see Sandra M. Gilbert and Susan Gubar, *The Madwoman in the Attic* (New Haven: Yale University Press, 1979), 642–50. Muddy boots are a prominent part of the description of the hero in Augusta Evans Wilson's best-selling *St. Elmo* (1867). For Wharton's use of conventions of the sentimentalists, see my "Edith Wharton's *Summer* and 'Woman's Fiction,'" *Essays in Literature* 11 (Fall 1984): 223–35.

44. Wharton gently mocks Poe in her early story "That Good May Come" (1894). His "The Raven," which borrows from Dickens's "Barnaby Rudge," is burlesqued in awful stanzas from "Boulterby Ridge." If Wharton declined to follow the example of writers like Willa Cather and Kate Chopin and directly acknowledge Jewett's influence, she did make the required pilgrimage to the Jewett home; in July of 1905, just before the publication of *The House of Mirth* and four years before Jewett's death, she took a car trip to South Berwick, Maine (Lewis, 150). For Jewett's influence on other writers, see Josephine Donovan, *Sarah Orne Jewett* (New York: Frederick Ungar Publishing Co., 1980), 135–40. The dangers of being associated with Jewett, even in 1990, are made clear by the recent outcry over Wharton's being called a "regionalist" by Susan Gubar (*New York Times Book Review*, 5 November 1989) and paired with Jewett by Brian Lee in *American Fiction 1865–1940* (Longman, 1987). See *Edith Wharton Newsletter* 6 (Fall 1989): 3, and *Edith Wharton Review* 7 (Spring 1990): 12.

45. For refutations of the idea that Wharton was a disciple or imitator of James, see Lewis, 131, and Howe, 6–7. Howe states, "The claim that Henry James exerted a major influence upon Mrs. Wharton's fiction, repeated with maddening regularity by literary historians, testifies to the laziness of the human mind" (6). As early as 1923, Fred Pattee pointed out major differences between Wharton and James as short-story writers. He says, "She is not so psychologically analytical as Henry James nor yet so scientific of method: where he worked notebook in hand she works with intuition, and often with more glow and passion. In rapidity, too, she greatly surpasses him, as she does in simplicity and naturalness of style." See *The Development of the American Short Story* (New York: Harper & Brothers, 1923), 375. I think "rapidity" is the key; Wharton preferred "compactness" and "vividness" to the slow analysis of James. Margaret B. McDowell contrasts Wharton and James as writers of ghost stories in "Edith Wharton's Ghost Stories," *Criticism* 12 (Spring 1970): 134–38.

Wharton's view of her indebtedness to James is perhaps expressed in her preachy story "The Debt" (1909). A scientist who refutes his mentor's theory claims that his debt requires solely that he "carry on the light. Do you suppose he'd have wanted me to snuff it out because it happened to light up a fact *he* didn't fancy? I'm using *his* oil to feed my torch with: yes, but it isn't really his torch or mine, or his oil or mine: they belong to each of us till we drop and hand them on" (2: 71).

46. Amy Kaplan, *The Social Construction of American Realism* (Chicago: University of Chicago Press, 1988), 71; hereafter cited in the text.

47. Louis Auchincloss, Introduction to *A Backward Glance* (New York: Charles Scribner's Sons, 1934), vii. Percy Lubbuck recalls that "she liked to be talked to as a man" in *Portrait of Edith Wharton* (New York: Appleton-Century-Crofts, 1947), 62.

48. Lewis, 31. Wharton's adolescent novella, entitled *Fast and Loose*, was published in 1977.

49. See Lewis, 71, 76–77.

50. Review of *The Greater Inclination*, *Academy* 57 (8 July 1899): 40.

51. See Anna McClure Sholl, "The Work of Edith Wharton," *Gunton's Magazine* 25 (November 1903): 426–32. This article is quoted in Tuttleton, 171.

52. Frederic Taber Cooper, *Some American Story Tellers* (New York: Holt, Rinehart & Winston, 1911), 178.

53. Louis Auchincloss, "Prefatory Note to 'The Pelican' and 'The Rembrandt,'" in *The Edith Wharton Reader*, ed. Louis Auchincloss (New York: Charles Scribner's Sons, 1965), 8.

54. Nevius made this point early on; for his discussion of the artist stories, see pp. 16–21.

55. Cynthia Griffin Wolff, *A Feast of Words: The Triumph of Edith Wharton* (New York: Oxford University Press, 1977), 395; hereafter cited in the text.

56. Plante criticizes this story at length, noting justly that it lacks depth and "does not really deal with any of the perennially important matters concerning the nature of man or the nature of art" (364).

57. Box 16, Edith Wharton Papers, Beinecke Library, Yale University.

58. Substantial discussion of the incest theme in Wharton can be found in the following works: Elizabeth Ammons, *Edith Wharton's Argument with America* (Athens: University of Georgia Press, 1980), 133–43, 182; Louise K. Barnett, "American Novelists and the 'Portrait of Beatrice Cenci,'" *New England Quarterly* 53 (June 1980): 168–83; Sandra M. Gilbert, "Life's Empty Pack: Notes toward a Literary Daughteronomy," *Critical Inquiry* 11 (March 1985): 355–84; Lewis, 524–26; Adeline R. Tintner, "Mothers, Daughters, and Incest in the Late Novels of Edith Wharton," in *The Lost Tradition: Mothers and Daughters in Literature*, ed. Cathy N. Davidson and E. M. Broner (New York: Frederick Ungar Publishing Co., 1980), 147–56; Adeline R. Tintner, "Mothers vs.

Daughters in the Fiction of Edith Wharton and Henry James," *AB Bookman's Weekly*, 6 June 1983, 4324–28; and Wolff, 379–80, 412–15.

59. Wolff, 307; Wharton, *A Backward Glance*, 2. Donovan suggests, 57, that the dead hand is the hand of the mother. It is entirely appropriate that Dr. Lombard recalls "some art-loving despot of the Renaissance" because the Italian Renaissance was notorious for open defiance of incest prohibitions and literature in which incest is taken lightly. See Donald Webster Cory and R. E. L. Masters, *Violation of Taboo: Incest in the Great Literature of the Past and Present* (New York: Julian Press, 1963), 5–6. See Barnett, "American Novelists," for discussion of references to Beatrice Cenci, a sixteenth-century incest victim, in the fiction of Hawthorne, Melville, and Wharton; Barnett concludes that "all found it a means of evoking the theme of incest, which contemporary canons of decorum kept from open discussion" (169).

60. Tintner uses the phrase "struggle for the father" in both her articles (p. 155 and p. 4328, respectively).

61. Sigmund Freud to Wilhelm Fliess, 1897, quoted in Judith Lewis Herman, *Father-Daughter Incest* (Cambridge: Harvard University Press, 1981), 10. For the explaining away of childhood sexual abuse, see especially Alice Miller, *Thou Shalt Not Be Aware: Society's Betrayal of the Child,* trans. Hildegarde and Hunter Hannum (New York: Farrar, Straus & Giroux, 1984). See also Florence Rush, *The Best Kept Secret: Sexual Abuse of Children* (Englewood Cliffs, N.J.: Prentice-Hall, 1980) and Jeffrey Moussaieff Masson, *The Assault on Truth: Freud's Suppression of the Seduction Theory* (New York: Farrar, Straus & Giroux, 1984).

62. Book-length personal narratives include the following: Maya Angelou, *I Know Why the Caged Bird Sings* (1969); Katherine Brady, *Father's Days* (1979); Charlotte Vale Allen, *Daddy's Girl* (1982); Eleanore Hill, *The Family Secret* (1985); Margaret Randall, *This Is About Incest* (1987); Sylvia Fraser, *My Father's House* (1988); and Louise M. Wisechild, *The Obsidian Mirror* (1988). A collection of writings by incest survivors is *Voices in the Night: Women Speaking about Incest,* ed. Toni A. H. McNaron and Yarrow Morgan (Pittsburgh: Cleis Press, 1982).

For an account of the effects of incestuous abuse on a renowned writer's life, see Louise DeSalvo, *Virginia Woolf: The Impact of Childhood Sexual Abuse on Her Life and Work* (Boston: Beacon Press, 1989). Woolf lived from 1882 to 1941, Wharton from 1862 to 1937. Rush (56) claims that there was a marked increase in sexual assaults on children during the Victorian era. Because of the secrecy surrounding incest and the effects of repression, it is very difficult to estimate the number of women who have suffered incestuous abuse. The most commonly cited contemporary statistics about childhood sexual abuse indicate that from 25 to 38 percent of American women were molested as children, most by someone they knew. See E. Sue Blume, *Secret Survivors: Uncovering Incest and Its Aftereffects in Women* (New York: John Wiley & Sons, 1990), xiv.

The most extensive surveys of incest victims, studies including both questionnaires and personal interviews, have been done by Judith Lewis Herman, cited above, and by Diana E. H. Russell, *The Secret Trauma: Incest in the Lives of Girls and Women* (New York: Basic Books, 1986).

63. The "post-incest syndrome" is so named by E. Sue Blume and other therapists. For description of the syndrome I have relied on personal narratives, plus the following sources, all of which agree as to the main characteristics of incest survivors: Blume; Herman; Russell; Denise J. Gelinas, "The Persisting Negative Effects of Incest," *Psychiatry* 46 (November 1983): 312–32; and Ellen Bass and Laura Davis, *The Courage to Heal* (New York: Harper & Row, 1988). The three broad patterns I listed might be thought to fit a large segment of the population, but the key in the survivor's life is the seeming lack of explanation for the problems.

64. Lewis, 53. Wolff claims that any marriage would have been disastrous because "the crisis of sexual intimacy . . . resurrected the bogies of childhood" (51). See Lewis, 52–54, and Wolff, 50–51.

65. *The Letters of Edith Wharton*, 139–40. All sources on the "post-incest syndrome" specify these symptoms. For Wharton's illnesses, see Lewis, 74–76 and 82–84, and Wolff, 75–91. She was once treated by the noted (or notorious) physician S. Weir Mitchell, whose "rest cure" was immortalized by Charlotte Perkins Gilman in "The Yellow Wallpaper" (1892). "The Portrait" was written during Wharton's "rest cure."

66. For an analysis, see Janet Goodwyn, "'Literature' or the Various Forms of Autobiography," chap. 6 in *Edith Wharton: Traveller in the Land of Letters* (New York: St. Martin's Press, 1990), 103–30. "Life and I," a 50-page manuscript, was probably written in 1920 or 1922 (Wolff, 417), *A Backward Glance* appeared in 1934, and "A Little Girl's New York" was published in *Harper's Magazine* in March 1938. "Life and I" is more revealing than the published works, apparently too revealing in Wharton's view because she presented a much expurgated version of her childhood in *A Backward Glance*. The extent to which she censored herself, even in "Life and I," is shown by an interesting revision in the manuscript. She begins a sentence, "I am often inclined—like most people—to blame my parents for" and then crosses out "blame" and "for," substituting "think," so that the final sentence reads, "I am often inclined—like most people—to think my parents might have brought me up in a manner more suited to my tastes and disposition" ("Life and I," 18).

67. Blume, 128. Blume also notes that survivors are "likely to be afraid of sleeping alone in the dark" (124).

68. Thus the most memorable images of Lucretia are her acid sayings—her criticisms of novelists, like the "common" Mrs. Beecher Stowe (*BG*, 68); her dry "Where did you pick *that* up?" in response to her daughter's newly

acquired slang, and her famous "icy comment" on Edith's first novel attempt, which included a reference to tidying up the drawing room: "Drawing-rooms are always tidy" (*BG*, 73).

69. See Goodman, 13–28. One explanation is offered in Janet Liebman Jacobs, "Reassessing Mother Blame in Incest," *Signs* 15 (Spring 1990): 500–514. A reality that should be noted is that, in spite of the drawing-room comment, it was the prosaic Lucretia who encouraged Wharton's writing, not the poetic George. Lucretia was the parent who actually promoted the "buds of fancy," listening to the child's stories, trying to write down the narratives she voiced, and eventually having her poems privately printed as *Verses* (1878) ("Life and I," 11 and 37; Lewis, 31).

70. Wendy Gimbel in *Edith Wharton: Orphancy and Survival* (New York: Praeger Publishers, 1984) deals with this aspect of Wharton's work.

71. Herman, 71. Russell notes that her "most startling finding" was that "girls reared in high-income families were more frequently victimized by incest than girls in lower-income families" (102; italics deleted). In her notes for a story to be entitled "The Family," Wharton describes an upper-class family that seems perfect on the surface. The reflector, who has just returned from a lonely life abroad, envies his sister's domestic happiness until her daughter commits suicide. It then comes out that his sister has had a series of affairs, her husband drinks, and both children's marriages are unhappy. Wharton ends her summary as follows: "Such is 'The Family.' The above is absolutely true, but if I were to use it as a subject all the critics would say it was not like real life, that such 'unpleasant' things may exist singly, but don't occur in one household, whereas that is just where & how they do occur, one source of corruption/Mrs. Catherwood in this case/infecting everything." "Subjects and Notes" (1918–23), Wharton Papers, Beinecke Library, Yale University.

72. Herman, 71 and 110–11. In "A Little Girl's New York" Wharton describes herself as "a much governessed and guarded little girl" (361).

73. Herman, 82; Miller, 63; Blume, 137.

74. Herman, 44. See also Bass and Davis, 125; Russell, 360–68; and Blume, 138.

75. Candace Waid, Introduction to *The Muse's Tragedy and Other Stories* (New York: New American Library, 1990), 9.

76. Marius Bewley, *Mask and Mirrors* (New York: Atheneum, 1964), 146–47.

77. The Raphael essays are "Kate Orme's Struggles with Shame in Edith Wharton's *Sanctuary*," *Massachusetts Studies in English* 10 (Fall 1986): 229–30; "Shame in Edith Wharton's *The Mother's Recompense*," *American Imago* 45 (Summer 1988): 187–203; and "Haunted by Shame: Edith Wharton's *The Touchstone*," *Journal of Evolutionary Psychology* 9 (August 1988): 287–96. See Alfred Bendixen, "The World of Wharton Criticism: A Bibliographic Essay,"

Edith Wharton Review 7 (Spring 1990): 20, for comments on the essays. For discussion of shame and incest, see Herman, 173, and Blume, chap. 7, "Spoiled and Soiled: Guilt, Shame, Self-Blame, and Self-Esteem," 109–19.

78. I myself have some reservations about offering the incest theory. A recent critic has questioned the "inquisitiveness about personal, especially sexual, matters" that she thinks characterizes much contemporary Wharton criticism; she thinks the unveiling of her letters to Fullerton, for instance, would have horrified Wharton (Joslin, 199). My concern is not so much what Wharton might think, for she deliberately left us evidence that she could have destroyed and she firmly believed in the advancement of knowledge (see my discussion of "The Debt"). But I do regret the uses that might be made of the theory by critics like those quoted in my Preface, who claimed that women are more likely than men to write out of personal maladjustment. Wharton no doubt posed as the "priestess of reason" (*Letters*, 483) and wrote a reserved autobiography because she wished to be remembered as a genius rather than a woman relieving emotional strain. If I thought her cover were effective, I would let matters stand, but as the waning of her literary reputation showed, it did not succeed. Thus, with the understanding that the artists described by Bewley include men as well as women, I offer an explanation of the deep center projected into Wharton's short stories.

79. R. W. B. Lewis, "Powers of Darkness," *Times Literary Supplement*, 13 June 1975, 644. Further references will be noted in the text.

80. For instance, Lewis, 85.

81. *The Letters of Edith Wharton*, 584.

82. Blume states, "Amnesia, or 'blocking,' is the most common feature of Post-Incest Syndrome" (81). She reports that about half her clients do not remember the abuse at first and that most have limited recall; see 81–99. See also Russell, 34, and Bass and Davis, 42.

83. Typically, Bass and Davis claim that the process of writing is itself "healing" (14).

84. Note the end of the passage, where Wharton identifies the book she was using for "making up" as a play about a prostitute. Whenever Wharton discusses her beginnings as a writer she introduces sex in some way. For other examples, see *A Backward Glance*, 24–25, 69–70, 75, and "Life and I," 7–8, 37.

85. See also the discussion of "The Lady's Maid's Bell" in the next section.

86. The Anson House will thus again "open on the universe" and lead to "all the capitals of Europe" (1: 245–46). We can compare Wharton's feelings on the publication of her first volume of short stories: "I felt like some homeless waif who, after trying for years to take out naturalization papers, and being rejected by every country, has finally acquired a nationality. The Land of Let-

ters was henceforth to be my country, and I gloried in my new citizenship" (*BG*, 119).

87. "Some Notable Books of the Year," *Independent*, 17 November 1910, 1089; Plante, 368–69.

88. Nevius, 123; see also Donovan, 45.

89. See, for instance, "Mrs. Wharton's Nativity," *Munsey's* 25 (June 1901): 436. Discussion of Wharton's depiction of men may also be found in Ammons, 15, and in Arthur H. Quinn, Introduction to *An Edith Wharton Treasury* (New York: Appleton-Century-Crofts, 1950), xxv.

90. Herrick, 40.

91. The priestess of sentimentalism, Lydia Huntley Sigourney, used this technique in her early short story "The Father" (1834). Wharton's contemporary, feminist theorist Charlotte Perkins Gilman, employed it frequently in her didactic fiction.

92. And Lewis considers the switch a "minor flaw" (1: xi).

93. See Kozikowski, 357–72.

94. When Eleanor on her deathbed exclaims that it was "worth it!" (2: 737), she can only mean that any man, however despicable, is better than none. I suspect that this was Wharton's own view, as also expressed in her comments that "nothing" has happened to a woman who has not experienced sexual intercourse. See, for instance, her characterization of old maids in "The Refugees" (2: 589) and "Duration" (2: 859–62). When she misses her chance for an affair, Margaret Ransom wonders "if any other woman had lived to whom *nothing had ever happened?*" (1: 646).

95. Ammons, 9; hereafter cited in the text.

96. Edith Wharton Papers, Beinecke Library, Yale University. Most of the short-story manuscripts in Wharton's papers date from the 1920s, making it difficult to study revisions of early stories. The manuscript showing a first-person narrator in "The Lamp of Psyche" is a two-page holograph scrap.

97. Auchincloss, "Prefatory Note," 8.

98. Kaplan, 439. The projection seems dependent on a reading of Ann Douglas's *The Feminization of American Culture* (1977).

99. See, for example, Goodman, 126–27, and Donovan, 48.

100. A different evaluation may be found in Theodore Ziolkowski, *Disenchanted Images: A Literary Iconology* (Princeton, N.J.: Princeton University Press, 1977), 140–43. Ziolkowski considers "The Moving Finger" Wharton's "most brilliant conflation" of art and ghost themes (140).

101. See Downey, Dwight, and Nevius, 154.

102. Adeline R. Tintner, "Fiction Is the Best Revenge: Portraits of Henry James by Four Women Writers," *Turn of the Century Women* 2 (Winter 1985): 46.

103. And has been so read by Allan Gardner Smith in "Edith Wharton

and the Ghost Story," in *Edith Wharton*, ed. Harold Bloom (New York: Chelsea, 1986), 97; hereafter cited in the text.

104. An early critic noted Wharton's frequent use of eye imagery; see Frances T. Russell, "Edith Wharton's Use of Imagery," *English Journal* 21 (June 1932): 457. The redness of the eyes also associates them with incest; Culwin has a "red blink" (2: 116), and the ghostly eyes are always described as having red lids (2: 120, 122, 126). In her two references to Beatrice Cenci, a sixteenth-century incest victim who had her father killed, Wharton calls her "pink-eyed" and "red-eyed" (see Barnett, 182).

105. Lewis, "Powers of Darkness," 644.

106. Whatever his individual qualities, the other man always seems weak (see "The Fullness of Life," "The Duchess at Prayer," "The Choice" [1908], "Kerfol," and "Joy in the House") because his antagonist is the husband as all-powerful father-parasite. No matter how improbable it may seem, as in "The Fullness of Life" and "The Choice," the husband-father wins because he cannot be gotten rid of.

107. Wharton gives Mary Boyne characteristics she considered quintessentially American. In *French Ways and Their Meaning* (1919) she criticizes the American child-wife's comparative ignorance of business and the general American tendency to cling to illusion: "'A tragedy with a happy ending' is exactly what the child wants before he goes to sleep: the reassurance that 'all's well with the world' as he lies in his cosy nursery. It is a good thing that the child should receive this reassurance; but as long as he needs it he remains a child" (65).

108. Lewis, 1:xix; Adeline R. Tintner, "'The Hermit and the Wild Woman': Edith Wharton's 'Fictioning' of Henry James," *Journal of Modern Literature* 4 (September 1974): 32–42.

109. Two years was approximately the duration of Wharton's sexual relationship with Morton Fullerton. Wharton shows typical prescience here, for she finished "The Hermit and the Wild Woman" in 1905 and began her affair in 1908. Wharton uses the metaphor of the erotic pool in a letter to Fullerton: "All I know is that I seem to have perennial springs of strength to draw on—& that they never flowed so freely as since my love for you had fed them." See Edith Wharton to W. Morton Fullerton, 24 March 1910, in *The Letters of Edith Wharton*, 206.

110. Blume, 28.

111. Lewis suggests that Wharton may have first heard around this time the rumor that she had been fathered by her brothers' English tutor. See Lewis's discussion of "His Father's Son," 253–54. The real father in the story is nice, the most positive portrait of a father Wharton offers. For fantasy fathers one should also note the ending of the early story "April Showers," where the heroine's literary failure is assuaged by the sympathy of her father. A good

father is the only compensation Wharton ever imagines for the rejection of a manuscript.

112. The giant mass of the past that forms a huge obstruction is similar to the image of the reef in Wharton's novel. *The Reef* was published the year after "Autres Temps . . ." For discussion of the image in the novel, see Gooder, 47.

113. By Lawson, "Edith Wharton," 318.

114. Waid, 18.

115. Interestingly, the reflector follows this statement by looking from Hermione to her father, who has been portrayed as a detached misogynist type, and thinking in the last sentence of the story that "he had perhaps worked better than he knew in placing them, if only for a moment, side by side" (1:615). This conclusion gives the odd impression that the fragrance drawn from corruption is less the marriage than the brief father-daughter reconciliation.

116. Lyde, 96. For a corrective to Stein's view, see especially 9–11, 16–17, 20, 176–78.

117. Ellen Kimbel, "The American Short Story: 1900–1920," in *The American Short Story, 1900–1945,* ed. Philip Stevick (Boston: Twayne Publishers, 1984), 33–69.

118. Gimbel, 20; Ammons, 168; Wilson, 27–28.

119. Margaret B. McDowell, "The Short Stories," chap. 6 in *Edith Wharton* (Boston: Twayne, 1976), 86; Walton, 166. See also Arthur Voss, *The American Short Story: A Critical Survey* (Norman: University of Oklahoma Press, 1973), 173.

120. In this respect Wharton's short stories are more satisfactory than her novels; because of the brevity of the short story we are less likely to miss her failure to suggest alternatives.

121. See, for example, Sandra M. Gilbert, "Soldier's Heart: Literary Men, Literary Women and the Great War," *Signs* 8 (1983): 422–50.

122. The observation that "she had a way of looking at you that made you feel as if there was something wrong with your hat" (2:215) recalls the kind of comment often made about Wharton herself. See, for instance, Lubbock, 28. In "'Xingu': Edith Wharton's Velvet Gauntlet," *Studies in American Fiction* 12 (Autumn 1984): 227–34, Judith E. Funston argues that Osric Dane is a portrait of James.

123. Ivy is as inarticulate as Mrs. Manstey and as incompetent as Mrs. Amyot of "The Pelican." Wharton's more sympathetic treatment prompts Donovan to note that the story "suggests a softening of Wharton's attitude toward femaleness and the female identity, which she previously rejected" (78).

124. For a good discussion of women's variation from the male pattern of

becoming more conservative with age, see Gloria Steinem, "Why Young Women Are More Conservative," in *Outrageous Acts and Everyday Rebellions* (New York: New American Library, 1983), 238–46.

125. Although the story was not published until 1926, it was written in 1923 (Lewis, 456).

126. See Edith Wharton to F. Scott Fitzgerald, 8 June 1925, *The Letters of Edith Wharton*, 482.

127. Richard H. Lawson discusses Wharton's reading of Nietzsche in "Nietzsche, Edith Wharton, and 'The Blond Beast,'" in *Actes du VII Congrès de l'Association Internationale . . . Literatures of America*, ed. Milan V. Dimic and Juan Ferrate (Stuttgart: Bieber, 1979), 170–72.

128. Arthur H. Quinn refers to "The Young Gentlemen" as "one of her finest efforts" in *American Fiction: An Historical and Critical Survey* (New York: D. Appleton-Century, 1936), 574.

129. "The Lady's Maid's Bell" is the only notable exception. Secretaries are the reflectors in "Full Circle" (1909), "The Blond Beast" (1910), and "The Triumph of Night" (1914), but they tend to be middle-class. In the interesting last half of "Full Circle" the wealthy character consistently misinterprets his secretary, whose only motive is to keep his job.

130. Louis Auchincloss, "Edith Wharton and Her Letters," *Hofstra Review* 2 (Winter 1967): 2. Jean Stafford's interest in writing a biography of Wharton has special significance because Stafford was probably an incest victim herself. See David Roberts, *Jean Stafford: A Biography* (Boston: Little, Brown, 1988), for discussion of a "secret" in Stafford's past. Although Roberts suggests venereal disease, there are numerous indications of the "post-incest syndrome."

131. See William T. Going, "Wharton's *After Holbein*," *Explicator* 10 (November 1951): Item 8.

132. Margaret B. McDowell, "Edith Wharton's 'After Holbein': 'A Paradigm of the Human Condition,'" *Journal of Narrative Technique* 1 (January 1971): 49. The characters' basic similarity is underlined by their continual projection. Thus Mrs. Jaspar thinks of Warley as ill and old, just as he considers her. The "dance" with Death is an appropriate image on several levels. For instance, the aristocratic characters seem like marionettes wound up by the servants.

133. Not only is he indolent and totally self-absorbed, but he says of Medford's impending visit, "I'll keep 'im 'ere all winter—a remarkable young man, Gosling—just my kind" (2: 531).

134. Elizabeth Ammons, "New Literary History: Edith Wharton and Jessie Redmon Fauset," *College Literature* 14 (Fall 1987): 213.

135. For discussion of atmosphere in the ghost stories, see McDowell, "Edith Wharton's Ghost Stories," especially 138 and 151.

136. By McDowell, in "Edith Wharton's Ghost Stories," 148.

137. Annette Zilversmit, "Edith Wharton's Last Ghosts," *College Literature* 14 (Fall 1987): 301.

138. Herman, 96.

139. The worst "terror" of Mr. Jones, it is explained in the story, is that "you couldn't ever answer him back" (2: 668). Ellen Powers Stengel notes that the "core" of Mrs. Clayburn's being has been breached by "trespasses against her space." See "Dilemmas of Discourse: Edith Wharton's 'All Souls' and the Tale of the Supernatural," *Publications of the Arkansas Philological Association* 15 (Fall 1989): 96, 100. The jargon of postmodernism that permeates this article has much in common with the language of writers on sexual abuse. Blume, for example, discusses the "shattering of boundaries" that violates the victim's personal space (86).

Female complicity in the violation is suggested by the figure of the "fetch," who comes to take the protective servants away. Lewis thinks the fetch represents Lucretia Jones ("Powers of Darkness," 645). In Wharton's mind her mother was at the least complicit because of her refusal to answer questions about sex.

140. Box 19, Edith Wharton Papers, Beinecke Library, Yale University.

141. *Voices in the Night*, p. 11. Note other titles like *Conspiracy of Silence* (Sandra Butler, 1978), *Silent Children* (Linda Tschirhant Sanford, 1980), and *I Never Told Anyone* (Ellen Bass and Louise Thornton, 1983).

142. The counterpart of Wharton's fog, snow, or white velvet in Virginia Woolf, another incest victim, is "cotton wool." See De Salvo, 103.

143. For discussion of a related theme, theory versus instinct, in "Joy in the House," see Miyoko Sasaki, "The Dance of Death: A Study of Edith Wharton's Short Stories," *Studies in English Literature* (Tokyo) 51, no. 1–2 (1974): 75–78.

144. "Joy in the House" was published in 1932. It appears that the outline and fragment of "Tradition" were written in 1933; clipped to a sheet dated 1933 that contains story ideas is a scrap referring to characters in "Tradition" (Box 19, f. 579, Edith Wharton Papers, Beinecke Library, Yale University). Goodwyn, 53, may be right that Wharton intended "Tradition" to be a novel, but the outline suggests a short story.

145. Edith Wharton, "Tradition," 1, Edith Wharton Papers, Beinecke Library, Yale University; hereafter cited in the text. This plot and Wharton's comment that the Old Respectables are "imposing themselves" on the French (2) reveal another side to Wharton's self-image; if in "Coming Home" she is the heroine who helps save France, here she is the imposter with a shameful past.

146. Thanks to Susan Koppelman for pointing out the significance of this story. The canary motif in "Bewitched" anticipates the destruction of the victim; the only way the canary can be freed is through death.

147. His name is Mr. Severance! Kate Spain, the woman who killed her

father, has a double, her servant Cassie, upon whom all the supposed results of the incest experience are projected. While Kate remains attractive and pleasant, Cassie hates men, overindulges in food, and becomes an alcoholic. She dies of a stroke, leaving Kate free to marry Mr. Severance. In Wharton's play version of the story ("Kate Spain," an unpublished manuscript), Cassie gets her revenge; Kate has to fulfill Cassie's dream and take her to Europe or she will produce evidence of the murder.

148. Thus, for those who demand closure the story "suffers by not being resolved." See Douglas Robillard, "Edith Wharton," in *Supernatural Fiction Writers: Fantasy and Horror*, ed. E. F. Bleiler, vol. 2 (New York: Scribner's, 1985), 787.

149. Leon Edel, "The Nature of Literary Psychology," *Journal of the American Psychoanalytic Association* 29, no. 2 (1981): 462–63. For other examples of Wharton's prescience, see "The Twilight of the God," where Oberville's circumstances are remarkably like Fullerton's (whom she hadn't yet met), "The Hermit and the Wild Woman," where she seems to foresee her affair with Fullerton, and "The Muse's Tragedy," where Mary Anerton's relationship with her lover after she is free from her husband anticipates Wharton's with Walter Berry.

150. Wolff, Introduction, x.

151. Lewis, 1: vii; Lawson, "Edith Wharton," 323. Voss calls her "one of the best American writers of the short story of manners and moral conduct" (173). For an opposite view, that Wharton's stories "contribute nothing to the enlargement of literature" and "have rightly not counted much in the revival of her reputation," see Kronenberger, 100.

Part 2

THE WRITER

Introduction

Wharton wrote two essays about the short story: "Telling a Short Story," which is chapter 2 in *The Writing of Fiction* (1925), and the Preface to *Ghosts* (1937), the collection of ghost tales she was working on at her death. The two essays, which are reprinted here, present in a straightforward manner Wharton's concept of the story and her literary attitudes and intentions. This section also contains selections from her autobiography, *A Backward Glance* (1934), in which she makes intriguing comments on her preparation for a literary career and beginnings as a short-story writer. Most of Wharton's writings about her craft come from late in her career when she had already won a Pulitzer Prize and was in her sixties and seventies. The selections from her early letters reveal a less confident Wharton, very different from the professional author in the late letters.

Telling a Short Story

Like the modern novel, the modern short story seems to have originated—or at least received its present stamp—in France. English writers, in this line, were slower in attaining the point to which the French and Russians first carried the art.

Since then the short story has developed and reached out in fresh directions, in the hands of such novelists as Mr. Hardy (only occasionally at his best in this form), of Stevenson, James, and Conrad, all three almost unfailingly excellent in it, of Mr. Kipling, past-master of the *conte,* and Sir Arthur Quiller-Couch, whose delightful early volumes, *Noughts and Crosses* and *I Saw Three Ships,* are less known than they deserve to be. These writers had long been preceded by Scott in "Wandering Willy's Tale" and other short stories, by Poe, the sporadic and unaccountable, and by Hawthorne; but almost all the best tales of Scott, Hawthorne, and Poe belong to that peculiar category of the eerie which lies outside of the classic tradition.

When the novel of manners comes to be dealt with, classification in order of time will have to be reversed, and in order of merit will be less easy; for even against Balzac, Tolstoi, and Turgenev the genius of the great English observers, from Richardson and Jane Austen to Thackeray and Dickens, will weigh heavily in the balance. With regard to the short story, however, and especially to that compactest form of it, the short short-story or *conte,* its first specimens are undoubtedly of continental production; but happily for English letters the generation who took over and adapted the formula were nursed on the Goethean principle that "those who remain imprisoned in the false notion of their own originality will always fall short of what they might have accomplished."

The sense of form—already defined as the order, in time and importance, in which the narrated incidents are grouped—is, in all the

Reprinted by permission of the Watkins/Loomis Agency, Inc., from *The Writing of Fiction* (New York: Charles Scribner's Sons, 1925), 33–58. Copyright 1925 by Charles Scribner's Sons; copyright renewed 1953 by William R. Tyler.

arts, specifically of the classic, the Latin tradition. A thousand years of form (in the widest disciplinary sense), of its observance, its application, its tacit acceptance as the first condition of artistic expression, have cleared the ground, for the French writer of fiction, of many superfluous encumbrances. As the soil of France is of all soils the most weeded, tilled, and ductile, so the field of art, wherever French culture extends, is the most worked-over and the most prepared for whatever seed is to be sown in it.

But when the great Russians (who owe to French culture much more than is generally conceded) took over that neat thing, the French nouvelle, they gave it the additional dimension it most often lacked. In any really good subject one has only to probe deep enough to come to tears; and the Russians almost always dig to that depth. The result has been to give to the short story, as French and Russian art have combined to shape it, great closeness of texture with profundity of form. Instead of a loose web spread over the surface of life they have made it, at its best, a shaft driven straight into the heart of human experience.

II

Though the critic no longer feels that need of classifying and sub-classifying the *genres* which so preoccupied the contemporaries of Wordsworth, there are, in all the arts, certain local products that seem to necessitate a parenthesis.

Such, in fiction, is the use of the supernatural. It seems to have come from mysterious Germanic and Armorican forests, from lands of long twilights and wailing winds; and it certainly did not pass through French or even Russian hands to reach us. Sorcerers and magic are of the south, the Mediterranean; the witch of Theocritus brewed a brew fit for her sister hags of the Scottish heath; but the spectral apparition walks only in the pages of English and Germanic fiction.

It has done so, to great effect, in some of the most original of our great English short stories, from Scott's "Wandering Willy" and Poe's awful hallucinations to Le Fanu's "Watcher," and from the "Thrawn Janet" of Stevenson to "The Turn of the Screw" of Henry James, last great master of the eerie in English.

All these tales, in which the effect sought is completely achieved, are models of the subtlest artifice. It is not enough to believe in ghosts, or even to have seen one, to be able to write a good ghost story. The greater the improbability to be overcome the more studied must be the approach, the more perfectly maintained the air of naturalness, the easy assumption that things are always likely to happen in that way.

One of the chief obligations, in a short story, is to give the reader an immediate sense of security. Every phrase should be a sign post, and never (unless intentionally) a misleading one: the reader must feel that he can trust to their guidance. His confidence once gained, he may be lured on to the most incredible adventures—as the Arabian Nights are there to show. A wise critic once said: "You may ask your reader to believe anything you can *make* him believe." It is never the *genii* who are unreal, but only their unconvinced historian's description of them. The least touch of irrelevance, the least chill of inattention, will instantly undo the spell, and it will take as long to weave again as to get Humpty Dumpty back on his wall. The moment the reader loses faith in the author's sureness of foot the chasm of improbability gapes.

Improbability in itself, then, is never a danger, but the appearance of improbability is; unless, indeed, the tale be based on what, in my first chapter, I called pathological conditions—conditions of body or mind outside the field of normal experience. But this term, of course, does not apply to states of mind inherited from an earlier phase of race culture, such as the belief in ghosts. No one with a spark of imagination ever objected to a good ghost story as "improbable"—though Mrs. Barbauld, who doubtless lacked the spark, is said to have condemned "The Ancient Mariner" on this ground. Most of us retain the more or less shadowy memory of ancestral terrors, and airy tongues that syllable men's names. We cannot believe *a priori* in the probability of the actions of madmen or neurasthenics, because their reasoning processes escape most of us, or can at best be imagined only as belonging to abnormal and exceptional people; but everybody knows a good ghost when he reads about him.

When the reader's confidence is gained the next rule of the game is to avoid distracting and splintering up his attention. Many a would-be tale of horror becomes innocuous through the very multiplication and variety of its horrors. Above all, if they are multiplied they should be cumulative and not dispersed. But the fewer the better: once the preliminary horror is posited, it is the harping on the same string—the same nerve—that does the trick. Quiet iteration is far more racking than the diversified assaults; the expected is more frightful than the unforeseen. The play of "Emperor Jones" is a striking instance of the power of simplification and repetition to excite in an audience a corresponding state of tension. By sheer voodoo practice it shows how voodoo acts.

In "The Turn of the Screw"—which stands alone among tales of the supernatural in maintaining the ghostliness of its ghosts not only through a dozen pages but through close on two hundred—the economy of horror is carried to its last degree. What is the reader made to expect? Always—all through the book—that somewhere in that hushed house of doom the poor little governess will come on one of the two figures of evil with whom she is fighting for the souls of her charges. It will be either Peter Quint or the "horror of horrors," Miss Jessel; no diversion from this one dread is ever attempted or expected. It is true that the tale is strongly held together by its profound, its appalling moral significance; but most readers will admit that, long before they are conscious of this, fear, simple shivering animal fear, has them by the throat; which, after all, is what writers of ghost stories are after.

III

It is sometimes said that a "good subject" for a short story should always be capable of being expanded into a novel.

The principle may be defendable in special cases; but it is certainly a misleading one on which to build any general theory. Every "subject" (in the novelist's sense of the term) must necessarily contain within itself its own dimensions; and one of the fiction writer's essential gifts is that of discerning whether the subject which presents itself to him, asking for incarnation, is suited to the proportions of a short story or of a novel. If it appears to be adapted to both, the chances are that it is inadequate to either.

It would be as great a mistake, however, to try to base a hard-and-fast theory on the denial of the rule as on its assertion. Instances of short stories made out of subjects that could have been expanded into a novel, and that are yet typical short stories and not mere stunted novels, will occur to everyone. General rules in art are useful chiefly as a lamp in a mine, or a hand rail down a black stairway; they are necessary for the sake of the guidance they give, but it is a mistake, once they are formulated, to be too much in awe of them.

There are at least two reasons why a subject should find expression in novel form rather than as a tale; but neither is based on the number of what may be conveniently called incidents, or external happenings, which the narrative contains. There are novels of action which might be condensed into short stories without the loss of their distinguishing qualities. The marks of the subject requiring a longer development are, first, the gradual unfolding of the inner life of its characters, and secondly the need of producing in the reader's mind the sense of the lapse of time. Outward events of the most varied and exciting nature may without loss of probability be crowded into a few hours, but moral dramas usually have their roots deep in the soul, their rise far back in time; and the suddenest-seeming clash in which they culminate should be led up to step by step if it is to explain and justify itself.

There are cases, indeed, when the short story may make use of the moral drama at its culmination. If the incident dealt with be one which a single retrospective flash sufficiently lights up, it is qualified for use as a short story; but if the subject be so complex, and its successive phases so interesting, as to justify elaboration, the lapse of time must necessarily be suggested, and the novel form becomes appropriate.

The effect of compactness and instantaneity sought in the short story is attained mainly by the observance of two "unities"—the old traditional one of time, and that other, more modern and complex, which requires that any rapidly enacted episode shall be seen through only one pair of eyes.

It is fairly obvious that nothing is more retarding than the marking of a time interval long enough to suggest modification in the personages of the tale or in their circumstances. The use of such an interval inevitably turns the short story into a long tale unduly compressed, the bald scenario of a novel. In the third chapter, where an attempt will be made to examine the technique of the novel, it will be needful to explore that central mystery—of which Tolstoy was perhaps the one complete master—the art of creating in the reader's mind this sense of passing time. Meanwhile, it may be pointed out that a third, and intermediate, form of tale—the *long* short story—is available for any subject too spreading for conciseness yet too slight in texture to be stretched into a novel.

The other unity, that of vision, will also be dealt with in considering the novel, in respect of which it becomes a matter much more complicated. Henry James, almost the only novelist who has formulated his ideas about his art, was the first to lay down the principle, though it had long (if intermittently) been observed by the masters of fiction. It may have occurred to other novelists—presumably it has—to ask themselves, as they sat down to write: Who saw this thing I am going to tell about? By whom do I mean that it shall be reported? It seems as though such a question must precede any study of the subject chosen, since the subject is conditioned by the answer; but no critic appears to have propounded it, and it was left to Henry James to do so in one of those entangled prefaces to the Definitive Edition from which the technical axioms ought some day to be piously detached.

It is clear that exactly the same thing never happens to any two people, and that each witness of a given incident will report it differently. Should some celestial task master set the same theme to Jane Austen and George Meredith the bewildered reader would probably have some difficulty in discovering the common denominator. Henry James, in pointing this out, also made the corollary suggestion that the mind chosen by the author to mirror his given case should be so situated, and so constituted, as to take the widest possible view of it.

One thing more is needful for the ultimate effect of probability; and that is, never to let the character who serves as reflector record anything not naturally within his register. It should be the storyteller's first care to choose this reflecting mind deliberately, as one would choose a building site, or decide upon the orientation of one's house, and when this is done, to live inside the mind chosen, trying to feel, see and react exactly as the latter would, no more, no less, and, above all, no otherwise. Only thus can the writer avoid attributing incongruities of thought and metaphor to his chosen interpreter.

IV

It remains to try to see what constitutes (in any permanent sense) the underlying norm of the "good short story."

A curious distinction between the successful tale and the successful novel at once presents itself. It is safe to say (since the surest way of measuring achievement in art is by survival) that the test of the novel is that its people should be *alive*. No subject in itself, however fruitful, appears to be able to keep a novel alive; only the characters in it can. Of the short story the same cannot be said. Some of the greatest short stories owe their vitality entirely to the dramatic rendering of a situation. Undoubtedly the characters engaged must be a little more than puppets; but apparently, also, they may be a little less than individual human beings. In this respect the short story, rather than the novel, might be called the direct descendant of the old epic or ballad—of those earlier forms of fiction in all of which action was the chief affair, and the characters, if they did not remain mere puppets, seldom or never became more than types—such as the people, for instance, in Molière. The reason for the difference is obvious. Type, general character, may be set forth in a few strokes, but the progression, the unfolding of personality, of which the reader instinctively feels the need if the actors in the tale are to retain their individuality for him through a succession of changing circumstances—this slow but continuous growth requires space, and therefore belongs by definition to a larger, a symphonic plan.

The chief technical difference between the short story and the novel may therefore be summed up by saying that situation is the main concern of the short story, character of the novel; and it follows that the effect produced by the short story depends almost entirely on its form, or presentation. Even more—yes, and much more—than in the construction of the novel, the impression of vividness, of *presentness*, in the affair narrated has to be sought, and made sure of beforehand, by that careful artifice which is the real carelessness of art. The short-story writer must not only know from what angle to present his anecdote if it is to give out all its fires, but must understand just *why* that particular angle and no other is the right one. He must therefore have turned his subject over and over, walked around it, so to speak, and applied to it those laws of perspective which Paolo Uccello called "so beautiful," before it can be offered to the reader as a natural unembellished fragment of experience, detached like a ripe fruit from the tree.

The moment the writer begins to grope in the tangle of his "material," to hesitate between one and another of the points that any actual happening thrusts up in such disorderly abundance, the reader feels a corresponding hesitancy, and the illusion of reality vanishes. The non-observance of the optics of the printed page results in the same failure to make the subject "carry" as the non-observance of the optics of the stage in presenting a play. By all means let the writer of short stories reduce the technical trick to its minimum—as the cleverest actresses put on the least paint; but let him always bear in mind that the surviving minimum is the only bridge between the reader's imagination and his.

V

Nietzsche said that it took genius to "make an end"—that is, to give the touch of inevitableness to the conclusion of any work of art. In the art of fiction this is peculiarly true of the novel, that slowly built-up monument in which every stone has its particular weight and thrust to carry and of which the foundations must be laid with a view to the proportions of the highest tower. Of the short story, on the contrary, it might be said that the writer's first care should be to know how to make a beginning.

That an inadequate or unreal ending diminishes the short tale in value as much as the novel need hardly be added, since it is proved with depressing regularity by the machine-made "magazine story" to which one or the other of half a dozen "standardized" endings is automatically adjusted at the four-thousand-five-hundredth word of whatsoever has been narrated. Obviously, as every subject contains its own dimensions, so is its conclusion *ab ovo*; and the failure to end a tale in accordance with its own deepest sense must deprive it of meaning.

Nonetheless, the short-story writer's first concern, once he has mastered his subject, is to study what musicians call the "attack." The rule that the first page of a novel ought to contain the germ of the whole is even more applicable to the short story, because in the latter case the trajectory is so short that flash and sound nearly coincide.

Benvenuto Cellini relates in his autobiography that one day, as a child, while he sat by the hearth with his father, they both saw a salamander in the fire. Even then the sight must have been unusual, for the father instantly boxed his son's ears so that he should never forget what he had seen.

This anecdote might serve as an apothegm for the writer of short stories. If his first stroke be vivid and telling the reader's attention will be instantly won. The " 'Hell,' said the Duchess as she lit her cigar" with which an Eton boy is said to have begun a tale for his school magazine, in days when Duchesses less commonly smoked and swore, would undoubtedly have carried his narrative to posterity if what followed had been at the same level.

This leads to another point: it is useless to box your reader's ear unless you have a salamander to show him. If the heart of your little blaze is not animated by a living, moving *something*, no shouting and shaking will fix the anecdote in your reader's memory. The salamander stands for that fundamental significance that made the story worth telling.

The arrest of attention by a vivid opening should be something more than a trick. It should mean that the narrator has so brooded on this subject that it has become his indeed, so made over and synthesized within him that, as a great draughtsman gives the essentials of a face or landscape in a half-dozen strokes, the narrator can "situate" his tale in an opening passage which shall be a clue to all the detail eliminated.

The clue given, the writer has only to follow. But his grasp must be firm; he must never for an instant forget what he wants to tell, or why it seemed worth telling. And this intensity of hold on his subject presupposes, before the telling of even a short story, a good deal of thinking over. Just because the limits of the form selected prevent his producing the semblance of reality by elaborating his characters, is the short story writer the more bound to make real the adventure in itself. A well-known French confectioner in New York was once asked why his chocolate, good as it was, was not equal to that made in Paris. He replied: "Because, on account of the expense, we cannot *work it over* as many times as the French confectioner can." Other homely analogies confirm the lesson: the seemingly simplest sauces are those that have been most cunningly combined and then most completely blent, the simplest-looking dresses those that require most study to design.

The precious instinct of selection is distilled by that long patience which, if it be not genius, must be one of genius's chief reliances in communicating itself. On this point repetition and insistence are excusable: the shorter the story, the more stripped of detail and "cleared for action," the more it depends for its effect not only on the choice of what is kept when the superfluous has been jettisoned, but on the order in which these essentials are set forth.

VI

Nothing but deep familiarity with his subject will protect the short-story writer from another danger: that of contenting himself with a mere sketch of the episode selected. The temptation to do so is all the greater because some critics, in their resentment of the dense and the prolix, have tended to overestimate the tenuous and the tight. Mérimée's tales are often cited as models of the *conte*; but they are rather the breathless summaries of longer tales than the bold fore-shortening of an episode from which all the significance it has to give has been adroitly extracted. It is easy to be brief and sharply outlined if one does away with one or more dimensions; the real achievement, as certain tales of Flaubert's and Turgenev's, of Stevenson's and of Maupassant's show, is to suggest illimitable air within a narrow space.

The stories of the German "romantic," Heinrich von Kleist, have likewise been praised for an extreme economy of material, but they should rather be held up as an awful warning against waste, for in their ingenious dovetailing of improbable incidents, the only economy practised is that of leaving out all that would have enriched the subject, visually or emotionally. One, indeed, "The Marquise d'O" (thrift is carried so far that the characters are known merely by their initials), has in it the making of a good novel, not unlike Goethe's "Elective Affinities"; but reduced to the limits of a short story it offers a mere skeleton of its subject.

The phrase "economy of material" suggests another danger to which the novelist and the writer of short stories are equally exposed. Such economy is, in both cases, nearly always to be advised in the multiplication of accidental happenings, minor episodes, surprises and contrarieties. Most beginners crowd into their work twice as much material of this sort as it needs. The reluctance to look deeply enough into a subject leads to the indolent habit of decorating its surface. I was once asked to read a manuscript on the eternal theme of a lovers' quarrel. The quarreling pair made up, and the reasons for dispute and reconciliation were clearly inherent in their characters and situation; but the author, being new at the trade, felt obliged to cast about for an additional, a fortuitous, pretext for their reunion—so he sent them for a drive, made the horses run away, and caused the young man to save the young lady's life. This is a crude example of a frequent fault. Again and again the novelist passes by the real meaning of a situation simply for lack of letting it reveal all its potentialities instead of dashing this way and that in quest of fresh effects. If, when once drawn to a subject, he would let it grow slowly in his mind instead of hunting about for arbitrary combinations of circumstance, his tale would have the warm scent and flavor of a fruit ripened in the sun instead of the insipidity of one forced in a hothouse.

There is a sense in which the writing of fiction may be compared to the administering of a fortune. Economy and expenditure must each bear a part in it, but they should never degenerate into parsimony or waste. True economy consists in the drawing out of one's subject of every drop of significance it can give, true expenditure in devoting time, meditation and patient labor to the process of extraction and representation.

It all comes back to a question of expense: expense of time, of patience, of study, of thought, of letting hundreds of stray experiences accumulate and group themselves in the memory, till suddenly one of the number emerges and throws its sharp light on the subject which solicits you. It has been often, and inaccurately, said that the mind of a creative artist is a mirror, and the work of art the reflection of life in it. The mirror, indeed, is the artist's mind, with all his experiences reflected in it; but the work of art, from the smallest to the greatest, should be something projected, not reflected, something on which his mirrored experiences, at the right conjunction of the stars, are to be turned for its full illumination.

Preface to *Ghosts*

"Do you believe in ghosts?" is the pointless question often addressed by those who are incapable of feeling ghostly influences to—I will not say the *ghost-seer*, always a rare bird, but—the *ghost-feeler*, the person sensible of invisible currents of being in certain places and at certain hours.

The celebrated reply (I forget whose): "No, I don't believe in ghosts, but I'm afraid of them," is much more than the cheap paradox it seems to many. To "believe," in that sense, is a conscious act of the intellect, and it is in the warm darkness of the prenatal fluid far below our conscious reason that the faculty dwells with which we apprehend the ghosts we may not be endowed with the gift of seeing. This was oddly demonstrated the other day by the volume of ghost stories collected from the papers of the late Lord Halifax by his son. The test of the value of each tale lay, to the collector's mind, not in the least in its intrinsic interest, but in the fact that someone or other had been willing to vouch for the authenticity of the anecdote. No matter how dull, unoriginal and unimportant the tale—if someone had convinced the late Lord Halifax that it was "true," that it "had really happened," in it went; and can it be only by accident that the one story in this large collection which is even faintly striking and memorable is the one with an apologetic footnote to the effect that the editor had not been able to trace it to its source?

Sources, as a matter of fact, are not what one needs in judging a ghost story. The good ones bring with them the internal proof of their ghostliness: and no other evidence is needed. But since first I dabbled in the creating of ghost stories. I have made the depressing discovery that the faculty required for their enjoyment has become almost atrophied in modern man. No one ever expected a Latin to understand a ghost, or shiver over it; to do that, one must still have in one's ears the

Reprinted by permission of the Watkins/Loomis Agency, Inc., from *Ghosts* (New York: Appleton-Century Co., 1937). Copyright 1937 by D. Appleton-Century Co.; copyright renewed 1965 by William R. Tyler.

hoarse music of the northern Urwald or the churning of dark seas on the outermost shores. But when I first began to read, and then to write, ghost stories, I was conscious of a common medium between myself and my readers, of their meeting me halfway among the primeval shadows, and filling in the gaps in my narrative with sensations and divinations akin to my own.

I had curious evidence of the change when, two or three years ago, one of the tales in the present volume made its first curtsy in an American magazine. I believe most purveyors of fiction will agree with me that the readers who pour out on the author of the published book such floods of interrogatory ink pay little heed to the isolated tale in a magazine. The request to the author to reveal as many particulars as possible of his private life to his eager readers is seldom addressed to him till the scattered products of his pen have been collected in a volume. But when "Pomegranate Seed" (which I hope you presently mean to read) first appeared in a magazine, I was bombarded by a host of inquirers anxious, in the first place, to know the meaning of the story's title (in the dark ages of my childhood an acquaintance with classical fairy lore was as much a part of our stock of knowledge as Grimm and Andersen), and secondly, to be told *how a ghost could write a letter, or put it into a letter-box.* These problems caused sleepless nights to many correspondents whose names seemed to indicate that they were recent arrivals from unhaunted lands. Need I say there was never a Welsh or a Scottish signature among them? But in a few years more perhaps there may be: for, deep within us as the ghost instinct lurks, I seem to see it being gradually atrophied by those two world-wide enemies of the imagination, the wireless and the cinema. To a generation for whom everything which used to nourish the imagination because it had to be won by an effort, and then slowly assimilated, is now served up cooked, seasoned and chopped into little bits, the creative faculty (for reading should be a creative act as well as writing) is rapidly withering, together with the power of sustained attention; and the world which used to be so *grand à la charté des lampes* is diminishing in inverse ratio to the new means of spanning it; so that the more we add to its surface the smaller it becomes.

All this is very depressing to the ghost-story purveyor and his publisher; but in spite of adverse influences and the conflicting attractions of the gangster, the introvert and the habitual drunkard, the ghost may hold his own a little longer in the hands of the experienced chronicler.

What is most to be feared is that these seers should fail; for frailer than the ghost is the wand of his evoker, and more easily to be broken in the hard grind of modern speeding-up. Ghosts, to make themselves manifest, require two conditions abhorrent to the modern mind: silence and continuity. Mr. Osbert Sitwell informed us the other day that ghosts went out when electricity came in; but surely this is to misapprehend the nature of the ghostly. What drives ghosts away is not the aspidistra or the electric cooker; I can imagine them more wistfully haunting a mean house in a dull street than the battlemented castle with its boring stage properties. What the ghost really needs is not echoing passages and hidden doors behind tapestry, but only continuity and silence. For where a ghost has once appeared it seems to hanker to appear again; and it obviously prefers the silent hours, when at last the wireless has ceased to jazz. These hours, prophetically called "small," are in fact continually growing smaller; and even if a few diviners keep their wands, the ghost may after all succumb first to the impossibility of finding standing room in a roaring and discontinuous universe.

It would be tempting to dwell on what we shall lose when the wraith and the fetch are no more with us; but my purpose here is rather to celebrate those who have made them visible to us. For the ghost should never be allowed to forget that his only chance of survival is in the tales of those who have encountered him, whether actually or imaginatively—and perhaps preferably the latter. It is luckier for a ghost to be vividly imagined than dully "experienced"; and nobody knows better than a ghost how hard it is to put him or her into words shadowy yet transparent enough.

It is, in fact, not easy to write a ghost story; and in timidly offering these attempts of mine I should like to put them under the protection of those who first stimulated me to make the experiment. The earliest, I believe, was Stevenson, with "Thrawn Janet" and "Markheim"; two remarkable ghost stories, though far from the high level of such wizards as Sheridan Le Fanu and Fitz James O'Brien. I doubt if these have ever been surpassed, though Marion Crawford's isolated effort, "The Upper Berth," comes very near to the crawling horror of O'Brien's "What Is It?"

For imaginative handling of the supernatural no one, to my mind, has touched Henry James in "The Turn of the Screw"; but I suppose a ghost novel can hardly be classed among ghost stories, and that tale

in particular is too individual, too utterly different from any other attempt to catch the sense of the supernatural, to be pressed into the
current categories.

As for the present day, I have ventured to put my own modest "om-
nibus" under the special protection of the only modern ghost evoker
whom I place in the first rank—and this dispenses with the need of
saying why I put him there. Moreover, the more one thinks the question over, the more one perceives the impossibility of defining the effect of the supernatural. The Bostonian gentleman of the old school
who said that his wife always made it a moral issue whether the mutton
should be roast or boiled, summed up very happily the relation of Boston to the universe; but the "moral issue" question must not be allowed to enter into the estimating of a ghost story. It must depend for
its effect solely on what one might call its thermometrical quality; if it
sends a cold shiver down one's spine, it has done its job and done it
well. But there is no fixed rule as to the means of producing this shiver,
and many a tale that makes others turn cold leaves me at my normal
temperature. The doctor who said there were no diseases but only patients would probably agree that there are no ghosts, but only tellers
of ghost stories, since what provides a shudder for one leaves another
peacefully tepid. Therefore one ought, I am persuaded, simply to tell
one's ghostly adventures in the most unadorned language, and "leave
the rest to Nature," as the New York alderman said when, many years
ago, it was proposed to import "a couple of gondolas" for the lake in
the Central Park.

The only suggestion I can make is that the teller of supernatural tales
should be well frightened in the telling; for if he is, he may perhaps
communicate to his readers the sense of that strange something un-
dreamt of in the philosophy of Horatio.

Selections from
A *Backward Glance*

The imagining of tales (about grown-up people, "real people," I called them—children always seemed to me incompletely realized) had gone on in me since my first conscious moments; I cannot remember the time when I did not want to "make up" stories. But it was in Paris that I found the necessary formula. Oddly enough, I had no desire to write my stories down (even had I known how to write, and I couldn't yet form a letter); but from the first I had to have a book in my hand to "make up" with, and from the first it had to be a certain sort of book. The page had to be closely printed, with rather heavy black type, and not much margin. Certain densely printed novels in the early Tauchnitz editions, Harrison Ainsworth's for instance, would have been my richest sources of inspiration had I not hit one day on something even better: Washington Irving's "Alhambra." These shaggy volumes, printed in close black characters on rough-edged yellowish pages, and bound in coarse dark-blue paper covers (probably a production of the old Galignani Press in Paris) must have been a relic of our Spanish adventure. Washington Irving was an old friend of my family's, and his collected works, in comely type and handsome binding, adorned our library shelves at home. But these would not have been of much use to me as a source of inspiration. The rude companion of our travels was the book I needed; I had only to open it for the Pierian fount to flow. There was richness and mystery in the thick black type, a hint of bursting overflowing material in the serried lines and scant margin. To this day I am bored by the sight of widely spaced type, and a little islet of text in a sailless sea of white paper.

Well—the "Alhambra" once in hand, making up was ecstasy. At any moment the impulse might seize me; and then, if the book was in reach, I had only to walk the floor, turning the pages as I walked, to be swept off full sail on the sea of dreams. The fact that I could not read added to the completeness of the illusion, for from those mysterious blank pages I could evoke whatever my fancy chose. Parents and nurses, peeping at me through the cracks of doors (I always had to be alone to "make up"), noticed that I often held the book upside down, but that I never failed to turn the pages, and that I turned them at about the right pace for a person reading aloud as passionately and precipitately as was my habit.

There was something almost ritualistic in the performance. The call came regularly and imperiously; and though, when it caught me at inconvenient moments, I would struggle against it conscientiously—for I was beginning to be a very conscientious little girl—the struggle was always a losing one. I had to obey the furious Muse; and there are deplorable tales of my abandoning the "nice" playmates who had been invited to "spend the day," and rushing to my mother with the desperate cry: "Mamma, you must go and entertain that little girl for me. *I've got to make up.*"

My parents, distressed by my solitude (my two brothers being by this time grown up and away) were always trying to establish relations for me with "nice" children, and I was willing enough to play in the Champs Elysées with such specimens as were produced or (more reluctantly) to meet them at little parties or dancing classes; but I did not want them to intrude on my privacy, and there was not one I would not have renounced forever rather than have my "making up" interfered with. What I really preferred was to be alone with Washington Irving and my dream.

The peculiar purpose for which books served me probably made me indifferent to what was in them. At any rate, I can remember feeling no curiosity about it. But my father, by dint of patience, managed to drum the alphabet into me; and one day I was found sitting under a table, absorbed in a volume which I did not appear to be using for improvisation. My immobility attracted attention, and when asked what I was doing, I replied: "Reading." This was received with incredulity; but on being called upon to read a few lines aloud I appear to have responded to the challenge, and it was then discovered that the work over which I was poring was a play by Ludovic Halévy, called "Fanny Lear," which was having a *succès de scandale* in Paris owing to the fact that the heroine was what ladies of my mother's day called "one of those women." Thereafter the books I used for "making up" were carefully inspected before being entrusted to me; and an arduous business it must have been, for no book ever came my way without being instantly pounced on, and now that I could read I divided my time between my own improvisations and the printed inventions of others. . . .

I used to say that I had been taught only two things in my childhood: the modern languages and good manners. Now that I have lived to see both these branches of culture dispensed with, I perceive that there are worse systems of education. But in justice to my parents I ought to have named a third element in my training; a reverence for the English language as spoken according to the best usage. Usage, in my childhood, was as authoritative an element in speaking English as tradition was in social conduct. And it was because our little society still lived in the reflected light of a long-established culture that my parents, who were far from intellectual, who read little and studied not at all, nevertheless spoke their mother tongue with scrupulous perfection, and insisted that their children should do the same.

This reverence for the best tradition of spoken English—an easy idiomatic English, neither pedantic nor "literary"—was no doubt partly due to the fact that, in the old New York families of my parents' day, the children's teachers were often English. My mother and her sisters and brother had English tutors and governesses, and my own brothers were educated at home by an extremely cultivated English tutor. In my mother's family, more than one member of the generation preceding hers had been educated at Oxford or Cambridge, and one of my own brothers went to Cambridge.

Even so, however, I have never quite understood how two people so little preoccupied with letters as my father and mother had such sensitive ears for pure English. The example they set me was never forgotten; I still wince under my mother's ironic smile when I said that some visitor had stayed "quite a while," and her dry: "Where did you pick *that* up?" . . .

This feeling for good English was more than reverence, and nearer: it was love. My parents' ears were wounded by an unsuitable word as those of the musical are hurt by a false note. My mother, herself so little of a reader, was exaggeratedly scrupulous about the books I read; not so much the "grown-up" books as those written for children. I was never allowed to read the popular American children's books of my day because, as my mother said, the children spoke bad English *without the author's knowing it*. You could do what you liked with the language if

145

you did it consciously, and for a given purpose—but if you went shuffling along, trailing it after you like a rag in the dust, tramping over it, as Henry James said, like the emigrant tramping over his kitchen oil-cloth—that was unpardonable, there deterioration and corruption lurked. I remember it was only with reluctance, and because "all the other children read them," that my mother consented to my reading "Little Women" and "Little Men"; and my ears, trained to the fresh racy English of "Alice in Wonderland," "The Water Babies" and "The Princess and the Goblin," were exasperated by the laxities of the great Louisa.

Perhaps our love of good English may be partly explained by the background of books which was an essential part of the old New York household. In my grand-parents' day every gentleman had what was called "a gentleman's library." In my father's day, these libraries still existed, though they were often only a background; but in our case Macaulay, Prescott, Motley, Sainte-Beuve, Augustin Thierry, Victor Hugo, the Brontës, Mrs. Gaskell, Ruskin, Coleridge, had been added to the French and English classics in their stately calf bindings. Were these latter ever read? Not often, I imagine; but they were there; they represented a standard; and perhaps some mysterious emanation disengaged itself from them, obscurely fighting for the protection of the languages they had illustrated.

A standard; the word perhaps gives me my clue. When I said, in my resentful youth, that I had been taught only languages and manners, I did not know how closely, in my parents' minds, the two were related. Bringing-up in those days was based on what was called "good breeding." One was polite, considerate of others, careful of the accepted formulas, because such were the principles of the well-bred. And probably the regard of my parents for the niceties of speech was a part of their breeding. They treated their language with the same rather ceremonious courtesy as their friends. It would have been "bad manners" to speak "bad" English, and "bad manners" were the supreme offence. . . .

The doing of "The Decoration of Houses" amused me very much, but can hardly be regarded as a part of my literary career. That began with the publishing, in "Scribner's Magazine," of two or three short stories. The first was called "Mrs. Manstey's View," the second "The Fulness of Life." Both attracted attention, and gave me the pleasant flutter incidental to first seeing one's self in print; but they brought me no nearer to other workers in the same field. I continued to live my old life, for my husband was as fond of society as ever, and I knew of no other existence, except in our annual escapes to Italy. I had as yet no real personality of my own, and was not to acquire one till my first volume of short stories was published—and that was not until 1899. This volume, called "The Greater Inclination," contained none of my earliest tales, all of which I had rejected as not worth reprinting. I had gone on working hard at the *nouvelle* form, and the stories making up my first volume were chosen after protracted consultations with Walter Berry, the friend who had shown me how to put "The Decoration of Houses" into shape. From that day until his death, twenty-seven years later, through all his busy professional life, he followed each of my literary steps with the same patient interest, and I doubt if a beginner in the art ever had a sterner yet more stimulating guide.

And now the incredible had happened! Out of the Pelion and Ossa of slowly accumulating manuscripts, plays, novels, and dramas, had blossomed a little volume of stories—stories which editors had wanted for their magazines, and a publisher now actually wanted for a volume! I had been astonished enough to see the stories in print, but the idea that they might in the course of time be collected in a book never occurred to me till Mr. Brownell transmitted the Scribner proposal.

I had written short stories that were thought worthy of preservation! Was it the same insignificant *I* that I had always known? Any one walking along the streets might go into any bookshop, and say: "Please give me Edith Wharton's book," and the clerk, without bursting into incredulous laughter, would produce it, and be paid for it, and the purchaser would walk home with it and read it, and talk of it, and pass it on to other people to read! The whole business seemed too unreal to be anything but a practical joke played on me by some occult humourist; and my friends could not have been more astonished and incredulous than I was. I opened the first notices of the book with trembling hands and a suffocated heart. What I had done was actually thought important enough to be not only printed but reviewed! With a sense of mingled guilt and self-satisfaction I glanced at one article after another. They were unbelievably kind, but for the most part their praise only humbled me; and often I found it bewildering. But at length I came on a notice which suddenly stiffened my limp spine. "When Mrs. Wharton," the condescending critic wrote, "has learned the rudiments of her art, she will know that a short story should always begin with dialogue."

Part 2

"*Always*"? I rubbed my eyes. Here was a professional critic who seemed to think that works of art should be produced by rule of thumb, that there could be a fixed formula for the design of every short story ever written or to be written! Even I already knew that this was ridiculous. I had never consciously formulated the principles of my craft, but during my years of experimenting I had pondered on them deeply, and this egregious commentary did me the immense service of giving my ponderings an axiomatic form. Every short story, I now saw, like every other work of art, contains within itself the germ of its own particular form and dimensions, and *ab ovo* is the artist's only rule. In an instant I was free forever from the bogey of the omniscient reviewer, and though I was always interested in what was said of my books, and sometimes (though rarely) helped by the comments of the professional critics, never did they influence me against my judgment, or deflect me by a hair's-breadth from what I knew to be "the real right" way.

Selections from
The Letters of Edith Wharton

To Edward L. Burlingame[1]

Florence
March 26 [1894]

Dear Mr. Burlingame,

I have just received your letter of March 13th, in which you tell me you don't like the story which I called "Something Exquisite."[2] Pray, by the way, have no tender hearted compunctions about criticizing my stories—Your criticism is most helpful to me & I always recognize its justice. . . .

I should like to bring out the book without adding many more stories, for I seem to have fallen into a period of groping, & perhaps, after publishing the volume, I might see better what direction I ought to take and acquire more assurance (the quality I feel I most lack). You were kind enough to give me so much encouragement when I saw you, & I feel myself so much complimented by the Messrs. Scribners' request that I should publish a volume of stories, that I am very ambitious to do better, & perhaps I could get a better view of what I have done & ought to do after the stories have been published. I have lost confidence in myself at present, & if you think "Judged"[3] a failure I shall feel I have made entirely "fausse route." Pray don't regard this as the wail of the rejected authoress—it is only a cry for help & counsel to you who have been so kind in giving me both.

Part 2

To Robert Grant[4]

> The Mount,
> Lenox, Mass.
> November 19 [1907]

Dear Mr. Grant,

It is very good of you to take time to write me such an interesting & really helpful analysis of my book.[5] . . .

I am very much pleased that you like the construction of the book, & I more than agree with you that I haven't been able to keep the characters from being, so to speak, mere *building-material.* The fact is that I am beginning to see exactly where my weakest point is.—I conceive my subjects like a man—that is, rather more architectonically & dramatically than most women—& then execute them like a woman; or rather, I sacrifice, to my desire for construction & breadth, the small incidental effects that women have always excelled in, the episodical characterisation, I mean. The worst of it is that this fault is congenital, & not the result of an ambition to do big things. As soon as I look at a subject from the novel-angle I see it in its relation to a larger whole, in all its remotest connotations; & I can't help trying to take them in, at the cost of the smaller realism that I arrive at, I think, better in my short stories. This is the reason why I have always obscurely felt that I didn't know how to write a novel. I feel it more clearly after each attempt, because it is in such sharp contrast to the sense of authority with which I take hold of a short story.—I think it ought to be a warning to stop; but, alas, I see things more & more from the novel-angle, so that I'm enclosed in a vicious circle from which I suspect silence to be the only escape.

To Rutger B. Jewett[6]

> January 31, 1931

Dear Mr. Jewett,

I have your letter of Jan. 17th, and return herewith a modified ending to "Pomegranate Seed," which ending will, I hope, be considered sufficiently explicit. I could hardly make it more so without turning a ghost story into a treatise on the sources of the supernatural. Oddly enough, when I wrote this story, last month, I read it aloud to five friends who were staying with me for Christmas. They all liked it, but all remarked with one accord: "Of course it's obvious from the first paragraph that the dead wife wrote the letters"; but they all agreed that the end was perfect.

As for the title, Mr. Schuyler[7] must refresh his classical mythology. When Persephone left the under-world to re-visit her mother, Demeter, her husband, Hades, lord of the infernal regions, gave her a pomegranate seed to eat, because he knew that if he did so she would never be able to remain among the living, but would be drawn back to the company of the dead.

I am so glad you like the last chapters of "The Gods Arrive," and I am sending you the two concluding chapters of Book II.

To Rutger B. Jewett

October 26, 1933

Dear Mr. Jewett,

I have delayed for some time to answer your letter of Sept. 29th, because I was so much taken aback by Miss Lane's communication that I did not know what to say.[8] When I think of my position as a writer I am really staggered at the insolence of her letter, and if it were possible to make any one of that kind understand what she had done, I should not be sorry to do so. My first impulse is to do nothing about selling "Duration" to another magazine, although I imagine that Ellery Sedgwick would be glad to have it for The Atlantic. I will think the matter over and let you know.

The fact is I am afraid that I cannot write down to the present standard of the American picture magazines. I am in as much need of money as everybody else at this moment and if I could turn out a series of potboilers for magazine consumption I should be only too glad to do so; but I really have difficulty in imagining what they want. I never supposed that their readers took much interest in my work, but I thought the magazine editors required a few well known names. If what they want is that I should write stories like those I see in their pages, I am afraid it is beyond my capacity.

I have just had a letter from Miss Giles, who asks to see me on behalf of the new editor of the Cosmopolitan. As you know I have held out firmly till now against the wiles of Mr. Hearst, but I have been the only one to do so. Many of my friends, for instance, Aldous Huxley and Louis Bromfield, appear to have succumbed at once, and I think you told me some time ago that in the case of the Cosmopolitan Hearst did not intervene personally. I have therefore decided to see Miss Giles and to ask point-blank what the situation is, and if I can reconcile it to my conscience I shall have to give them one of the stories you have in hand.

Many thanks for your letter of Oct. 6th, telling me that you have sent "Kouradjine Limited" to Miss Lane.[9] I confess I should not have done it if you had consulted me; I see no reason for taking her orders in that way and would much rather simply keep "Duration" for my next volume.

Notes

1. Edward Livermore Burlingame, editor of *Scribner's Magazine* from its first issue in January 1887 until his resignation in 1914.

2. "Something Exquisite" was revised and renamed "Friends."

3. No story of this title was ever published.

4. Robert Grant, novelist, short-story writer, and distinguished Boston jurist.

5. *The Fruit of the Tree.*

6. Rutger Bleecker Jewett, Wharton's editor at D. Appleton and Co., who often acted as her agent.

7. Loring Schuyler, editor of the *Ladies' Home Journal.*

8. Gertrude Lane, editor of the *Woman's Home Companion*, had informed Jewett that the magazine would not be able to run Wharton's story "Duration."

9. "Kouradjine Limited" was sold to Hearst's *Cosmopolitan* for a good figure and published as "Bread Upon the Waters."

Part 3

THE CRITICS

Introduction

Wharton's biographer, R. W. B. Lewis, was the first scholar to collect her stories, and his Introduction to the collection has become the classic treatment of Wharton's short stories. The selection from his Introduction deals with the marriage/divorce stories. Recent criticism, which has concentrated on the ghost tales, is well represented by the selection from Sandra M. Gilbert and Susan Gubar's *Sex Changes*, vol. 2 of *No Man's Land*. The title of the feminist critics' chapter on Wharton, "Angel of Devastation: Edith Wharton on the Arts of the Enslaved," indicates the tenor of much contemporary criticism.

R. W. B. Lewis

The situations she chose so to treat and to enlarge upon are not, at first glance, very original or unusual ones. In "Telling a Short Story," Mrs. Wharton quotes with approval Goethe's contention that "those who remain imprisoned in the false notion of their own originality will always fall short of what they might have accomplished." Mrs. Wharton, who entertained no such false notion, was content with the received forms and conventions of the short story; and she did not attempt to apply the art of storytelling to any hitherto unheard-of subject. There was, however, one area of experience which she was perhaps the first *American* writer to make almost exclusively her own: even more, I dare say, than Henry James, who would in any event be her only rival in this respect. This is what, in the loose groupings of stories appended to this introduction, I call the marriage question.

I have collected almost two dozen titles under this head, but the list could be much longer: several of those gathered under "Art and Human Nature" and nearly all those under "Ghosts" and "Romance and History" could be said to belong there as well. To point to so persistent a concern may seem only to stress the resolutely traditional cast of Mrs. Wharton's imagination; for while American fiction in the nineteenth century (before Howells and James) had not much focused on the marriage question, that question had provided the theme of themes for a whole galaxy of English, French and Russian writers. A generation for whom the marriage question tends to be sporadic and peripheral is likely to forget its former centrality, and to suppose that for Jane Austen, for Trollope, for Stendhal, for Tolstoi, the question was *merely* the occasion for some far more arresting human drama. And a generation that does so may find it difficult to appreciate how much Mrs. Wharton, examining the question over the years, managed to make of it.

She made, one might say, almost everything of it. It is not only that she explored so many phases and dimensions of the question: the very grounds for marrying, and premarital maneuvering, in "The Quicksand," "The Dilettante," "The Introducers" and others; the stresses and strains, the withering hopes and forced adjustments of the marital relation in "The Fullness of Life," "The Lamp of Psyche," "The Letters," "Diagnosis" and elsewhere; the intricate issue of divorce in "The Last Asset," "The Other Two," "Autres Temps . . ."; the emotional and psychological challenge of adultery in "Souls Belated," "Atrophy," "The Long Run," and so on; the phenomenon of illegitimacy in "Her Son," "Roman Fever" and with gentle mockery in "His Father's Son"; the ambiguous value of children in the piercingly satirical "The Mission of Jane." It is not only that her treatment of the question, in these multiple phases, displays so broad a range of tone and perspective, and so keen an eye for the dissolving and emergent structures of historical institutional and social life with which the question was enmeshed. It is that the question, as Mrs. Wharton reflected on it, dragged with it all the questions about human nature and conduct to which her generous imagination was responsive.

There are of course urgent biographical reasons for Edith Wharton's near obsession with the perplexities of marriage, though, as I shall suggest, her deeper and more private passions found covert expression in ghost stories and romances. The chief cluster of stories bearing upon marriage, divorce and adultery were written during the years (up to 1913) when her personal problems in those regards were most pressing: when, among other things, her own marriage was becoming unbearable to her, when her husband Edward Robbins ("Teddy") Wharton was succumbing to mental illness and given ever more frequently to bouts of disjointed irascibility, and when her relation to Walter Berry (the international lawyer who was her mentor and romantic idol) arrived at one peak of intensity. But whatever the immediate causes, the whole domain of the marriage question was the domain in which Edith Wharton sought the truth of human experience; it was where she tested the limits of human freedom and found the terms to define the human mystery.

"Souls Belated" is an excellent case in point. The situation there is that of Mrs. Lydia Tillotson, who has abandoned her husband and come to Europe with her lover Ralph Gannett to spend a year wandering through Italy and then to settle for a time, registered as man and wife, at a resort hotel on one of the Italian lakes. Her divorce decree is at this moment granted, and the lovers are free to marry; but Lydia, to Gannett's astonishment, is passionately opposed to remarrying. She is appalled at the thought of yielding to that conventional necessity, of returning to the social fold and eventually of being received by the very people she had hoped to escape. "You judge things too theoretically," Gannett tells her. "Life is made up of compromises." "The life we ran away from—yes!" she replies. To this Gannett remarks with a smile: "I didn't know that we ran away to found a new system of ethics. I supposed it was because we loved each other." One of the merits of "Souls Belated" is the author's delicate division of sympathy between Lydia's anguished impulse to escape and Gannett's readiness to compromise (just as one of this early story's minor flaws is a certain shiftiness in point of view); but it is evident that on this occasion Gannett speaks for Edith Wharton. The impossibility of founding a new ethic— of a man and woman arranging their life together on a new and socially unconventional basis—was one of Mrs. Wharton's most somber convictions, and a conviction all the stronger because (partly out of her own anguish) she tested it again and again in her stories.

Edith Wharton's moral imagination, as it exercised itself on this fundamental theme, may be usefully contrasted with that of D. H. Lawrence. Writing about Anna Karenina and Vronsky (in his posthumously published *Study of Thomas Hardy*), Lawrence argued that, in effect, Tolstoi had let his characters down; that "their real tragedy is that they are unfaithful to the greater unwritten morality" (greater, that is, than conventional social morality), "which would have bidden Anna be patient and wait until she, by virtue of greater right, could take what she needed from society; would have bidden Vronsky detach himself from the system, become an individual, creating a new colony of morality with Anna." In *Women in Love* and *Lady Chatterley's Lover,* Lawrence presents us with couples who do detach themselves from the system and do seek to create just such a new colony. Neither Birkin and Ursula nor Connie Chatterley and Mellors meet with much success; the site of the new colony is not located within the bounds of the two novels. But given Lawrence's apocalyptic view of modern industrial society, and his intense belief that no genuine human relation can be consummated within it, it is the continuing search that Lawrence espoused.

For Edith Wharton, the effort was utterly doomed from the start; society, crushing as it might be, was all there was. "I want to get away with you," Newland Archer tells Ellen Olenska in *The Age of Innocence,* "into a world . . . where we shall be simply two human beings who love each other, who are the whole of life to each other." Mme. Olenska's reply is poignant and final. "Oh my dear—where is that country? Have you ever been there?" So it is in "Souls Belated": Lydia tries to leave Gannett, but she knows she has literally no place to go; she comes wearily back to him, and at the story's end they are heading for Paris and the ceremony which will marry them back into respectable society.

The relation between man and woman—whether marital or extra-marital—was, in Mrs. Wharton's sense of it, beset by the most painful contradictions. "I begin to see what marriage is for," Lydia Tillotson says in "Souls Belated." "It's to keep people away from each other. Sometimes I think that two people who love each other can be saved from madness only by the things that come between them—children, duties, visits, bores, relations. . . . Our sin," she ends up, is that "we've seen the nakedness of each other's souls." But such dire proximity, such exposed nakedness—which Mrs. Wharton seems to have ardently desired and fearfully shrunk from—could occur within marriage as well.

Her consciousness of the dilemma was made evident in the exchange that took place a good many years after the writing of "Souls Belated" between Mrs. Wharton and Charles Du Bos, the gifted French essayist and student of French and English literature, who had known her since 1905, when he undertook to translate *The House of Mirth*. On an afternoon in the summer of 1912, driving through the French countryside, the two of them had been comparing their favorite literary treatments of married life. In fiction, they agreed upon George Eliot's *Middlemarch*, and Du Bos quoted the words of the heroine, Dorothea Brooke, that "marriage is so unlike anything else—there is something even awful in the nearness it brings." But if Mrs. Wharton assented to that, she also—after an interval, during which they selected Browning's "By the Fireside" and his "Any Wife to Any Husband" as the best poetic examples—went on to exclaim, with a kind of desolation, "Ah, the poverty, the miserable poverty, of any love that lies outside of marriage, of any love that is not a living together, a sharing of all!"

It is because of some such principle that Halston Merrick, in "The Long Run" (a story written a few months before the exchange just quoted), sends away his mistress Paulina Trant, when the latter offers to abandon her dreary husband and run off with him. In the course of their dialogue about the risks and sacrifices that might be in store for them, Paulina had observed with sad irony that "one way of finding out whether a risk is worth taking is *not* to take it, and then to see what one becomes in the long run, and draw one's inferences." What becomes of Halston and Paulina, as they retreat into the conventional, is in its well-cushioned manner not much less dreadful than what becomes of Ethan Frome and Mattie Silver. (One notes in passing that more often than not Edith Wharton's destroyed characters survive to take the full measure of their destruction.) Halston, who once had serious inclinations to literature, turns into a joyless bachelor, the manager of his father's iron foundry. Paulina, after her husband's death, marries "a large glossy man with . . . a red face," and is seen regularly at dinner parties, listening to the banal conversations with "a small unvarying smile which might have been pinned on with her ornaments," ready at the proper moment to respond with the proper sentiment. This superb and gruesome story adds to the impression that, for Edith Wharton, if the individual is offered any real choice in life, it is usually a choice between modes of defeat.

Of course, the human condition envisaged is not always so bleak in Edith Wharton's short stories, nor the alternatives so desperate; she was not so driven by a theory of life that she remained blind to variety both in experience and in narrative. In "The Letters," when Lizzie Deering discovers that her husband had not even opened the tender letters she had written him years before during the time of their courtship, she does not yield to her first impulse—to take their child and to leave him. She is stricken by the deception and by all that it implies, but she slowly adjusts "to the new image of her husband as he was." He was not, she realizes, "the hero of her dreams, but he was the man she loved, and who had loved her." The situation she now takes in and accepts—in a "last wide flash of pity and initiation"—is that "out of mean mixed substances" there had, after all, been "fashioned a love that will bear the stress of life." And in an altogether different mood, there is "The Mission of Jane," wherein Mrs. Lethbury (a woman "like a dried sponge put in water; she expanded, but she did not change her shape") and her elegant, helplessly embarrassed husband adopt a baby girl. This unspeakable child, as she grows up, assumes as her mission the relentless reform of the entire household. She fulfills that mission at last, and after hair-raising hesitation, by marrying and departing— thus allowing her parents to come together on the common ground of enormous relief, joining in fact and spirit as they had never done in two decades of marriage.

One of the seeming options for the domestically harried and entrapped, under the circumstances of modern American life, was, need-less to say, the act of divorce; and it is not surprising that Mrs. Wharton (whose decree was granted in 1913) dealt with this alternative a num-ber of times. For some years before Mrs. Wharton began writing, di-vorce had been "an enormous fact . . . in American life," as William Dean Howells had remarked when he was writing *A Modern Instance* (1882), a novel of which "the question of divorce" was to be "the mov-ing principle." Howells complained that "it has never been treated seriously"; but following his lead, Edith Wharton did so in some of her most successful stories—among them, "The Reckoning," "The Last Asset," "Autres Temps . . ." and "The Other Two." She caught at the subject during the period when divorce was changing from the scan-dalous to the acceptable and even the commonplace; and it is just the shifting, uncertain *status* of the act on which Mrs. Wharton so know-ingly concentrated. In her treatment, it was not so much the grounds for divorce that interested her (though she could be both amusing and bitter on this score), and much less the technicalities involved. It was the process by which an individual might be forced to confront the fact itself—especially in its psychological and social consequences—as something irreversible and yet sometimes wickedly paradoxical. (The contemporary reader, for whom, again, divorce may seem little more than tangential to the main business of the personal life, can enjoy a shock of recognition in reading the stories cited.) Divorce, thus consid-ered, was also the source of a revelation: about manners and the stub-born attitudes they may equally express or conceal; about the essential nature of the sexual relation; about the lingering injuries to the psyche that divorce, given certain social pressures and prejudices, may inflict on all concerned.

It is all those things that Julia Westall is driven to understand in "The Reckoning." Julia had been a young woman with "her own views on the immorality of marriage"; she had been a leading practitioner, in New York Bohemia, of "the new dispensation . . . *Thou shalt not be unfaithful—to thyself.*" She had only acted on her own foolishly selfish ideas when she brusquely demanded release from her first husband; now she is reduced to hysteria and almost to madness when her second husband, who had been her disciple in these matters, makes the same demand of her. "The Reckoning" is somewhat overwritten, and it is uneven in tone; it is an anecdote, really, about the biter bit, though by no means unmoving. A richer and more convincingly terrible story is "Autres Temps . . . ," the account of Mrs. Lidcote's forced return

Part 3

from a dream of freedom to "the grim edges of reality," a reality here
constituted by the social mores, at once cheerfully relaxing and cruelly
fixed, about divorce. Years before (the story was written in 1916), Mrs.
Lidcote had suffered disgrace and exile because she had been divorced
and remarried. Now it appears that times must have changed, for her
daughter has done the very same thing without arousing the faintest
social disapproval. Mrs. Lidcote dares to return to America; but after
two experiences of profoundest humiliation, she learns that for her the
times and the mores will never change. Few moments in Edith Wharton's short stories are as telling in their exquisite agony as those in
which first Mrs. Lidcote's daughter and then her kindly would-be lover
acknowledge by a slow, irrepressible and all-devouring blush the truth
of *her* situation. Those moments have the more expansiveness of
meaning, because few of Edith Wharton's heroines accept the grim
reality with greater courage or compassion for their destroyers. And in
few stories are the radical ironies of social change more powerfully
handled.

"The Other Two" is a yet more brilliant dissection of the mannered
life, and it is very likely the best story Mrs. Wharton ever wrote. It can
stand as the measure of her achievement in the short story form; for it
has scarcely any plot—it has no real arrangement of incidents, there
being too few incidents to arrange—but consists almost entirely in the
leisurely, coolly comic process by which a situation is revealed to those
involved in it. It is revealed in particular to Waythorn, his wife's third
husband, who discovers himself in mysterious but indissoluble league
with "the other two," as exceedingly different in background or in style
as all three are from one another. Waythorn comes by degrees to perceive that the wife he adores, and who had seemed to him so vivid and
above all so unique a personality, is in fact (and in a disconcertingly
appropriate figure) " 'as easy as an old shoe'—a shoe that too many feet
had worn. . . . Alice Haskett—Alice Varick—Alice Waythorn—she had
been each in turn, and had left hanging to each name a little of her
privacy, a little of her personality, a little of the inmost self where the
unknown god abides."

Those last echoing phrases add up to a splendid formulation, and
they contain a good deal of Edith Wharton's basic psychology. But for
the most part, the rhetoric of "The Other Two" does not need or attempt to rise to such overt and summary statement. Everything is communicated, rather, by the exact notation of manners—of dress and
gesture and expression: of Haskett's "made-up tie attached with an

elastic," and Waythorn's uneasy distaste for it; of Varick sitting by Mrs. Waythorn at a ball and failing to rise when Waythorn strolls by; of Mrs. Waythorn absent-mindedly giving her husband cognac with his coffee. The story's last sentence brings an exemplary little comedy of manners (which could serve as a model in any effort to define the genre) to a perfect conclusion. The three husbands are together for the first time, in the Waythorn drawing room. Mrs. Waythorn enters and suggests brightly, easily, that everyone must want a cup of tea.

> The two visitors, as if drawn by her smile, advanced to receive the cups she held out.
> She glanced about for Waythorn, and he took the third cup with a laugh.

Sandra M. Gilbert

Obviously the paradox of saying the unsayable, of speaking the unspeakable, infuses and energizes the very genre of the ghost story, a genre of which Wharton, like James, was one of America's most brilliant practitioners. Because both were novelists of manners and psychological "realists," neither would seem to have been a major candidate for such a role. Yet James arguably turned to the genre in an effort to examine the inchoate wellsprings of character, while Wharton was driven to it by precisely the bleak skepticism that kept her from fantasizing, as so many of her feminist contemporaries did, about changes in sex roles and social rules. Like the "Life Apart" that she had with Morton Fullerton, the ghost story offered her a literature apart in which, for once, she could allow herself to imagine transcending the limits of the possible and liberating desires for which there was no appropriate place in her culture.

The importance of this genre to the writer who felt that "Life is the saddest thing there is, next to death" should not be underestimated. For Wharton, ghost stories were not only frequently about the powers of unsayable words. They themselves, more than any other kind of writing, incarnated the power of the *forbidden* word, the word that refuses to be limited by the "laws" of nature and culture. "'Till I was twenty-seven or eight," she confessed in an extraordinary canceled passage from *A Backward Glance*, "I could not sleep in a room with a book containing a ghost-story; and . . . I have frequently had to burn books of this kind, because it frightened me to know that they were downstairs in the library!" Some of her own best ghost stories illuminate one source of her terror: the unleashing of female rage as well as the release of female desire. Others document another source of fear: the expression of female pain at the repression of rage and the killing of desire.

Reprinted by permission of Yale University Press from "Angel of Devastation: Edith Wharton on the Arts of the Enslaved," chap. 4 in Sandra M. Gilbert and Susan Gubar, *Sex Changes*, vol. 2 of *No Man's Land: The Place of the Woman Writer in the Twentieth Century* (New Haven, Conn.: Yale University Press, 1989), 159–64. Copyright 1989 by Yale University Press.

Most, in one way or another, indicate that what may have been especially terrifying to Wharton about the ghost story was the fact that it consistently made possible just the transgressive protest against "reality" that she secretly longed to mount.

"Kerfol" (1916), one of Wharton's most famous supernatural tales, focuses, like a number of her other works in this genre, on what she saw as the mortal, or indeed even immortal, "knots" of "the marriage tie." Visiting "the most romantic house in Brittany" (S II 282) which also seems to him like "the loneliest place in the whole world," the narrator encounters a pack of eerily silent dogs, about whom he later learns that, according to the local peasantry, they appear once a year and "are the ghosts of Kerfol." When he investigates, he is given the transcript of the seventeenth-century murder trial of a certain Anne de Cornault. As he reads through it, he discovers the bizarre story of the marriage between the wealthy, middle-aged lord of Kerfol and a young woman who came from a family that was "much less great and powerful" than his but whom he locked up like a rare treasure in his great mansion, where her only companions were a series of dogs that he strangled one by one after deciding she had been unfaithful to him. When the husband died under mysterious circumstances—"He had been dreadfully scratched and gashed about the face and throat, as if with curious pointed weapons; and one of his legs had a deep tear in it which had cut an artery" (291)—his wife had been arraigned for murder, but she had insisted (rightly, the story suggests) that the true killers were "my dead dogs" (299). Yet of course, as Wharton surely meant to imply, the animals were themselves agents of their mistress's unspeakable and deadly desire, a fury that erupts at the center of the tale when the courtroom transcript has the young wife describing what she heard during the murder: "dogs snarling and panting . . . once or twice he cried out. I think he moaned once . . . then I heard a sound like the noise of a pack when the wolf is thrown to them—gulping and lapping" (298).

What gives this tale its weird authority is its odd blending of the superhuman (ghosts) and the subhuman (dogs), a juxtaposition that enables "Kerfol" to dramatize with special intensity the importance to Wharton of a genre in which she could say the unsayable. For just as she associated ghost stories with fearful and unspeakable transgression, this writer who was all her life an impassioned dog lover connected animals with the fear and fascination of that which could not speak or be spoken. In one of the earliest passages in *A Backward Glance* she remembered how her first dog awoke in her "that long ache of pity for animals, and for all inarticulate beings, which nothing has ever stilled" (BG 4). To be sure, the fantasy of supernatural or quasi-supernatural vengeance that is played out in "Kerfol" recurs in a number of Wharton stories. "Miss Mary Pask" (1926), for example, records a punitive encounter between a self-satisfied bachelor and a "dowdy old mai[d]"— a kind of Gerty Farish—whom he has always patronized in the past but who now terrifies him because he mistakenly thinks she is dead. Similarly, "The Eyes" (1910) documents the haunting (by a pair of sinister red-rimmed eyes) that devastates another smug bachelor after he has twice, in different ways, betrayed a young woman who is in love with him. But "Kerfol" brings together the elements of the vengeful tale— in particular the elements of unspeakable oppression and unsayable rage—with singular force.

At the same time, "Kerfol" does allow the dead Anne de Cornault, who after her husband's demise had spent the rest of her life imprisoned in "the keep of Kerfol . . . a harmless madwoman" (S II 300), to speak from beyond the grave. Testifying in the transcript that the narrator then transcribes and that Wharton ultimately publishes, Anne reveals the secret history of subordination and insubordination that still haunts "the most romantic house in Brittany" and that may, by implication, haunt romance itself. Because of this, her story represents not only one of Wharton's central strategies for fantasizing that moment in which the worm/woman turns on her master but also one of the writer's major devices for simultaneously saying the unsayable and enacting its unsayability.

Far more than "Kerfol" does, two other brilliant Wharton ghost stories—"Mr. Jones" (1930) and "Pomegranate Seed" (1936)—depend on portrayals of women who speak from beyond the grave, in one case to articulate pain at a life that is like a death and in another to exact tribute that is due from a living man. The main action of "Mr. Jones" is a piece of collaborative detective work by Lady Jane Lynke, a travel writer, and an older friend named Edward Stramer, a Jamesian-sounding novelist who likes "to settle down somewhere in the country where he could be sure of not being disturbed" when he is finishing a novel (S II 604). Together, these surrogates of Wharton and her mentor learn that Bells, a beautiful Sussex estate that Lady Jane has inherited, is ruled by the ghost of one "Mr. Jones," an old family retainer—indeed, the amanuensis of a Regency aristocrat who was one of the last heirs of Bells actually to use the estate. This historical personage is introduced in a parodic passage that provides a key to the story's theme. Strolling among the family monuments, Lady Jane comes upon a

> plain sarcophagus . . . surmounted by the bust of a young man with a fine arrogant head, a Byronic throat and tossed-back curls.
>
> "Peregrine Vincent Theobald Lyncke, Baron Clouds, fifteenth Viscount Thudeney of Bells, Lord of the Manors of Thudeney, Thudeney-Blazes, Upper Lynke, Lynke-Linnet—" so it ran, with the usual tedious enumeration of honors, titles, court and country offices, ending with: "Born on May 1st, 1790, perished of the plague at Aleppo in 1828." And underneath in small cramped characters, as if crowded as an afterthought into an insufficient space: "Also His Wife."
>
> That was all. No names, dates, honors, epithets, for the Viscountess Thudeney.[1]

The oppressive silencing and dehumanizing of "Also His Wife" is, of course, the real subject of this chilling tale, in which Wharton ultimately gives a name and a voice to an anonymous, speechless woman. Exploring the house despite the spectral interdictions of Mr. Jones (who manifests his will through the present-day servants, all of whom are his descendants), Lady Jane and Stramer discover, first, a portrait of "Juliana, Viscountess Thudeney, 1818"—"Also His Wife"—whose "long fair oval" face looks "dumbly" out at them "in a stare of frozen beauty" (606), and then a pile of papers that the dead Mr. Jones had hidden, including a poignant letter from "Also His Wife" in which, though her text reveals that she was literally deaf and dumb, the "frozen" Juliana is at last granted the release of speech, if only speech to the future. Complaining to a husband who is perpetually absent that "Mr. Jones persists—and by your express orders, so he declares—in confining me," she protests that "to sit in this great house alone, day after day, month after month . . . is a fate more cruel than I deserve and more painful than I can bear" and begs to be allowed to make "the acquaintance of a few of your friends and neighbors" (613).

As the story makes plain, the unfortunate Juliana was never granted her wish in life, and, as it also reveals, she was imprisoned in this way because she was an object of exchange: the daughter of a rich East India merchant who apparently sought a connection with the aristocracy, she brought a vast dowry to her husband, who was ashamed of her speech impediment (and therefore imprisoned her) but needed her money to carry on a career of gambling and womanizing. The secret that is at the center both of the story and of the patriarchal estate of Bells is thus a horrifying one, a secret of the silencing of woman and of the traffic in women. And the relentlessly analytic author of *The House of Mirth* insists, with her usual pessimism, that the revelation of such social ills will not necessarily cure them; at the end of the tale, the spirit of Mr. Jones, the faithful servant of patriarchal authority, still tenaciously inhabits Bells. Yet that the estate has come into the hands of a literary woman who has purloined the letters that record its inequities and who has at last liberated the words of "Also His Wife" suggests some hope of a transformation which, though unsayable here, might be speakable in the future.[2]

Despite such guarded optimism, however, "Mr. Jones" mainly uses the convention of speech from beyond the grave to examine the same reification of woman that Wharton studied in so many novels. By contrast, "Pomegranate Seed" turns to this convention in order to explore the enigma associated with the inscription of female desire. Charlotte Ashby, the second wife of the "heartbroken widower" Kenneth Ashby, notices immediately after her honeymoon that her husband has begun to receive a series of mysterious letters, which are "always the same— a square grayish envelope with 'Kenneth Ashby, Esquire' written on it in bold but faint characters" (S II 764). After reading these, he behaves oddly, complains of headaches, and has "the look of a man who [has] been so far away from ordinary events that when he returns to familiar things they seem strange" (765). Finally, when he has received nine letters, he disappears, leaving Charlotte and his mother—who, on being shown the latest missive, recognizes the handwriting of her former daughter-in-law—with the dreadful realization that all the communications have come from his dead wife, whom he has now gone to join.

In the story's wonderful final scene, the two living women struggle to interpret the script from beyond the grave which has exerted such triumphant control over Kenneth Ashby, though it seems to them to be "only a few faint strokes, so faint and faltering as to be nearly undecipherable" (785). Cries the mother-in-law: "we're going mad— we're both going mad. We both know such things are impossible." But her daughter-in-law replies: "I've known for a long time now that everything was possible." If not in life, Wharton here implies, then in death, beyond the boundaries of logic and the logic of boundaries, a kind of female victory becomes possible, albeit a cryptic and problematic one.[3] And, not insignificantly, though she examined such cryptic victories in the greatest detail in her ghost stories, this otherwise skeptical writer also alluded to them in her more "realistic" fictions, notably in the early novella *The Touchstone* (1897) and in *The House of Mirth*.

As we argued in *The War of the Words*, *The Touchstone* explores a number of issues relating to the female affiliation complex,[4] but the central *donnée* of the story is the unearthly triumph of Margaret Aubyn, whose posthumously published letters ultimately convince their onetime recipient, the weak-spirited Glennard, that he must change his life because her dead "presence"—morally instructive, powerfully maternal—is now "the one reality in a world of shadows."[5] (Indeed, the affinity of *The Touchstone* with the supernatural tale was recognized by its English publisher, who renamed the work *A Gift from the Grave*, a title whose sensationalism Wharton disliked but whose accuracy she did not seriously dispute [BG 125–26].) Similarly, in *The House of Mirth*, the dead "semblance of Lily Bart" (HM 338) speaks the unsayable to Lawrence Selden, uttering the enigmatic "word which made all clear." Although Lily's world has reduced her to a kind of dead letter, a signifier who signifies nothing in the society she inhabits, after death—and only after death—she does manage cryptically to rebuke the novel's "negative hero" for his unmanliness. In her depiction of Lily's death, and of the body language through which this heroine speaks from beyond the grave, Wharton may be covertly alluding to Tennyson's "Elaine," the episode in *The Idylls of the King* that recounts the fate of the "*lily* maid of Astolot," who, rejected by Sir Lancelot, died and floated downstream on a barge, in one lifeless hand a lily, in the other a reproachful letter confessing "I loved you, and my love had no return. / And therefore my true love has been my death."[6] But also, precisely because Lily's dead "semblance" speaks of a love that can *have* "no return" in the Veblenesque economy of *The House of Mirth*, her author may be incorporating this dead heroine into an extended "ghost story" of female desire, a tale that Edith Wharton would continue telling all her life.

Notes

1. In *A Backward Glance* Wharton recalls James's parodic improvisations on English genealogies, improvisations that may well have inspired this passage in "Mr. Jones": motoring through the countryside around Lamb House, James "would murmur [quaint names] over and over to himself in a low chant, sometimes creating characters to fit them, and sometimes whole families, with

their domestic complications and matrimonial alliances, such as the Dymmes of Dymchurch, one of whom married a Sparkle, and was the mother of little Scintilla Dymme-Sparkle, subject of much mirth and many anecdotes" (249).

2. It is interesting, here, to consider that "Jones" was Wharton's "maiden" (that is, her patrilineal) name, and that, as a long-time admirer of the works of Poe, she had always been fascinated by the trope of "purloined letters"; see, for instance, her use of letters not only in *The House of Mirth* (where Bertha Dorset's letters are crucial to the plot) but also in such a novella as *The Touchstone* and such stories as "The Muse's Tragedy" (1899), "The Letter" (1904), "The Letters" (1910), and "Pomegranate Seed" (1936).

3. To be sure, the first wife in "Pomegranate Seed" is not presented as especially sympathetic: Wharton characterizes her as a "distant, self-centered woman" (S II, 763).

4. See *The War of the Words*, chap. 4.

5. Wharton, *Madame de Treymes and Others: Four Novelettes by Edith Wharton* (New York: Scribner's, 1970), p. 61.

6. See Alfred Lord Tennyson, "Lancelot and Elaine," in *The Idylls of the King, The Complete Poetical Works of Tennyson* (Boston: Houghton Mifflin, 1898), p. 398, lines 1268–69. For an exploration from a very different perspective of the "unsayability" or undecidability associated with Lily Bart, see Frances L. Restuccia, "The Name of the Lily: Edith Wharton's Feminism(s)," *Contemporary Literature* 28 (Summer 1987): 223–38.

Chronology

1862   Edith Jones born New York City, 24 January, the last of three children and only daughter of Lucretia Stevens Rhinelander and George Frederic Jones.

1866–1872   Lives and travels in Europe with family.

1877   Completes novella, *Fast and Loose*.

1878   *Verses* privately printed at Lucretia Jones's expense; one of the poems is published in the *Atlantic Monthly*.

1879   Makes social debut.

1882   George Frederic Jones dies.

1885   Marries Edward "Teddy" Wharton.

1891   Publishes first short story, "Mrs. Manstey's View," in *Scribner's*.

1894–1895   Suffers extended nervous breakdown after years of symptoms.

1899   *The Greater Inclination*, first collection of stories.

1901   *Crucial Instances*. Lucretia Jones dies.

1902   Begins friendship with Henry James. Moves into a new home, The Mount, in Lenox, Massachusetts.

1904   *The Descent of Man and Other Stories*.

1905   *The House of Mirth* (novel).

1907   Starts living part of the year in Paris.

1908   *The Hermit and the Wild Woman and Other Stories*. Begins affair with Morton Fullerton.

1910   *Tales of Men and Ghosts*.

1911   *Ethan Frome* (novella). Separates from Edward Wharton, sells The Mount, and leaves the United States.

1912   *The Reef* (novel).

1913   *The Custom of the Country* (novel). Divorces Edward Wharton.

1914–1917   Organizes war relief in France.

1916   *Xingu and Other Stories*. Is made Chevalier of the Legion of Honor by the President of France. Henry James dies.

1917   *Summer* (novella).

1919   Moves into Pavillon Colombe, a villa north of Paris.

1920   *The Age of Innocence* (novel).

1921   Awarded the Pulitzer Prize for *The Age of Innocence*.

1923   Receives honorary doctor of letters from Yale University (the first honorary degree given a woman by a major university) during her last visit to the United States.

1924   *Old New York* (novellas). Receives the Gold Medal of the National Institute of Arts and Letters.

1925   *The Writing of Fiction* (nonfiction).

1926   *Here and Beyond*.

1930   *Certain People*. Is elected to the American Academy of Arts and Letters.

1932   Several short stories are rejected; at least one story is turned down by all editors.

1933   *Human Nature*.

1934   *A Backward Glance* (autobiography).

1936   *The World Over*.

1937   Has a stroke in June and dies 11 August at Pavillon Colombe; is buried in Versailles. *Ghosts* published posthumously.

Selected Bibliography

Primary Works

Published Stories

The stories are listed in alphabetical order. The abbreviations that follow the statement of first publication refer to the short-story collections, listed in the next section, in which each story appears. No references are made in this section to *The Collected Short Stories of Edith Wharton* because it contains all the stories.

"After Holbein." *Saturday Evening Post* 200 (5 May 1928): 6–7. *BSS, CP, EWT, RF, SEW.*

"Afterward." *Century* 79 (January 1910): 321–39. *GS, G, MT, TMG.*

"All Souls'." First published in *G. GS, SEW.*

"The Angel at the Grave." *Scribner's* 29 (February 1901): 158–66. *BSS, CI, RF.*

"April Showers." *Youth's Companion* 74 (18 January 1900): 25–26.

"Atrophy." *Ladies' Home Journal* 44 (November 1927): 8–9. *CP, SEW.*

"Autres Temps. . . ." *Century* 82 (July 1911): 344–52; (August 1911): 587–94 (under title "Other Times, Other Manners"). *BSS, EWT, MT, RF, SEW, X.*

"The Best Man." *Collier's* 35 (2 September 1905): 14–17. *HWW.*

"Bewitched." *Pictorial Review* 26 (March 1925): 14–16. *GS, G, HB.*

"The Blond Beast." *Scribner's* 48 (September 1910): 291–304. *TMG.*

"The Bolted Door." *Scribner's* 45 (March 1909): 288–308. *TMG.*

"A Bottle of Perrier." *Saturday Evening Post* 198 (27 March 1926): 8–10 (under title "A Bottle of Evian"). *CP, EWR, EWT, G.*

"Charm Incorporated." *Hearst's International-Cosmopolitan* 96 (February 1934): 28–31 (under title "Bread upon the Waters"). *SEW, WO.*

"The Choice." *Century* 77 (November 1908): 32–40. *X.*

"Coming Home." *Scribner's* 58 (December 1915): 702–18. *X.*

"Confession." *Storyteller* 58 (March 1936): 64–85 (under title "Unconfessed Crime"). *WO.*

"The Confessional." *CI.*

"Copy." *Scribner's* 27 (June 1900): 657–63. *CI, MT.*

"A Coward." *GI.*

"A Cup of Cold Water." *GI.*

"The Daunt Diana." *Scribner's* 46 (July 1909): 35–41. *TMG.*

Selected Bibliography

"The Day of the Funeral." *Woman's Home Companion* 60 (January 1933): 7–8; (February 1933): 15–16 (under title "In a Day"). *HN*.
"The Debt." *Scribner's* 46 (August 1909): 165–72. *TMG*.
"The Descent of Man." *Scribner's* 35 (March 1904): 313–22. *DM, MT*.
"Diagnosis." *Ladies' Home Journal* 47 (November 1930): 8–9. *HN*.
"Dieu d'Amour." *Ladies' Home Journal* 45 (October 1928): 6–7. *CP*.
"The Dilettante." *Harper's* 108 (December 1903): 139–43. *DM, MT*.
"The Duchess at Prayer." *Scribner's* 28 (August 1900): 153–69. *CI*.
"Duration." *WO*.
"Expiation." *Hearst's International-Cosmopolitan* 36 (December 1903): 209–222. *DM, MT*.
"The Eyes." *Scribner's* 47 (June 1910): 671–80. *EWR, GS, G, MT, TMG*.
"Friends." *Youth's Companion* 74 (23 August 1900): 405–406, (30 August 1900): 417–18.
"Full Circle." *Scribner's* 46 (October 1909): 408–419. *TMG*.
"The Fullness of Life." *Scribner's* 14 (December 1893): 699–704. *MT*.
"A Glimpse." *Saturday Evening Post* 205 (12 November 1932): 16–17. *HN*.
"The Hermit and the Wild Woman." *Scribner's* 39 (February 1906): 145–56. *HWW*.
"His Father's Son." *Scribner's* 45 (June 1909): 657–65. *MT, TMG*.
"The House of the Dead Hand." *Atlantic Monthly* 94 (August 1904): 145–60.
"The Introducers." *Ainslee's* 16 (December 1905): 139–48; (January 1906): 61–67.
"In Trust." *Booklover's* 7 (April 1906): 432–40. *HWW*.
"A Journey." First published in *GI*. *MT*.
"Joy in the House." *Nash's Pall Mall* 90 (December 1932): 6–9. *HN*.
"Kerfol." *Scribner's* 59 (March 1916): 329–41. *GS, G, X*.
"The Lady's Maid's Bell." *Scribner's* 32 (November 1902): 549–60. *DM, EWT, GS, G, MT*.
"The Lamp of Psyche." *Scribner's* 18 (October 1895): 418–28.
"The Last Asset." *Scribner's* 36 (August 1904): 150–68. *BSS, HWW, MT, RF, SEW*.
"The Legend." *Scribner's* 47 (March 1910): 278–91. *MT, TMG*.
"The Letter." *Harper's* 108 (April 1904): 781–89. *DM* (English edition only).
"The Letters." *Century* 80 (August 1910): 485–92; (September 1910): 641–50; (October 1910): 812–19. *SEW, TMG*.
"The Line of Least Resistance." *Lippincott's* 66 (October 1900): 559–70.
"The Long Run." *Atlantic Monthly* 109 (February 1912): 145–63. *SEW, X*.
"The Looking Glass." *Hearst's International-Cosmopolitan* 99 (December 1935): 32–35 (under title "The Mirrors"). *GS, WO*.
"Les Metteurs en Scène." *Revue des Deux Mondes* 67 (October 1908): 692–708.
"Miss Mary Pask." *Pictorial Review* 26 (April 1925): 8–9. *GS, G, HB*.
"The Mission of Jane." *Harper's* 106 (December 1902): 63–74. *DM, MT, SEW*.

"The Moving Finger." *Harper's* 102 (March 1901): 627–32. *CI, EWT.*
"Mr. Jones." *Ladies' Home Journal* 45 (April 1928): 3–5. *CP, GS, G.*
"Mrs. Manstey's View." *Scribner's* 10 (July 1891): 117–22.
"The Muse's Tragedy." *Scribner's* 25 (January 1899): 77–84. *GI, MT.*
"The Other Two." *Collier's* 32 (13 February 1904): 15–20. *BSS, DM, EWT, MT, RF, SEW.*
"The Pelican." *Scribner's* 24 (November 1898): 620–29. *EWR, GI, MT, SEW.*
"Permanent Wave." *Redbook* 64 (April 1935): 20–23 (under title "Poor Old Vincent"). *WO.*
"Pomegranate Seed." *Saturday Evening Post* 203 (25 April 1931): 6–7. *BSS, EWR, GS, G, SEW, WO.*
"The Portrait." *GI.*
"The Potboiler." *Scribner's* 36 (December 1904): 696–712. *HWW.*
"The Pretext." *Scribner's* 44 (August 1908): 173–87. *HWW.*
"The Quicksand." *Harper's* 105 (June 1902): 13–21. *DM.*
"The Reckoning." *Harper's* 105 (August 1902): 342–55. *DM, SEW.*
"The Recovery." *Harper's* 102 (February 1901): 468–77. *CI.*
"The Refugees." *Saturday Evening Post* 191 (18 January 1919): 3–5. *CP.*
"The Rembrandt." *Hearst's International-Cosmopolitan* 29 (August 1900): 429–37. *CI, EWR.*
"Roman Fever." *Liberty* 11 (10 November 1934): 10–14. *BSS, EWT, RF, WO.*
"The Seed of the Faith." *Scribner's* 65 (January 1919): 17–33. *HB.*
"Souls Belated." First published in *GI. BSS, MT, RF.*
"The Temperate Zone." *Pictorial Review* 25 (February 1924): 5–7. *HB.*
"That Good May Come." *Scribner's* 15 (May 1894): 629–42.
"The Triumph of Night." *Scribner's* 56 (August 1914): 149–62. *GS, G, MT, X.*
"The Twilight of the God." *GI.*
"The Valley of Childish Things." *Century* 52 (July 1896): 467–69.
"Velvet Ear-pads." *HB.*
"A Venetian Night's Entertainment." *Scribner's* 34 (December 1903): 640–51. *DM.*
"The Verdict." *Scribner's* 43 (June 1908): 689–93. *HWW.*
"Writing a War Story." *Woman's Home Companion* 46 (September 1919): 17–19.
"Xingu." *Scribner's* 50 (December 1911): 684–96. *BSS, EWT, MT, RF, X.*
"The Young Gentlemen." *Pictorial Review* 27 (February 1926): 29–30. *HB.*

Selected Story Collections

BSS   The Best Short Stories of Edith Wharton. Edited by Wayne Andrews. New York: Scribner's, 1958. Contains "Roman Fever," "Xingu," "The Other Two," "Pomegranate Seed," "Souls Belated," "The Angel at the Grave," "The Last Asset," "After Holbein," and "Autres Temps . . ."
CI   Crucial Instances. New York: Scribner's, 1901. Reprint, New York: AMS

Press, 1969. Contains "The Duchess at Prayer," "The Angel at the Grave," "The Recovery," "Copy," "The Rembrandt," "The Moving Finger," and "The Confessional."

CP *Certain People.* New York: D. Appleton, 1930. Contains "Atrophy," "A Bottle of Perrier," "After Holbein," "Dieu d'Amour," "The Refugees," and "Mr. Jones."

The Collected Short Stories of Edith Wharton. Edited by R. W. B. Lewis. 2 vols. New York: Scribner's, 1968. Reprint, New York: Macmillan, 1987–89. Contains all the stories.

DM *The Descent of Man and Other Stories.* New York: Scribner's, 1904. Contains "The Descent of Man," "The Mission of Jane," "The Other Two," "The Quicksand," "The Dilettante," "The Reckoning," "Expiation," "The Lady's Maid's Bell," and "A Venetian Night's Entertainment."

EWR *The Edith Wharton Reader.* Edited by Louis Auchincloss. New York: Scribner's, 1965. Reprint, New York: Macmillan, 1989. Contains "The Pelican," "The Rembrandt," "The Eyes," "A Bottle of Perrier," and "Pomegranate Seed."

EWT *An Edith Wharton Treasury.* Edited by Arthur H. Quinn. New York: Appleton-Century-Crofts, 1950. Contains "After Holbein," "A Bottle of Perrier," "The Lady's Maid's Bell," "Roman Fever," "The Other Two," "The Moving Finger," "Xingu," and "Autres Temps . . . ."

G *Ghosts.* New York: Appleton-Century, 1937. Contains "All Souls'," "The Eyes," "Afterward," "The Lady's Maid's Bell," "Kerfol," "The Triumph of Night," "Miss Mary Pask," "Bewitched," "Mr. Jones," "Pomegranate Seed," and "A Bottle of Perrier."

GI *The Greater Inclination.* New York: Scribner's, 1899. Reprint, New York: AMS Press, 1969. Contains "The Muse's Tragedy," "A Journey," "The Pelican," "Souls Belated," "A Coward," "The Twilight of the God," "A Cup of Cold Water," and "The Portrait."

GS *The Ghost Stories of Edith Wharton.* Illustrated by Laszlo Kubinyi. New York: Scribner's, 1973. Contains "The Lady's Maid's Bell," "The Eyes," "Afterward," "Kerfol," "The Triumph of Night," "Miss Mary Pask," "Bewitched," "Mr. Jones," "Pomegranate Seed," "The Looking Glass," and "All Souls'."

HB *Here and Beyond.* New York: D. Appleton, 1926. Contains "Miss Mary Pask," "The Young Gentlemen," "Bewitched," "The Seed of the Faith," "The Temperate Zone," and "Velvet Ear-pads."

HN *Human Nature.* New York: D. Appleton, 1933. Contains "The Day of the Funeral," "A Glimpse," "Joy in the House," and "Diagnosis."

HWW *The Hermit and the Wild Woman and Other Stories.* New York: Scribner's, 1908. Contains "The Hermit and the Wild Woman," "The Last Asset," "In Trust," "The Pretext," "The Verdict," "The Potboiler," and "The Best Man."

MT   *The Muse's Tragedy and Other Stories.* Edited by Candace Waid. New York: New American Library, 1990. Contains "The Fullness of Life," "The Muse's Tragedy," "A Journey," "The Pelican," "Souls Belated," "Copy," "The Descent of Man," "The Mission of Jane," "The Other Two," "The Dilettante," "Expiation," "The Lady's Maid's Bell," "The Last Asset," "His Father's Son," "The Legend," "The Eyes," "Afterward," "Xingu," "Autres Temps . . . ," and "The Triumph of Night."

RF   *Roman Fever and Other Stories.* New York: Scribner's, 1964. Reprint, with introduction by Cynthia Griffin Wolff, New York: Collier, 1987. Contains "Roman Fever," "Xingu," "The Other Two," "Souls Belated," "The Angel at the Grave," "The Last Asset," "After Holbein," and "Autres Temps . . . ."

SEW *The Stories of Edith Wharton.* Edited by Anita Brookner. New York: Carroll & Graf, 1990. Contains "The Pelican," "The Other Two," "The Mission of Jane," "The Reckoning," "The Last Asset," "The Letters," "Autres Temps . . . ," "The Long Run," "After Holbein," "Atrophy," "Pomegranate Seed," "Charm Incorporated," and "All Souls'."

TMG *Tales of Men and Ghosts.* New York: Scribner's, 1910. Contains "The Bolted Door," "His Father's Son," "The Daunt Diana," "The Debt," "Full Circle," "The Legend," "The Eyes," "The Blond Beast," "Afterward," and "The Letters."

WO   *The World Over.* New York: Appleton-Century, 1936. Contains "Charm Incorporated," "Pomegranate Seed," "Permanent Wave," "Confession," "Roman Fever," "The Looking Glass," and "Duration."

X   *Xingu and Other Stories.* New York: Scribner's, 1916. Contains "Xingu," "Coming Home," "Autres Temps . . . ," "Kerfol," "The Long Run," "The Triumph of Night," and "The Choice."

Other Works

The Age of Innocence. New York: D. Appleton, 1920. Novel.

Artemis to Actaeon and Other Verse. New York: Scribner's, 1909. Poetry.

A Backward Glance. New York: Appleton-Century, 1934. Autobiography.

The Buccaneers. New York: Appleton-Century, 1938. Novel.

Bunner Sisters, in *Xingu and Other Stories.* New York: Scribner's, 1916. Novella.

The Children. New York: D. Appleton, 1928. Novel.

The Custom of the Country. New York: Scribner's, 1913. Novel.

The Decoration of Houses (with Ogden Codman, Jr.). New York: Scribner's, 1897. Nonfiction.

Ethan Frome. New York: Scribner's, 1911. Novella.

Fighting France, from Dunkerque to Belfort. New York: Scribner's, 1915. Nonfiction.

French Ways and Their Meaning. New York: D. Appleton, 1919. Nonfiction.

Selected Bibliography

The Fruit of the Tree. New York: Scribner's, 1907. Novel.
The Glimpses of the Moon. New York: D. Appleton, 1922. Novel.
The Gods Arrive. New York: D. Appleton, 1932. Novel.
Her Son, in *Human Nature.* New York: D. Appleton, 1933. Novella.
The House of Mirth. New York: Scribner's, 1905. Novel.
Hudson River Bracketed. New York: D. Appleton, 1929. Novel.
In Morocco. New York: Scribner's, 1920. Nonfiction.
Italian Backgrounds. New York: Scribner's, 1905. Nonfiction.
Italian Villas and Their Gardens. New York: Century, 1904. Nonfiction.
Madame de Treymes. New York: Scribner's, 1907. Novella.
The Marne. New York: D. Appleton, 1918. Novella.
The Mother's Recompense. New York: D. Appleton, 1925. Novel.
A Motor-Flight through France. New York: Scribner's, 1908. Nonfiction.
Old New York: False Dawn, The Old Maid, The Spark, New Year's Day. 4 vols.
    New York: D. Appleton, 1924. Novellas.
The Reef. New York: D. Appleton, 1912. Novel.
Sanctuary. New York: Scribner's, 1903. Novella.
A Son at the Front. New York: Scribner's, 1923. Novel.
Summer. New York: D. Appleton, 1917. Novella.
The Touchstone. New York: Scribner's, 1900. Novella.
Twelve Poems. London: The Medici Society, 1926. Poetry.
Twilight Sleep. New York: D. Appleton, 1927. Novel.
The Valley of Decision. 2 vols. New York: Scribner's, 1902. Novel.
Verses. Newport: C. E. Hammett, 1878. Poetry.
The Writing of Fiction. New York: Scribner's, 1925. Nonfiction.

Secondary Works

Sources I have not seen are indicated by an asterisk (*).

Bibliography

Bendixen, Alfred. "A Guide to Wharton Criticism, 1974–1983." *Edith Wharton Newsletter* 2 (Fall 1985): 1–8.
———. "Recent Wharton Studies: A Bibliographic Essay." *Edith Wharton Newsletter* 3 (Fall 1986): 8–9.
———. "Wharton Studies, 1986–1987: A Bibliographic Essay." *Edith Wharton Newsletter* 5 (Spring 1988): 5–8, 10.
———. "The World of Wharton Criticism: A Bibliographic Essay." *Edith Wharton Review* 7 (Spring 1990): 18–21.
Brenni, Vito J. *Edith Wharton: A Bibliography.* Morgantown, W. V.: McClain Printing, 1966.

Garrison, Stephen. *Edith Wharton: A Descriptive Bibliography.* Pittsburgh: University of Pittsburgh Press, forthcoming.*

Lauer, Kristin O., and Margaret P. Murray. *Edith Wharton: A Secondary Bibliography.* New York: Garland Publishing, 1990.*

Sklepowich, Edward A. "Edith Wharton." *American Literary Realism* 8 (Autumn 1975): 331–40. Survey of dissertations on Wharton.

Springer, Marlene. *Edith Wharton and Kate Chopin: A Reference Guide.* Boston: G. K. Hall, 1976.

Springer, Marlene, and Joan Gilson. "Edith Wharton: A Reference Guide Updated." *Resources for American Literary Study* 14, no. 1–2 (1984): 85–111.

Tuttleton, James W. "Edith Wharton: An Essay in Bibliography." *Resources for American Literary Study* 3 (Autumn 1973): 163–202. Expanded version appears as "Edith Wharton" in *American Women Writers: Bibliographical Essays,* ed. Maurice Duke, Jackson R. Bryer, and M. Thomas Inge, 71–107. Westport, Conn.: Greenwood Press, 1983.

Zilversmit, Annette. "Bibliographical Index." *College Literature* 14 (Fall 1987): 305–9.

Biography and Collected Criticism

Bloom, Harold, ed. *Edith Wharton.* New York: Chelsea House, 1986.

Howe, Irving, ed. *Edith Wharton: A Collection of Critical Essays.* Englewood Cliffs, N.J.: Prentice-Hall, 1962.

Lewis, R. W. B. *Edith Wharton: A Biography.* New York: Harper & Row, 1975.

Lubbock, Percy. *Portrait of Edith Wharton.* New York: Appleton-Century-Crofts, 1947.

Wolff, Cynthia Griffin. *A Feast of Words: The Triumph of Edith Wharton.* New York: Oxford University Press, 1977.

Short-Story Criticism

Bell, Millicent. "A James 'Gift' To Edith Wharton." *Modern Language Notes* 72 (March 1957): 182–85. "The Pretext."

Bement, Douglas. *Weaving the Short Story.* New York: Farrar & Rinehart, 1931.

Bendixen, Alfred. Introduction to *Haunted Women: The Best Supernatural Tales,* 1–12. New York: Ungar, 1985. "The Fullness of Life" and "Pomegranate Seed."

Blackall, Jean Frantz. "Edith Wharton's Art of Ellipsis." *Journal of Narrative Technique* 17 (Spring 1987): 145–62.

Blum, Virginia L. "Edith Wharton's Erotic Other World." *Literature and Psychology* 33, no.1 (1987): 12–29.

Caws, Mary Ann. "Framing in Two Opposite Modes: Ford and Wharton." *Comparativist* 10 (May 1986): 114–20. "The Other Two."

Chu, Li-Min. "The Ghostly Stories of Edith Wharton." *Bulletin of National Taiwan University* 26 (1977): 417–48.*

Conn, Peter. "Edith Wharton." In *The Divided Mind: Ideology and Imagination in America, 1898–1917*, 173–96. Cambridge: Cambridge University Press, 1983. "Souls Belated."

Cooper, Frederic Taber. "Edith Wharton." In *Some American Story Tellers*, 168–95. New York: Holt, Rinehart, and Winston, 1911.

Donovan, Josephine. *After the Fall: The Demeter-Persephone Myth in Wharton, Cather, and Glasgow.* University Park: Pennsylvania State University Press, 1989.

Downey, June E. "Comparative Discussion." In *Creative Imagination: Studies in the Psychology of Literature*, 202–208. New York: Harcourt Brace, 1929. "The Duchess at Prayer."

Dwight, Eleanor. "Edith Wharton and 'The Cask of Amontillado.'" In *Poe and Our Times: Influences and Affinities*, ed. Benjamin Franklin Fisher IV, 49–57. Baltimore: Edgar Allan Poe Society, 1986. "The Duchess at Prayer."

Edel, Leon. "The Nature of Literary Psychology." *Journal of the American Psychoanalytic Association* 29, no.2 (1981): 447–67. Also in *Stuff of Sleep and Dreams: Experiments in Literary Psychology*, 36–41. New York: Harper and Row, 1982. "All Souls'."

French, Marilyn. Introduction to *Roman Fever and Other Stories*. London: Virago, 1985.

Funston, Judith E. "'Xingu': Edith Wharton's Velvet Gauntlet." *Studies in American Fiction* 12 (Autumn 1984): 227–34.

Gerlach, John. *Toward the End: Closure and Structure in the American Short Story.* University: University of Alabama Press, 1985. "Roman Fever."

Gilbert, Sandra M., and Susan Gubar. *No Man's Land: The Place of the Woman Writer in the Twentieth Century.* 2 vols. New Haven: Yale University Press, 1988–89.

Going, William T. "Wharton's 'After Holbein.'" *Explicator* 10 (November 1951): Item 8.

Gooder, Jean. "Unlocking Edith Wharton: An Introduction to *The Reef*." *Cambridge Quarterly* 15, no.1 (1986): 33–52.

Gordon, Mary. Introduction. In *Ethan Frome and Other Short Fiction*, vii–xviii. New York: Bantam, 1987.

Greenwood, J. V. "The Implications of Marital Status in Edith Wharton's Short Stories and *Nouvelles*." *Kobe College Studies* 5 (February 1959): 9–28.*

———. "The Importance of Milieu in Edith Wharton's Short Stories and *Nouvelles*." *Kobe College Studies* 5 (October 1958): 9–28.*

———. "The Nature and Results of Conflict in Edith Wharton's Short Stories and *Nouvelles*." *Kobe College Studies* 6 (June 1959): 1–27.*

Howells, William Dean. *Great Modern American Stories.* New York: Boni & Liveright, 1921. "The Mission of Jane."

Kaplan, Amy. "Edith Wharton's Profession of Authorship." *ELH* 53 (Summer 1986): 433–57. A slightly revised version appears as chap. 3 in *The Social Construction of American Realism,* 65–87. Chicago: University of Chicago Press, 1988.

Kimbel, Ellen. "The American Short Story: 1900–1920." In *The American Short Story, 1900–1945,* ed. Philip Stevick, 33–69. Boston: Twayne, 1984.

Kozikowski, Stanley J. "Unreliable Narration in Henry James's 'The Two Faces' and Edith Wharton's 'The Dilettante.'" *Arizona Quarterly* 35 (Winter 1979): 357–72.

Kronenberger, Louis. "Mrs. Wharton's Literary Museum." *Atlantic Monthly* 222 (September 1968): 98–102.

Lawson, Richard H. "Edith Wharton." In *American Short-Story Writers, 1880–1910,* ed. Bobby Ellen Kimbel, 308–23. Detroit: Gale Research, 1989.

———. "Nietzsche, Edith Wharton, and 'The Blond Beast.'" In *Actes du VII Congrès de l'Association Internationale . . . Literatures of America,* ed. Milan V. Dimic and Juan Ferrate, 169–72. Stuttgart: Bieber, 1979.

———. "The Short Stories." in *Edith Wharton,* 77–89. New York: Frederick Ungar, 1977.

Lewis, R. W. B. Introduction. In *The Collected Short Stories of Edith Wharton,* vol. 1, vii–xxv. New York: Charles Scribner's Sons, 1968. Reprinted in *Women Writers of the Short Story,* ed. Heather McClave, 32–49. Englewood Cliffs, N.J.: Prentice-Hall, 1980. Also reprinted as "A Writer of Short Stories" in *Edith Wharton,* ed. Harold Bloom, 9–28. New York: Chelsea House, 1986.

———. "Powers of Darkness." *Times Literary Supplement,* 13 June 1975, 644–45.

Lyde, Marilyn Jones. *Edith Wharton: Convention and Morality in the Work of a Novelist.* Norman: University of Oklahoma Press, 1959.

McDowell, Margaret B. "Edith Wharton's 'After Holbein'": 'A Paradigm of the Human Condition.'" *Journal of Narrative Technique* 1 (January 1971): 49–58.

———. "Edith Wharton's Ghost Stories." *Criticism* 12 (Spring 1970): 133–52.

———. "The Short Stories." In *Edith Wharton,* 84–91. Boston: Twayne, 1976 (rev. 1990).

Murray, Margaret P. "The Gothic Arsenal of Edith Wharton." *Journal of Evolutionary Psychology* 10 (August 1989): 315–21. "Pomegranate Seed."

Nevius, Blake. *Edith Wharton: A Study of Her Fiction.* Berkeley: University of California Press, 1953.

O'Brien, Edward J. *The Advance of the American Short Story.* New York: Dodd, Mead, 1923.

O'Neal, Michael J. "Point of View and Narrative Technique in the Fiction of Edith Wharton." *Style* 17 (Spring 1983): 270–89. "Roman Fever."

Pattee, Fred Lewis. *The Development of the American Short Story.* New York: Harper and Brothers, 1923.

———. Introduction to *Century Readings in the American Short Story,* 424–31. New York: Century, 1927. "The Choice."

Petry, Alice Hall. "A Twist of Crimson Silk: Edith Wharton's 'Roman Fever.'" *Studies in Short Fiction* 24 (Spring 1987): 163–66.

Plante, Patricia R. "Edith Wharton as a Short Story Writer." *Midwest Quarterly* 4 (Summer 1963): 363–79.

Price, Alan. "Edith Wharton's War Story." *Tulsa Studies in Women's Literature* 8 (Spring 1989): 95–100. "Coming Home."

Quinn, Arthur Hobson. "Edith Wharton." In *American Fiction: An Historical and Critical Survey,* 550–81. New York: D. Appleton-Century, 1936.

———. Introduction to *An Edith Wharton Treasury,* v–xxvii. New York: Appleton-Century-Crofts, 1950.

———. "Mrs. Wharton as a Writer of Short Stories." *Book News Monthly* 26 (November 1907): 179–81.

Robillard, Douglas. "Edith Wharton." In *Supernatural Fiction Writers: Fantasy and Horror,* ed. E. F. Bleiler, vol. 2, 738–88. New York: Scribner's, 1985.

Ross, Danforth. *The American Short Story.* Minneapolis: University of Minnesota Press, 1961.

Sasaki, Miyoko. "The Dance of Death: A Study of Edith Wharton's Short Stories." *Studies in English Literature* (Tokyo) 51, no. 1–2 (1974): 67–90.

Scarborough, Dorothy. *The Supernatural in Modern English Fiction.* New York: G. P. Putnam, 1917.

Schriber, Marysue. "Darwin, Wharton, and 'The Descent of Man,'" *Studies in Short Fiction* 17 (Winter 1980): 31–38.

Singley, Carol J., and S. E. Sweeney. "Forbidden Reading and Ghostly Writing: Anxious Power in Wharton's 'Pomegranate Seed.'" Forthcoming in *Women's Studies.*

Smith, Allan Gardner. "Edith Wharton and the Ghost Story." In *Gender and Literary Voice: Women and Literature I,* ed. Janet Todd, 149–59. New York: Holmes and Meier, 1980. Reprinted in *Edith Wharton,* ed. Harold Bloom, 89–97. New York: Chelsea House, 1986.

Stein, Allen F. *After the Vows Were Spoken: Marriage in American Literary Realism.* Columbus: Ohio State University Press, 1984.

Stengel, Ellen Powers. "Dilemmas of Discourse: Edith Wharton's 'All Souls'' and the Tale of the Supernatural." *Publications of the Arkansas Philological Association* 15 (Fall 1989): 85–104.

———. "Edith Wharton Rings 'The Lady's Maid's Bell.'" *Edith Wharton Review* 7 (Spring 1990): 3–9.

Tintner, Adeline R. "Fiction Is the Best Revenge: Portraits of Henry James by Four Women Writers." *Turn-of-the-Century Women* 2 (Winter 1985): 42–49.

———. " 'The Hermit and the Wild Woman': Edith Wharton's 'Fictioning' of Henry James." *Journal of Modern Literature* 4 (September 1974): 32–42.

———. "Jamesian Structures in *The Age of Innocence* and Related Stories." *Twentieth Century Literature* 26 (Fall 1980): 332–47.

———. "Mothers vs. Daughters in the Fiction of Edith Wharton and Henry James." *AB Bookman's Weekly,* 6 June 1983, 4324–28.

———. "Wharton and James: Some Literary Give and Take." *Edith Wharton Newsletter* 3 (Spring 1986): 3–5, 8.

Vita-Finzi, Penelope. *Edith Wharton and the Art of Fiction.* New York: St. Martin's, 1990.*

Voss, Arthur. *The American Short Story: A Critical Survey.* Norman: University of Oklahoma Press, 1973.

Waid, Candace. Introduction. In *The Muses's Tragedy and Other Stories,* 7–19. New York: New American Library, 1990.

Walton, Geoffrey. *Edith Wharton: A Critical Interpretation.* Rutherford, N.J.: Fairleigh Dickinson University Press, 1970. Rev. ed., 1982.

Wiiliams, Blanche Colton. "Edith Wharton." In *Our Short Story Writers* (1922), 337–57. Freeport, N.Y.: Books for Libraries Press, 1969.

Wolff, Cynthia Griffin. Introduction. In *Roman Fever and Other Stories,* ix–xx. New York: Macmillan, 1987.

Woollcott, Alexander. "An Afterword on 'The Lady's Maid's Bell.' " In *Woollcott's Second Reader,* 31–33. New York: Viking, 1937.

Wright, Austin McGiffert. *The American Short Story in the Twenties.* Chicago: University of Chicago Press, 1961.

Zilversmit, Annette. "Edith Wharton's Last Ghosts." *College Literature* 14 (Fall 1987): 296–305.

Ziolkowski, Theodore. *Disenchanted Images: A Literary Iconology.* Princeton, N.J.: Princeton University Press, 1977. "The Moving Finger."

Index

"Fate," 53
"Hamatreya," 54–55
"Nature," 53
Eyes, as literary motif, 65, 67, 69

Fate, as literary theme, 53, 54–56
Father/daughter relationship, as
  literary theme, 32, 38–42, 49,
  103–4, 120n111
Fern, Fanny, 32
Fitzgerald, F. Scott, 108n2
  "Beatrice Bobs Her Hair," 84
  The Great Gatsby, 90
Flaubert, Gustave, 29, 136
Freeman, Mary Wilkins, 29–33
  "A New England Nun," 30, 54,
  55
  "Old Woman Magoun," 104
Freud, Sigmund, 42
Fuller, Henry Blake, 29
Fullerton, Morton, 18, 19, 22, 43,
  66, 67, 164

Gale, Zona, 108n2
Gerlach, John, 11
Ghost stories
  early, 28, 40
  Gilbert on, 164–69
  incest situation in, 68, 101–3,
  104–6
  late, 96–99
  middle, 57, 64–70, 72–73, 76
  Wharton on, 129–31, 139–42
Gilbert, Sandra, 98, 99
Gilligan, Carol
  In a Different Voice, 80, 81
Gilman, Charlotte Perkins, 116n65,
  119n91
Goethe, Johann von, 128, 156
Gooder, Jean
  "Unlocking Edith Wharton," 48
Goodman, Susan, 32, 45, 46
Grant, Robert, 6, 150
Green world, as literary theme, 30,
  32
Greenwood, Grace, 32, 33
Gubar, Susan, 98, 99

Halevy, Ludovic
  Fanny Lear, 144
Hardy, Thomas, 29, 128
Hawthorne, Nathaniel, 29, 31, 36,
  56, 128
Hearst's International-Cosmopolitan
  (periodical), 84, 151
Hemingway, Ernest, 90
Henry, O., 8
Holbein, Hans, 93, 95
Homosexuality, as literary theme,
  65–67
Howells, William Dean, 29, 156
  A Modern Instance, 161

Incest, as literary theme, 40–42, 44,
  48, 49–50, 67, 85–86, 89, 101–6
International theme, 78, 83, 103–4
Irving, Washington, 112n41, 144
  The Alhambra, 143

James, Henry, 5, 18–19, 27, 81, 128,
  146
  as critic of Wharton stories, 28, 85
  Daisy Miller, 10
  influence of, 29, 31, 33, 36, 78
  as model for characters, 67,
  71–72, 87
  point of view, 4, 12, 132–33
  The Turn of the Screw, 129, 131,
  141–42
Jewett, Rutger B., 150–52
Jewett, Sarah Orne, 29–33
  "The Foreigner," 89
  "A White Heron," 30
Jones, George Frederic, 40, 41,
  44–47, 67, 68, 93
Jones, Lucretia Rhinelander, 45–47,
  69, 123n139

Kaplan, Amy
  *The Social Construction of American
  Realism*, 31, 62
Keys and locks, as literary motif,
  39–40, 48, 53
Kimbel, Ellen
  "The American Short Story:
  1900–1920," 81

185

Index

The Author

Barbara A. White is associate professor of women's studies at the University of New Hampshire. She received her Ph.D. in English from the University of Wisconsin and has written extensively about American women writers. Her books include *Growing Up Female: Adolescent Girlhood in American Fiction* (1985) and *Hidden Hands: An Anthology of American Women Writers, 1790–1870* (1985), coedited with Lucy M. Freibert. She is also the author of two bibliographies, *American Women Writers: An Annotated Bibliography of Criticism* (1977) and *American Women's Fiction, 1790–1870: A Reference Guide* (1990).

The Editor

Gordon Weaver earned his Ph.D. in English and creative writing at the University of Denver, and is currently professor of English at Oklahoma State University. He is the author of several novels, including *Count a Lonely Cadence, Give Him a Stone, Circling Byzantium*, and most recently *The Eight Corners of the World*. His short stories are collected in *The Entombed Man of Thule, Such Waltzing Was Not Easy, Getting Serious, Morality Play, A World Quite Round*, and *Men Who Would Be Good*. Recognition of his fiction includes the St. Lawrence Award for Fiction (1973), two National Endowment for the Arts fellowships (1974 and 1989), and the O. Henry First Prize (1979). He edited *The American Short Story, 1945–1980: A Critical History* and is currently editor of the *Cimarron Review*. Married and the father of three daughters, he lives in Stillwater, Oklahoma.